Dear Mama:

Lessons on Race, Grace, and the Wisdom to Overcome

Shawn Schwaner, Ph. D.

ISBN: 978-0692666241
ISBN-13: 0692666249

Today I chose Happiness,

So, I inhaled love

And exhaled your memory

(Michelle Morgan @ Michelle's Scriptures, 2015)

This book is dedicated to my guardian angel, Bertha Lee (Mama) Green,

and all who oppose hatred in its various and destructive forms.

TABLE OF CONTENTS

A Letter to Mama:

Dear Mama,

The time has come for me to open the doors to the Temple that you and I have shared for so long. As I write, my life has fallen on hard times and there are few places to turn. Not many people can understand me like you, and I extend my hand to you, my guardian angel, to help me through this turmoil.

Though I have stayed true to your lessons and have fed the hungry freely and without judgment, life has thrown me significant challenges. I know that God is looking after this fool but you are the one that gave me life, protected me, and paved the possibility of being human in this mortal place. Without you, I could have never become a man, father, or teacher.

Mama, I am hungry. I seek your nourishment so that I can garner the strength to relieve the demons that inhabit my soul. It is time for me to share your stories of abuse, my mother's abuse, and my abuse so that I can take your message of love and tolerance to light the path of hope for others. It is time to take my "million-dollar personality," as you called it, and share your wisdom.

As our world has changed in the 20 years since your death, your lessons remain invaluable and needed more than ever. I am simply a messenger and wish to resist my selfishness in remembering you in my heart, only, and allow the world to know your beauty. Countless friends and families have told me that your story was worth telling and I am ready to share; this is a tribute to you and my thank you note for giving me a chance. I trust that you would be honored in this most genuine retelling of our story.

Your story is worthy of life and it will save me, my children, and unknown friends, once again.

I love you and seek to make you proud.

Your "little white baby,"

Shawn

i

PROLOGUE

"I was born a poor black child."

History has a way of bringing seemingly unrelated people and events into public discourse and consciousness. In a typical day, few draw upon the past to understand how it shapes the present condition. My life was formed, defined, and brought to being by a woman who dropped out of school in the third grade, was physically and sexually abused by her step-father, picked cotton and fought in bare knuckle boxing matches for survival, and developed a wisdom beyond that which is common. The life of Bertha Lee (Mama) Green, rife with pain, burned a flame that lit a path for her "little white baby" and subsequently the life and thinking of nearly 10,000 students. These overlaps between the darkness born of hate and the lightness birthing love are curious, indeed.

When Steve Martin proclaimed in the 1976 classic movie, The Jerk, that "I was born a poor black child," I sat amazed that someone understood my position in the world. While watching the rhythm less Martin dance foolishly on the front porch of the rural shack, it reverberated truth to me. Though my biological parents were white, I was born a poor black child and my Mama was an African-American Creole Cherokee mountain of strength and kindness.

Some would define her as a babysitter or, in the more modern vernacular, nanny; but she was much more. Mama was a matriarch who ruled with an iron fist and loved with a tender heart. My young childhood friend, Chris Strock, remembered her as "an intimidating woman who loved us kids." She was an amalgamation of experience, abuse, racial discrimination, and hatred; she was a plurality of history, family, and disadvantage. Mama was a queen borne from a cruel world. The mix she brought to life was a brew of wisdom beyond the common day. Mama Green was both the past and the present and lives

2

on today through the grace of storytelling.

As I compose this manuscript from the depths of my personal despair, I remember her wisdom fondly. As I dwell in my *"Temple of Pain,"*, as she called it, I am lifted by her memory, sayings, and experience of triumph. She once said that, *"As long as I have a breath, I will love you."* Well, she breathes through these parables and is blessing my life once again. In writing her story, my life and career as a college professor is a reflection of a physical body twenty plus years deceased, yet a soul that is alive and fresh today. Her memory burns bright and it is my duty to share her journey and wisdom, it is my duty to deliver her message, it is my duty to live and acknowledge that she saved me once and is doing so again. I can hear her saying now, *"The Lord works in mysterious ways"* – maybe I am finally starting to understand what she meant.

This story is about Mama Green, her *"little white baby,"* and the power of persistence, perseverance, and patience. It is a shared history of two people that, by typical structural circumstances, should never have met. Instead, our lives are intertwined in a historical formation of love that transcends time and space in a most unique fusion. My pilgrimage to the mecca of understanding starts and ends with the woman who raised me from *"three weeks and one day old"* to the aging man who *"will always be Mama's Baby."*

The stories and quotations used in this book are true and reflect her renderings and my personal recollections. To say the least, there is blood, sex, abuse, and pain scattered herein. This is a dark treatise bearing light where life lessons, guidance, charm, and wit serendipitously converge. This book bears tolerance, understanding, and a tacit view that *"Only love can save the world."* In the end, her ultimate message to me was simple: *"Live with purity of purpose and always be at peace"*.

In the spring of 1988, several Denison University students and I, including Lisa Coleman, the current Chief Diversity Officer at Harvard

3

University, had dinner with Maya Angelou at the Buxton Inn in Granville, Ohio. The quiet literary giant shared some anecdotes of her work but was more interested in hearing from the students attending. This dinner occurred in the aftermath of a major student protest/sit-in at Denison University regarding race, and Dr. Tony Stoneburner, A Denison University English professor, mentioned that I had an interesting view on the subject. When she asked to hear it, I shared the story of me and Mama Green. When I finished telling the complex story of love and sacrifice, she noted that, "You should write a book about your life with Mrs. Green." Nearly three decades have since passed and I surmise that now is time. In reference to Maya Angelou, I can attest that, "I know why the caged bird sings."

These reflections are a call for love through sacrifice, strength through vulnerability, and the acknowledgement that greatness sleeps within the rubble of personal adversity. "Dear Mama" is my story as shaped by the life and guidance of Mama Green. In a most philosophical way, this collection is a living representation of how a stream of past events produce current consciousness and knowledge that is used in daily life. This book is a spirited connection between the history of sharecropping and cotton picking to the coming of age of a man and educator. Our meeting and relationship represents the quintessential notion that if a butterfly flaps its wings in New York it can cause a tsunami in Japan and how history and destiny are an unfolding process of becoming. It's an exchange between tradition, luck, and serendipity. Under this umbrella, everyone, even Mama Green, can make a difference to humanity's history. The essence of my life blended together with hers shows that we are all interconnected through an untold bond invisible by sight, but transcendent nonetheless.

I've learned from Mama that people are more similar than they are different and that it is through the social construction of moral and ethical boundaries that hate emerges and destroys the concept of possibility. External hate explodes in violence manifest; internal hate eviscerates the perfection of untainted souls. The possibility of peace, love, and happiness are rendered helpless through abuse, impropriety, and illusion. Hope can only survive through the suspension of indifference and the realization that within each person is a shared thread of humanness. Mama taught me two simple lessons that have shaped my life, 1. **Never hate.** 2. **Never judge another unless you have walked in their shoes.** Such wisdom is a testament that no matter the hardship, no matter the despair, we can all learn lessons from one another if, and only if, we are open to the wisdom of a Mama.

This is Mama's story; this is my story; this is our truth.

SECTION ONE: MAMA'S LIFE

Chapter 1: Bullets Blazing Glory

"I'll kill all of you mutha fuckas."

Bullets blazed into the descending dusk sky as Old Man Dank bled from the three holes in his back. Stumbling through the broken door he rolled down the stairs and onto the dirt and gravel covered street. Stones and topsoil penetrated into his wounds as he writhed in pain. He roared out, "I'm gonna kill that bitch! I'm gonna kill that bitch. Goddammit, I'm gonna kill that fucking bitch."

Mama Ladd ran through the field with her red "do-rag" waving in the air. Running with her newborn baby Pauline, she hurdled the cotton harvest. "Oh, it's murder; it's murder. She's gonna kill everyone. Murder." The screams faded as she disappeared into the horizon. Her ragged dress fell from her thick and blackened shoulders. "Murder, I say, murder." "Police, help, murder."

As R.L. stumbled in the stones he yelled, "She's gone crazy! She's gone crazy." "Oh Lawd, my sister has gone crazy."

On the porch, Bertha yelled, "I'll kill all you mutha fuckas!," as the smoke from the gun huffed a furious storm. Hate raged from the bowels of her despair. Repressed anger lurched into the acrimonious air as tears flowed from her stoic face. "I'll kill all you mutha fuckas." And then, the gun dropped to the decaying wooden porch floor with a pristine thump.

Though that summer day preceded my biological birth by some 40 years, it set in motion a series of transformational events that redefined time in a transcendent form. Bertha Lee Green had shot her stepfather - her villain - her captor - her misery - in the back, and fate changed forevermore. The "meanest man" in the south could not abuse his way to controlling the will of his unbridled step-daughter any longer. Instead, he created a Socratic philosopher that would change the lives of all who crossed her path; indeed, those three bullets travelled through destiny and gave me life. In a most spiritual way, our two souls were melded together in perpetuity that day.

Chapter 2. Blytheville

Born the granddaughter of a slave, Mama Green was entrenched in a life of brutality. Forced into servitude, ragged and wretched, Mama was a giant. She carried the tenderness of a saint and wrote the original soundtrack to the School of Hard Knocks. Standing at a squat 5'4" and weighing in at a solid 260, Bertha Green was both intimidating and gentle. With the hands the size of Julius "Dr. J" Erving, she was a feminist in courage and strength but a mean and "take no prisoner" street fighter by experience. Raised in a climate of omnipresent violence, Bertha was forced into a life of wretchedness.

Pundits of the Southern Subculture of Violence theory have evidence showing that rates of homicide are, and have been, highest in the Deep South. The preservation of honor has been paramount to defining power and masculinity. The expression of violence was highest in counties in which levels of economic disparity between rich whites and poor blacks were the highest. Importantly, and contrary to popular opinion, patterns of homicide have been high in many rural areas, especially at the turn of the 20th century.

The South was built around an agrarian economy; competition in the south was fierce and children, especially black ones, were treated as economic assets rather than "precious youth." Jim Crow segregation was legal, strong, and derisive. Black adults were forced to step off of sidewalks for young white children and relegated to a subordinate position. African-Americans lived in fear of lynching and Ku Klux Klan assaults as more whites lived in the rural counties than blacks with a caste system built around a sharecropping economy. Bertha Green was born into this blistering climate in 1908 in Tupelo, Mississippi.

By the year 1910, before Bertha could walk, her father picked up the family and moved to Blytheville, Arkansas. Rebuilding Chicago following the destructive "Great Fire" of 1871 pushed the lumber industry in communities along the Mississippi River, such as Blytheville,

Arkansas, to grow. In combination with a stable cotton production system, the railroads expanded to transport lumber and cotton to the Northern industrial cities. The quality of the land was rich soil from centuries of an overflowing Mississippi River and drew black migrants to the area.

Blytheville had a majority comprised of whites who owned the railroads, stores, and saloons. The economy trickled upward from the black sharecroppers to the wealthy landowners; at the time, black farmers were in competition with "Mexicans" to obtain low skilled jobs. Sadly, in an amalgamation of historical precedence, locals believed that the "Mexicans" were diseased and openly hated by blacks in the area. In fact, historical records show that Spanish colonists in the pre-Louisiana Purchase era spread European disease killing off significant swaths of indigenous population. The cultural inability to see variation in the Hispanic population therefore defined all Hispanics as Mexican in the half century wake of the Mexican-American War.

Natural gas did not reach the Blytheville until 1950, making coal and firewood the heating sources for local residents. Interestingly (and sadly), the wealthy landowners, during cotton harvest time, created "athletic" competitions to see which sharecropper could pick the most cotton in a day. White businessmen gathered in a stadium type of formation and watched "the contests" as blacks picked the harvest, solidifying the strong and obvious racial divide in the region.

Downtown Blytheville was constructed around a disreputable saloon culture. Given the massive influx of immigrants, fueling a 1000% growth rate in the decade, the infrastructure could not keep up with local civil demand. Competition for jobs was cutthroat and competitive and the rowdy night life, drinking, and lewd behavior lit up the night sky. Blytheville was one of the most dangerous "cities" in Arkansas and Bertha, whose father died while she was a small child, was thrust into a violent, hierarchical, and deeply competitive rural environment. Given the small 27 square mile community, there were few secrets, no hiding, and everyone "knew each other." Blytheville's culture was steeped in poverty, socio-economic division, and violence while being built around internal economic cooperation, even if that cooperation came through coercion and corrupt political influence. The underground economic system thrived there and produced a subculture of violence and suspicion.

Bertha and her brother, R.L., were born to their father, Mr. Franklin. Bertha was told by her mother that she was born in 1908. Shortly after R.L. was born, they moved from Tupelo, MS to Blytheville. In this context, Bertha was regarded as an economic asset and not a little girl; the consequences of that choice on her life were profound.

After her father passed away, Bertha's mother, Mama Laura, sought out domestic jobs as they became available, as she was a strong, sturdy, and humorous woman which gave her access to a competitive job market. At some point, she met Will Henry Ladd - aka "Mr. Dank", a bitter and tyrannical man, and they married. He was a regarded as a hyper-masculine male who was fully entrenched in a competitive and violent subculture with a willingness to kill at the slightest provocation. Deeply embedded in the Blytheville saloon culture, Mr. Dank was a gambler, drunk, and "bastard", who ruled his household out of fear and violence.

Bertha was forced to quit school by her Mr. Dank because of her strength in cutting down trees and her victories at the annual Blytheville cotton picking contests, which earned her $.25 per bushel. Sadly, Old Man Dank stole all of Bertha's hard earned money and used it to drink and gamble, rendering her labor stolen and effectively worthless.

Mr. Dank's internalization of the conflict culture "justified" his controlling family members through violence and created a home of fear, humiliation, and abuse. Bertha, and other children like her, were trapped in an overlap of poor external economic conditions and internal family strife. In the midst of this conflict, and as World War I raged, Old Man Dank had shot and killed a white man in downtown Blytheville for whistling at his wife, forcing him to flee into the uninhabited "Blytheville Swamp" to avoid lynching, castration, or both at the hands of the local

Klansmen. Fearing for both their lives, Mr. Dank persuaded Mama Laura to move to Joiner, Arkansas (pop. 300), to avoid retaliation. Bertha's witnessing of a lynching in her youth, in combination with fear of the Klan, especially with its resurgence from 1910 until 1925, created an external wall of general distrust.

Further, by the late 1920s, the lumber industry in the region had begun to decline. Investments in real estate by landowners was growing due to easy to access bank loans when, suddenly, commodity prices began to fall. The value of cotton plummeted during the late 1920's preventing the Roaring 20's culture from fully expressing itself in the region. Instead, economic hardship reigned. The Depression had reached Arkansas years before it touched the remainder of the country. The foreclosure of property and despondence of locals created a context where an underground economic system and a culture of "ready, aim, fire" proliferated.

By 1932, the threat of lynching peaked and economic devastation roared through the region. The Great Flood of 1927 destroyed the entire area and sent agriculture into chaos, as most cities in northeast Arkansas were under water for months. President Hoover called the flood "the greatest peacetime disaster" that was felt by "Arkansas planters and residents of river lowlands and was of epic proportions." The already poor citizens of Blytheville, Leporta, and Joiner, Arkansas (places where Mama would live before moving to Toledo, Ohio) were decimated. The breakdown of community structures pushed gambling, the illegal distribution of alcohol, and a Blues music culture into the forefront. Blytheville jumped. Music within the tavern culture built for a dynamic social climate as route 61 connected Bluesy Memphis to St. Louis. For a time, Mama earned a living playing the piano with her brother in speakeasies from Memphis to Missouri.

The Great Depression, which added economic insult to injury, forced residents to live in Red Cross Tent Cities as people like Mama found work with the WPA, the Civilian Conservation Corps, and the new canning kitchens. Those who didn't migrate to Chicago and other northern cities found work under these Federal work relief programs. Mama learned her canning skills as she worked in those kitchens, picked cotton when possible, and learned to cook as a part-time employee in local hotels. Mama always maintained her own garden and grew her own food, "just in case." The government rationing cards that Mama showed me, often didn't provide enough food for family survival. In its totality, Mama Green was raised in this most tumultuous, economically depraved, and violent culture which was, sadly, all she knew; it was a place where the proverbial theory of "the strongest survive" was actually true.

Mama Green told me that she grew up in Hell.

In reflection, Mama's pain, ironically, was my salvation. Mama would survive and grow to become my guardian angel, even as she lives through me now. Her pain was a temple from which she fed the hungry and I ate ravenously and freely from that place. As I grew older she always said, **"Listen to your Mama"** and I am doing just that, right now. Her experience and placement in my life saved me from the physical aggression of a tyrant's descendant and is saving it again from the internal tyrant of anger and stolen dreams.

Chapter 3: The Temple of Pain

By the time Mama was 10 years old, her father had died and her mother had re-married "Old Man Dank." World War I was exploding abroad but imploding within their home as well. By this time, Mama Green had been forced to leave school to chop down trees for winter fire wood as she picked cotton in the summer and fall. She had always regretted losing the opportunity to attend school, with all of her higher level thinking.

Fortunately, Mama had learned how to read and write by the time she dropped out in the third grade. She attended a small country school in a one room shack that was designed for grades K-8. The kindergartners sat in the front row and the eighth graders in the back. There was one chalk board in the front of the room and each student had a tiny desk of their own. In total, 40 kids were in the class.

The teacher was a kind woman whose name is unknown. She had a quiet charm but was stern in her approach. One "peep" would land a student in the corner wearing a dunce cap; Bertha wore it once and vowed to never do so again. The humiliation burned throughout her young body. She excelled in writing and math and was regarded as a good and smart student. In the winter, she was permitted to put wood into the 'pot-belly' stove that sat in the back of the room for heat.

Mama Green lived about two miles away from the school and had to walk each day whether there was rain, sleet, or snow. She owned one or two dresses that were used for school, work, church, and for sleeping. She washed her clothes on a washboard and tore her fingers on a bi-weekly basis. She collected water for the family, tended to the animals, and worked the fields after school. Her cardboard shoes miraculously withheld the pressure. All of the kids were poor and black and had similar work and clothes issues. In Blytheville, graduating from eighth grade was an accomplishment for a chosen few; she would not be one. She loved school, but being the eldest of three forced her to earn a living instead.

Though she never talked about her biological father, she was keenly aware of the existence of her stepfather, Old Man Dank. According to legend, he was the "meanest man in the world" and refused earthly departure while lying on his death bed. It was said that he laid there for six months just to torment the family and when he died, his ghost haunted the house until they were forced to move to Leporta, Arkansas. Mr. Dank has been widely regarded by his descendants as an original gangster, known to have shot and killed two people.

One day, after gambling and drinking at a nearby saloon, Old Man Dank returned home hungry and angry. He smelled of a local distillery had lost hundreds of dollars. Mama Green's brother, R.L., was just a baby and Pauline had not yet been born. Mama Ladd was out looking for a house cleaning job as there were few good jobs available. When he arrived at home, Dank yelled, "Bertha, get in this house, I need you to cook me something to eat." Sweaty and tired from picking cotton, she perspired as a man in a factory or a worker in a sweatshop. She was ten years old and her hands were torn from the sharp husks that held the cotton fiber. "Cook me some goddamned food, you stupid ass bitch. Can't you see that I'm hungry."

At the time, Bertha had never cooked and was forced from being a child into a mother's role. She tried to make a breakfast though it was late in the day, but it turned out like a prisoner's discarded meal. She didn't use enough flour for the pancakes, added too much milk to the batter, and was clueless to the use of baking powder. The eggs ran like a stream and the oats were overcooked and hardened like a big rock. When the slimy cream colored imitation of food hit the table Old Man Dank slammed his fist down, shaking the kitchen. "Get in here, dog, and eat this shit."

When the dog came into the room, Mr. Dank put the plate on the floor beside him. The dog sniffed the "shit" and walked away. As Mama Green later told me, "I was such a bad cook when I was young that the dog wouldn't even eat it." Though she later became a famous cook, at ten years old she was, as she used to say it, *"Still shittin' yellow shit [as a baby would]."*

Enraged and drunk, Old Man Dank ripped Mama Green's Dress from her small but strong frame. He then tore off his belt and proceeded to beat her. He started by slamming her sweaty face onto the kitchen table and pounded it until she stopped squirming. Bloodied welts raised from her back and legs. After unleashing countless lashes, later he took his forearm to the back of her neck and wrapped her arms so they were immobile.

He raped her that day; thus, Mama's innocence was lost forever.

Childhood sexual assault destroys. Though Bertha Green never was a child, she was no longer a human, either. Uncertain as to what exactly happened or why she had been assaulted, the incident shred her inner light. After a period of darkness, she witnessed Dank beat her brother R.L., at which time she chose to protect her powerless brother by taking the beating meant for him and to ensure that her newborn sister would never experience such tragedy. The one time beating of her brother brought to life the strongest willed woman I have ever known. Her desire to protect the weak was stronger than her will to avoid her own brutal experience.

It is in this context that she developed her most famous saying which was, *"Never let your left hand know what your right hand is doing."* She also proclaimed that, *"Sometimes you have to stand up for the weak"* and *"If you can't stand up for yourself, why should anyone else?"* These philosophies of strength were her survival cries. They guided her through muddied waters and also launched her into violence that could have been avoided. Yet her anguish became her strength and anger, the driver of goodness. Her brutal childhood found its purpose through a love of humanity. When respected, she was a friend for life; when crossed, she bore teeth like a guard dog at Hades gate.

15

Without having a teacher at school to turn to, and a mother intermittently seeking domestic employment (requiring to live at her employer's home for periods of time), Dank's physical and sexual abuse became routine. She never told her mother; her brother only knew of the physical abuse and her sister never saw any of that trauma, only experiencing the broad-based despair associated with absolute poverty. Bertha's childhood was stolen away in that summer of war.

She did, however, build a temple out of her pain. Whenever her stepfather would abuse her, she would bury the pain and create illusions. Bertha would take out an ax and imagine Old Man Dank as the tree as she thrashed at its restorative (the wood was used as heat in the winter) power; she later said that, all she wanted to do was, *"Slap the cow-walking piss out of his mouth."* Instead, she picked cotton faster than anyone in her town to show that she had great skill and was not defeated. She also learned to cook, to prove her worthiness. Mama went to war as a child and the victory she won was self-esteem.

Even when Mr. Dank began to use foreign instruments (such as a broom handle), to engage in his felonious sexual penetration, she would clean even harder to dismiss the pain emanating from the broom's handle. She began to hit stones with broom sticks in the street, in order to exorcise the demons. During the summer she would lift bales of hay in the barn to develop muscular strength. Mama's pain became her drive; her pain became her conviction and her pain was Socrates as her philosophies on distrust, perseverance, and standing up for the weak were born. Even when she was denied food, she made overcoming hunger a pursuit of strength over defeat. She would tell me that, *"My pain is my temple and I gain strength there."*

She didn't know it then, but as she endured those horrible beatings, deliberate hunger, and significant aggression, but she was developing a recipe of strength and tolerance that impacted the world. Intelligent beyond belief, she taught herself to read with the smallest of schooling she had earned from the one room shack. She would proclaim, *"I may be a third grade dropout, but nobody can outsmart me."*

The beatings continued behind an invisible screen and Bertha became a master of wearing and constructing masks. When her mama came home, she cooked a wizardry of food, when available. Bertha was close to her mother's love but she, too, was physically and emotionally abused. Mama Ladd may have been a large, strong, and robust woman, but the seeds of abuse can render the strongest incapable during the siege of violence. In order to protect her mother, Bertha buried her own horrors.

I believe her experience as a survivor and witness of abuse is the reason why she and my mother got along so famously. Both had endured levels of abuse that movies fail to depict. Based upon their experiences, I am certain that real abuse is not sanitized; it smells; it hurts; it stings; it laments. Real abuse destroys souls and lights infernos. It rips at the soul in a darkened hour or lights a warrior's path to battle. Unfortunately, it destroys innocence and places it on unintended paths; that is where Mama learned that, "***God gives me strength.***"

Upon reflection, I've come to realize that the Temple of Pain is a sacred place that houses one's authentic being. Over time, individuals learn how to wear social masks to preserve face and to protect their presentation of self. Our lives become an ongoing struggle to preserve that which is good within our souls against the ridicule of a deeply competitive world.

In some instances, the use of physical, emotional, and sexual abuse has the power to destroy oneself. Assuming that abuse occurs in a relationship (be it friend, spouse or family), the bonds of trust are tattered and shredded by those entrusted to protect our life, freedom, and pursuit of happiness. The outcome of such transgressions builds a temple that can either become significantly isolated and lonely or a fuel for strength. The individual response cannot be positively predicted but the impact is significant nonetheless. The ongoing response of making sense of vulnerability, loss of control, and the unwarranted adversity destroys core selves; the mind goes to work in constructing a coping system in order to persevere.

In Mama Green's case, she took her pain and built a fortress. Few people would contest her ability to survive in the face of challenge. She could, *"Make a meal out of nothing"* while assuring that **"No one ever left her home hungry."** She believed that, at the end of the day, we can either be strong and stand up, or disappear. For her, she always proclaimed that one should, *"Never start a fight, but make sure you end it."*

By extension, one's strength in the face of adversity changes the world. Those who manage the potential devastation of a spoiled identity can extend their strength to others by touching upon the altar in the Temple. Lighting a candle from one's own heart can illuminate a path to salvation for those who hide behind masks themselves. When at terms with the pain, we are connected and can feed each other from a table of love. Unfortunately, the storms of despair are strong and can only be weathered by the buffer of confidence and esteem.

Therefore, given that everyone has a temple of pain, an invitation to enter into another person's Temple is the highest level of respect; it is the place where survivors break bread every day. The temple is where wisdom is used to feed the weary. As a child, when I was weak or under duress, Mama allowed me entry into **her** Temple; her love and understanding lit my path and it was Mama's resolve that paved my journey to the career of professor and a life as teacher.

Chapter 4. Riding the Bull and Other Childhood Fun

Life in Jim Crow Mississippi was shaped by the sharecropper economy. Having been born on a plantation, Mama Green's mother, Mama Ladd, had grown up picking cotton much as her grandmother did prior to Lincoln's Emancipation Proclamation. Driven by a deeply devout Christian Baptist background, Mama Ladd was a strong believer in predetermination and the acceptance that today's world was shaped by God's hand. Though she was a strong matriarch, as was common among black families in the south, she was also cognizant of the clear and precise distinction between man and women's role within the family system.

Bertha was indoctrinated into the Baptist church when she was a young child, prior to her father's death. Her belief in God was deep and strong, and she worried mightily about sin and doing what was right by God's word. Reading the Bible and singing hymns were a sure way of learning to read and share the message of the Lord. Poverty, however, had a direct impact on developing her understanding that survival was in God's plan and that adversity was manageable with patience, perseverance, and persistence. When she saw corn and beans grown in the fields, she saw life. When she observed cotton grown on the plantations, she saw textile warmth. Mama was pure in her optimism and simply believed that, **"God lives in all things."**

She often wondered why life was so hard given her mother's effort to make it better. Though she never questioned the work of God, she always maintained a survivor's edge. Given the difficult financial times in Mississippi, Mama Ladd moved to Blytheville, Arkansas to live with her emigrating extended family in order to find work. There were some jobs in agriculture and the timber industry that gave hope to many black southern families, as life in the south was hard and the economic and social barriers between white and black were clear and without ambiguity.

Life in Blytheville was challenging, and fun was self-generated. Bertha and her cousins played traditional games, such as hide and seek. They also created their own curious and dangerous contests, however.

Though Mama was working adult hours in the fields, she and her cousins found time to play. Their favorite game, though remarkably dangerous, was "Riding the Bull." She and her two male cousins had either cut or found a piece of barbed wire and used it as a rein to put in the bull's mouth. Typically, they would creep up to a bull that was grazing beside a fence, put the wire into its mouth, and hopped on for the ride. The goal was to see who could stay on the raging bull the longest. Though the bull would buck and try to throw the kids, they held on. Finally, as they fell, the goal was to run and jump over the fence.

On one occasion, she and her cousins had climbed a tree centered in the middle of the field. As they shimmied over the branch to make way to the bull, a snake came creeping across a branch overhead. When it dangled by Bertha's neck, she heard a hiss. She turned and saw the snake opening its mouth to bite her neck. Instantaneously, she fell eight or ten feet to the ground. Startled, the bull dashed into a full sprint forward, and she and the cousins went running to the fences. Once they had jumped the fence, the play of climbing a tree had ended forever. Mama never rode a bull or climbed a tree from that point on.

To her consternation, snakes were known to sneak into and under her shack as the fall gave way to the winter. In search of warmth, snakes were known to creep under beds, under the porch of the house, and into the outhouse. It was through her countless encounters of butchering snakes with knives that led her to hate the slippery creatures. Once, a snake slipped out from under her bed while she slept and Mama went into a panic scaring everyone in the house. By the time her mother had arrived in the room the snake had been carved to pieces. It was so bad that Mama was unable to watch a snake that even appeared on television and her fear became an obsession.

Eventually, their sense of fun shifted from the danger of bull riding to playing the parachute game. Essentially, she and her cousins would climb on top of her house and jump to the ground beneath. Bertha wanted to see their dress open as a parachute. Remarkably, neither she nor her cousins ever got hurt from the "Danger Games." They did learn, though, that *"God watches over all fools."*

In reflection, fun and fear are constructed within a local context. For Mama, the "Danger Games" were actually "toughening games" reinforcing and validating bravery, courage, and strength. Even amidst her deeply devoted work life, she and her cousins were seduced into danger. It was in the games that children learned to cope with their surroundings and adapt to adversity. I can only imagine that riding a bull or jumping off of a house shaped a level of bravery and courage to deal with the ongoing squalor of everyday life. More than anything, Mama Green learned to take scraps and transform them into a usable form. Bertha was indeed, clever, creative, and courageous.

Chapter 5. Growing up in Tornado Alley

Poor black children in the south were relegated to one room school houses, playing in farming lands, and riding bulls for fun. Rolling tumbleweeds were common in Blytheville and Joiner, Arkansas. Dry and arid summers killed the grass as the western winds commonly blew balls of hay through the barren lands.

Wretched poverty and limited factory work caused economic struggles. Most of the young children and able-bodied men picked cotton in the fields. Mama did so earning $.25 a bushel. Even at her young age she was able to pick 2-3 bushels per day. Never mind the pain of the pods cutting her hands, daily, to the point of bleeding. The money earned was needed to guarantee that food made it on the table.

Though economic strife was widespread, she loved school. According to her, the one room school house sat several miles away from her home. And though it is cliché, she wore, when times were hard, shoes made of cardboard. Though she was not alone, owning only one dress and wearing such shoes always struck her as a travesty. She vowed, even at a young age, that if she ever had kids *"they would never attend a country school; I would drive to Memphis if I had to."*

The school had one pot belly stove in the center for heat in the winter and little else. The chalkboard on the wall was meager but was used by grades K-8. Most of the kids were, as she noted, frazzled. The shortage of money was evident in most households though the dreams of a better life persisted. Mama loved math so that she could count money. Her mantra was that one should, *"**Always know how to count your money so you don't end up like Joe Louis.**"* Though she could do math by long hand Mama always thought it was more powerful to count in the head. So, in math class, which was taught by one teacher for 8 different grades, she excelled. She was a brilliant woman. Mama never used paper and pencil preferring to do problems in her head instead.

Once while in the second row (second grade) she refused to write out her work. The teacher, "Mrs. Go Sit in the Corner," forced her to sit in the corner for not following the rules after a swift rap to the knuckles with a ruler. Young Bertha refused to go to the corner as she had gotten the answer right. "Wham," she was whacked again. After the third time, she begrudgingly went to the corner where she spent the entire day without permission to eat lunch or play at recess.

When she arrived home and told her mother what had happened, Mama Ladd responded with a reply of sympathy. Her stepfather, Old Man Dank, exploded. "Dammit, Bertha, you are a hard-headed son of a bitch." Then, before she could reply, his belt was ripped through its loops that securely held the weapon of psychological destruction close to his waist. With a powerful swat across her exposed buttocks, he ordered her to do the math right or stay home and work. Unable to properly sit in her desk at school the next day, her teacher thought she had to urinate.

"No ma'am, I do not have to urinate."

The teacher replied with, "Then why are you twitching around so much? Are you disrespecting me?"

"No ma'am," she responded.

The teacher, using a humiliation tactic, ordered Bertha to the board to write out the math problem. "Get up there and do your problem, Bertha." Having walked two miles in her makeshift shoes magnified the pain from her previous day's beating. Thinking Bertha was continuing to be defiant, the teacher pulled Bertha up by her dress and tore the weakened and frayed fabric. Though it was not destroyed and hung together humbly, it was noticeable. After spending the remainder of the school day in the corner, Mama went home.

That fall day changed Bertha's life forever. Half way into the fall of the third grade, Mr. Dank beat her mercilessly for embarrassing him at the school. After beating Bertha to the point where she needed hospitalization (though he refused to get her medical help), he forced her to stay home and drop out of school. Bertha would never return to the little schoolhouse again.

And so it was, Mama spent the winter of 1916-1917 chopping down trees in the nearby woods, breaking them down for fire wood, and was charged with keeping the family warm. When I would ask, "Mama, why are your hands so big?" She would always reply, "Because I had to chop down trees and chop wood to make a fire to keep my family warm." She sold the excess wood so that the family had enough money to eat.

Mr. Dank was a saloon keeper and known as a drunk. He oversaw the gambling operations in the back of the saloon where the nightly poker table was located. When he wasn't working, he was gambling and drinking. Wildly popular at the local tavern, he was a brutal dictator at home. Ms. Ladd was a kind, gentle, and strong soul who loved her children. After her first husband Mr. Franklin left, she met William "Dank" Ladd. Mama Green had no memories of her birth father and didn't even know his name. When she tried to find it, the birth certificate records had been burned in a fire at the Jackson, MS, courthouse where vital statistics were stored. Her knowledge of her father, as well as her official birth date, were gone. Her mother had always said she was born on October 20, 1908 but the "official record," which was destroyed, said 1910. Mama always believed her mother.

Publicly, Mr. Dank was an affable man, but in private he was a tormentor. Because Bertha was the eldest, she bore the brunt of his anger. Little is known of his background other than his father was an alcoholic and a strong arm disciplinarian. Regardless, his anger was directed at and absorbed by Bertha, who over time, developed a disposition of independence at any cost, control of self, and distrust of others. After being beaten, molested, and forced into childhood labor by her brutal disciplinarian, she developed the mantra that, *"If you can't stand up for yourself, no one else will."*

Her mother had taught Bertha the same lessons that were passed on to me. For them, severe weather was a constant threat. In one incident, circa 1919, the family had been caught off guard while eating supper. Mama had looked out the window and yelled, "The clouds are rolling. Run!"

As they fled the kitchen and ran out the door, a massive F-4 tornado was bearing down. As they ran to the storm shelter located some 50 yards away from the shack, wooden projectiles from the nearby woods became deadly. Mama Ladd pulled open the cellar door and rather than climbing down the stairs into the cramped 8'x8' box, everyone jumped. Mama was the last to go and as she jumped into the cellar, the steam engine winds passed overhead, shearing the doors off its hinges. As she looked up through the now missing door, she saw the cyclone pass overhead while ducking as if enemy fighters were bombing their bunker.

That event shaped her respect of the weather and strengthened her belief in God. It was her belief that she, her brother, and mother were spared death that day because of His plan. She confided in me after one particular storm in Toledo, that her life was spared in 1919 because it was in God's will that she survived to share her love with me and protect my life.

In general, though, her weather stories made me laugh. Once, as a storm was approaching, she told me of the time when it rained fish while they lived in Arkansas. She had proclaimed that the storm was so strong that fish fell from the sky. Being a child I said, "And did it rain cats and dogs, too?"

She laughed, thinking that my little five-year-old joke was clever. She replied with, "Baby, I would never lie to you. It rained fish."

I simply said, "Okay, Mama."

Over time she taught me about the tumbleweeds and how those showed that the weather was so dry it caused drought conditions. On another occasion, she had discussed how every once in a while she and her brother, R.L., saw balls of lightning roll down the street. Her belief was that God made the trees, the grass, and the weather and we, as humans, were finite before God's infinite power. She'd say, *"Tomorrow is never promised to anyone."*

Once, while attending Ohio State University as a graduate student, I saw a documentary on strange but real weather phenomenon that included rolling balls of lightning and fish falling from the sky. Though I cannot remember the exact physics behind the phenomenon, I did understand that powerful updrafts from waterspouts and storms over the Gulf of Mexico had the ability to transport fish into the cold upper clouds. It wasn't until warmer updrafts thawed the air, or the fish became too heavy to maintain their buoyancy, that they fell back to Earth.

After watching the documentary, I thought, "I'll be damned, Mama was telling the truth all along." When I called her on the phone and told her of the story, and she replied, "I have never lied to you."

Upon reflection, the documentary confirmed that Mama had, in fact, always been truthful; that knowledge saddened me. All of the bizarre stories that I learned from Mama Green, such as the one room school houses in Arkansas, riding bulls, jumping from houses, boxing, and physical and sexual abuse were all true. Her life had become redefined for me from a story of love and sacrifice to one that was spiritual and inspiring. The viciousness of Mama Green's childhood with her stepfather, amid segregation and racism, fueled her quest of tolerance for the weak and alienated. I was saddened that she had experienced such pain in her youth but thankful that Mama had learned how to use it for good and persevere through adversity.

Though I was always aware of her impact on my life, it became clear to me that our connection was far more spiritual. Her stories were riveting; her humor was enervating; her ability to transcend adversity was inspiring; her compassion for others, humbling. Mama Green and her various and sundry experiences were my greatest teacher, and

26

ironically, prepared me for life in a private school better than any formal education could. She was a living well of truth and wisdom. In time, Mama became my moral compass that has guided my major life decisions well into adulthood. Mama taught me to harness love, how to read people, and to respond to emotional turmoil with compassion.

Chapter 6. Hay Stacks, Knives, and George Washington

As a baby, I wasn't blessed with sleeping in a crib. Mama and Daddy Green emptied a dresser drawer for me and put a blanket in it for warmth. I suppose that is why I like to sleep on floors, in cramped spaces, and closets. For me, sleeping has always been a unique experience.

Mama Green and Daddy Green's bedroom was a place of safety for me. The walls were barren except for a calendar with the picture of Dr. Martin Luther King. It hadn't been turned since 1963 and stayed on November until 1979 when Mama finally moved to 1234 Girard Street, a few years after Daddy had passed away.

The room was simple. There were no paintings on the wall and the white paint had long turned gray from the fierce coal furnace air. The curtains were drab and there were two windows. Given the isolation of the house within a ghetto-like area, they served as lookout posts during break-in attempts. For years, Mama trained me to walk me around the house in the dark and how to peek outside without moving the curtains, and to keep the lights off so people could not see in. I was taught how to roll off the bed, at a moment's notice, with the phone in order to dial 0 for the police. The green carpet was old and worn to the point of being little more than flooring itself and smelled foul when my body would come crashing onto its surface.

Before I could walk, Mama had a stuffed black cat named "Boo Boo Kitty" and a toy leopard that I played with constantly. I loved those cats and would pet them as though they were real, though it mystified me when Boo Boo Kitty's eye popped out. There was nothing more enjoyable during those days than to mountain climb on Mama Green and Erma Jean's (Mama Green's daughter) stomachs. For a baby, those mounds were a source of adventure. Erma Jean always laughed at how much my hard shoes would hurt as I tried to crawl over her.

Because I was always so curious about exploring and not really interested in sleep, Mama was permitted to put one drop of beer into my formula at bedtime. She was taught as a child that it was healthy and an effective way to calm restless babies. Mama was not a major proponent of modern medicine and much preferred to use "horse liniment" on her ailing muscles; she used castor oil or gargled with warm salt water for a sore throat; and, when someone had a cold she mixed honey, whiskey, and lemon together to produce a powerful elixir. After gagging on its nasty taste, I always felt better.

Mama was the local dentist as well. She had a magic way of pulling loose teeth without causing pain. She would wiggle it ever so slightly, give a deceptive cough, and yank, out came the tooth. Back in those days, the tooth fairy tended to leave a dime or a quarter.

Having grown up during the Great Depression, Mama Green became a money savant. Her ability to generate income was magical. And, when she earned it, she kept it. Mama used to always tell me, *"Baby, save all of your pennies because they will add up to dollars."* Although most people would walk by a penny laying on the ground, she would say, *"Pick up your pennies because you didn't have them when you woke up this morning."*

When she was a little girl, Old Man Dank was renowned for gambling, drinking, and losing money. He would come home, beat Mama or worse, and go to bed. In addition, he would deny the kids food. Bertha and R.L., especially, often went hungry. As she aged, she made it her mantra to **"N***ever let a person leave your home hungry."* She fed everyone. On some occasions, Old Man Dank would come home a gambling winner, but he was too drunk to know how much he had won or lost. So, at night, Mama would sneak into his bedroom and rummage through his pockets and take money.

Once she found $800, a significant amount of money in the 1920s. Bertha stole the money and hid it in genius places. She would take the knob off of her bed post and store some of the money in the frame. Some of the money was hidden in piles of hay in the barn; even though she feared snakes, it was not enough to prevent her from crawling under the porch to hide money behind a board in the foundation of the house. At the end of the day, she took enough money to buy Mama Laura, R.L., and Pauline clothes from Mr. Anonymous, a local white grocery store owner. She hid cheese and crackers in the hay of the barn and would crawl into the chicken coops to steal eggs.

Uncle R.L. had learned in school that "George Washington had never told a lie." So, on one occasion when Mama had told him how she purchased the food to feed the hungry duo, R.L. decided to tattle and tell Mr. Dank. Old Man Dank tried to kill Bertha, but she was strong enough by the age of 12 or 13 to fight back. She lost the fight, but got away as she fled the shack and ran through the cotton fields. Soon, thereafter Old Man Dank began to bare knuckle box with Mama instead of beating her.

In time, she had developed the strength of a man and Dank became more brutal. To get back at Bertha, he began to beat Mama's mother, Mama Ladd. It was intolerable. Over time, he had become so mean that Bertha, tired of the sexual assault and physical abuse, was straddling the edge of sanity. By then, she had no school friends to turn to; cousins were instructed to stay away from the "meanest man in the world", and Mama Ladd tried to buffer as best she could, but Bertha had become an island standing at the eye of the hurricane's rage.

Mama Green would not relent. In her teens she began stretching daily to develop her flexibility. The ax and the hoe were used to develop strength. Soon, her arms grew to the size of a grown man's. Dank was still capable of beating her but the fighting and boxing became more competitive. Eventually, Mama began to learn where to punch and, essentially, trained herself as a bare knuckle boxer. One fight, around the age of 15, in 1923, ended with Dank on the ground and Bertha stomping him. It was here that she implemented her belief to, "*Never wrestle a man when they are down, they may have a knife. Stomp them.*" Mama Ladd begged Bertha to stop. With tears flowing like the nearby mighty Mississippi, she pulled away.

Soon thereafter, when Bertha and R.L. returned home, Old Man Dank was brandishing a switch blade while he was sharpening a straight razor. He said simply, "We're not going to have any more problems, are we Bertha?"

"No sir." She rarely ever spoke to Old Man Dank again.

Later that summer, R.L. again threatened to tell Mr. Dank that Bertha had stolen money to feed them. He said to Bertha, "I have to tell Mr. Dank since, like George Washington, I cannot tell a lie." Mama whipped around and said, *"Dammit, R.L.,* **you don't know your ass from a hole in the ground.** You don't have any common sense. If you tattle on me, I am going to **feed you some of this big African soup bone."** Having witnessed Bertha and Old Man Dank box in the house, and not wanting her "soup bone" fist on to his face, R.L. relented. "OK, Bertha, I won't tell on you. But I want to." And that was the last time R.L. and Bertha ever had an issue with R. L. telling Old Man Dank anything. He was hungry and had to eat.

Most notably, once R.L.'s sentiment shifted, the nature of the domestic civil war changed as well. Survival was now the children's battle cry.

Chapter 7. Mr. Anonymous and his Six Friends

The owner of the nearest country store (referred to as Mr. Anonymous), had a long time crush on Bertha. A white man of privilege (who, Bertha said, had a house that with a push of a button, could elevate and rotate) whose name I have never known, saw the light inside her spirit. He was well aware of the misery that she endured in her small ramshackle home some miles away. After all, he was the man who sold Bertha survival disguised as cheese, bread, and crackers.

After noting that Bertha was the real provider for her brother, Mr. Anonymous began to inquire into her life. Though she insisted that her purchases were to feed R.L. and herself, and that she quit school to earn a living, Mr. Anonymous eventually learned of Bertha's physical abuse and emotional torment. Armed with the knowledge that she was a top producing cotton picker in the region, Mr. Anonymous saw the star of goodness shine from her massive hands. At the taverns, he saw Old Man Dank act out of his scurrilous nature.

One robust spring morning, Mr. Anonymous called Bertha into his store office. He declared that he was aware of Mr. Dank's abusive manner and could not sit back and witness the dimming possibility of her future. Though she could not figure out how he knew of the abuse at the time, as she always lived by the adage, *"Keep your tongue"* and *"A still tongue makes for a wise head,"* she later learned that Old Man Dank bragged of his domestic means of control; Bertha confirmed the truth of Dank's boasting to Mr. Anonymous.

In his numerous drunken excursions, Old Man Dank proudly professed that Bertha had to be forcefully controlled as she was too "wild." He extolled the idea that she was worthless and was little better than the hogs in the pen. Mr. Anonymous had long noted that it was Bertha who was feeding the kids and it was apparent that there was a disparity between the two stories. I suppose that given the racial divide in the Deep South during that era and the economic devastation from the failing lumber and cotton industries and post-flood strife, having a rich old white man noticing her good qualities gave Bertha a unique perspective on guardian angels. She would always tell me, *"Never turn your back on anyone, not even a bum; they may be your guardian angel."* She always had a deep respect for Mr. Anonymous.

As a child, she was convinced that Mr. Dank would find out her life-saving secrets, thievery, and hidden booty. She was convinced that she could, *"Never let her right hand know what her left hand was doing,"* otherwise, she was certain that she would die at the hands of her mother's husband. One morning, after the great flood had receded, Mr. Anonymous handed Bertha a gun loaded with six bullets. Given Dank's reputation and disdain for Bertha, he knew that her death was imminent. "Bertha," he said, "If you are ever in a fight for your life, use this to shoot Old Man Dank."

Soon, she would find that Mr. Anonymous' words would ring true. It was life or death and no one else could do it for her. She learned from Mr. Anonymous that, *"If you can't stand up for yourself, why should anyone else?"* It wasn't long before the gun's protection would fire its seething revenge.

Chapter 8. The Chicken and the Pie Crust

Ever since I was young, I loved Mama's apple pies, her sweet potato pies, and her "goopy" and legendary peach cobbler. Her mastery of culinary arts came with age and the threat of abuse from the hand of a ruthless dictator. Working as a cook in local hotels and restaurants allowed her to learn the finer details of southern cooking.

One scorching hot day in July or August, 1928, Dank had set off for work. Pauline, R.L., and Mama Ladd were in the front room just off from the porch as Mama was "whipping up" her fried chicken masterpiece. She typically would put her salt, pepper, and other secret spices on the chicken to baste hours before actually frying. She always said that it was important to let the seasoning get into the meat of the food; *"Never be afraid of your spices"* she'd say, and she was right as her food was of world class quality.

As her chicken marinated, Mama would take her flour and make pie crusts. She had a piece of plastic that she would unroll and put a covering of flour on it to prevent sticking. Then she would spread the crust out using a whisky bottle that doubled as a rolling pin. True to form, her crust was always flaky, light, airy, and perfectly tender to the bite.

On this particular day, despite the always imminent threat from Dank, she was at peace with her mother and siblings. As she was rolling her crust, a chicken flew in through the window, landed on the crust and started walking and pecking at it. Angered by the fowl's poor choice of landing locations, she grabbed it by the leg and flung it out the window and onto the dirt road. The sudden and unexpected toss broke the chicken's leg, and as it hobbled in a circle in the dirt road in front of the house, it clucked loudly from its unanticipated agony.

Dank soon came home and walked into the kitchen with an angry glare.

"Bertha, do you know what happened to that chicken's leg?" he said.

Bertha ignored him while rolling a new pie crust.

"Bertha, do you know what happened to that chicken's leg," he said more aggressively.

She replied with a simple, "I don't know what you're talking about."

"Bertha, I know you broke that chicken's leg, didn't you, you fucking bitch," he angrily retorted as he walked closer.

Bertha, out of years of anger and with little care or concern about the chicken, turned and responded with a forceful, "Mother fucker, if you say I broke the chicken's leg, then I broke the fucking chicken's leg."

With the speed of a gazelle, Dank pulled out his straight blade razor and flipped it open with a furious speed. "I'm gonna beat your ass once and for all, you little heathen."

Just as he struck at Bertha with his razor, she grabbed a "cane bottom chair" and swung it across the top of his head. The dried chair shattered into a thousand pieces, covering the kitchen floor. Bertha ran to her bedroom to grab her gun as Dank's razor blade slid across the floor, knocked loose by Bertha's mighty blow. Dank tried to grab her by the ankle but missed. As he stumbled to his feet, and the others stared at the raucous in terror, Bertha dove into the bedroom and reached into the mattress of her bed. Her six bullet defense provided by Mr. Anonymous was in hand.

When Dank said, "I'm gonna kill you, you little fucking bitch," she pulled the trigger to freedom. Missing on the first shot, Dank turned and ran toward the front door, yelling, "The bitch has gone crazy." As Bertha ran after him, Mama Ladd had already sprinted out the door with Pauline as R.L. jumped from the porch. Bertha fired three more shots into Dank's back. The first hit his upper right shoulder and the other two in his back. He fell awkwardly out of the front door as Mama Ladd ran straight through the field; R.L. took off down the road.

Mama Green unloaded the last two bullets into the air while she raised her hands to the Lord for forgiveness as she ranted, "I'll kill all you mutha fuckas." She cried one stoic tear, stood as a marble statue of strength, and changed the course of her destiny.

Bertha stood that day at the intersection of a turning point and a crossroad. She was no longer the abused victim in a home of despair. She had faced the hand of Satan himself and struck him down, mightily. The demons of abuse and despair emitted from her body; she was born again and God, in His Almighty ability, renewed her life. Bertha would never again be physically, sexually, or emotionally abused. The meanest man in the world was neutered and Bertha never traveled without a gun or a knife again.

As dusk set on Joiner, and Old Man Dank crawled in the scathing dirt, a black car pulled up to whisk Bertha away. Mr. Anonymous had heard of the shooting, closed his store, and came to rescue Mama that day. In hindsight, when he picked up Mama from her dungeon of a shack, he unknowingly saved my life that day as well. His choice to save a battered girl paved the philosophical path to my own salvation. Paying it forward, I have learned, has a cumulative effect on history.

In the most philosophical and endearing of terms, I was born that day. The gift of Mr. Anonymous' bullet filled gift to Bertha released the serpents that blocked my spirit's entry into this world. As Mr. Dank laid in a puddle of blood, the universe redefined the direction of the world. Mama's experience that day, her rebirth, was the day that changed my life; I would not have been born without those three shots; I would have remained a spirit, unborn, seeking entry into the world.

Mama's story of pain had a purpose. Her pain shaped her philosophy; her mind provided wisdom, her strength bore illumination to a darkened life. I write today because her pain and experience occurred just as they did; without accident or mistake. Her life blazed the way for my existence and I teach now, today, from a sacred place that my students can only start to know and utilize in their lives. The sacrifice of a chicken's life has meaning beyond my comprehension, beyond my proclamation that life is good and that pain is necessary. I know that with *"The purity of purpose, one can find peace."*

Chapter 9. Bladey Mae and the Six Corner Brawl

In Bertha's childhood days, alcohol was normal fare as Prohibition did little to stop its flow.

Mama Green was a regular at taverns from Memphis to Saint Louis along the Route 61 corridor. In her early 20s, she and her friends would drive over the Mississippi River and go into the "coloreds only" taverns. She and R.L. had long been known as party generating musicians. In response to the need for money after the Great Flood of 1927, she and her brother R. L. regularly played duets together at local bars and taverns during the Blues' rise to prominence. Amazingly, both played the piano by ear.

In the movie Ray, starring Jamie Foxx, it was shown that a local tavern owner had showed Ray Charles how to play the piano. Bertha and R.L. were similarly trained. After years of a detached, though still abusive relationship with Mr. Dank, the ongoing poverty forced them to adapt to hostile conditions. Bertha's favorite response was playing Boogie Woogie beats in Memphis clubs and speakeasies.

The era of the Harlem Renaissance had made its way to Memphis and surrounding small towns. The crowds were rowdy, intoxicated, and danced tirelessly and effortlessly. Money flowed.

Evidently, Bertha was a crowd favorite. Her gift of story and joke-telling were only matched by her piano mastery. Even though she liked to sing in the local Baptist church choir, the night life had great appeal. She actually reveled in the jubilation of the club atmosphere. Because of her size, Bertha had a high tolerance for alcohol. Always stone faced from the years of abuse, behind the mask rested a comedian. She could get a crowd laughing like few others. Her stories of barbed wire bull-riding, the parachute dress, and the chickens walking on a pie crust stories were favorites. Her use of profanity was oddly accepted as normal parlance and added a Redd Foxx appeal to her delivery. Erma Jean often compared Bertha to the 1960's comedy sensation Mom's

Mabley, for her raw style of humor.

Bertha loved to dress well for the exciting night life. She wore stylish hats with beautiful dresses as her piano earnings allowed her to expand her wardrobe, which symbolized her feeling of triumph. In spite of her emerging sense of style, she never left home without a gun or switch blade knife.

On one occasion, she and her boyfriend at the time, Freddie Bennett, a Negro League baseball star, arrived at a "white's only" club. After Freddie, Bertha, R.L. and his girlfriend entered through the "'colored" door in the back, Bertha and R. L. approached the bar to purchase drinks. As they neared the liquid dispensary, some upscale white women took it upon themselves to enforce Jim Crow by saying, "Look at this high society [sic] nigger. She's dressed like a country nigger-bitch."

Without hesitation, Bertha spun and said, "I guess you must be interested in a visit to the hospital tonight, mutha fucka. Come on over here and get some of this nigga- bitch, bitch."

Just then (and as she had told me repeatedly when you're going to fight more than one person), *she threw her back into a corner,* and snapped out her knife, Bladey-Mae. Bertha was fond of nicknaming cars and weapons. As the story goes, after she threw herself into the corner every woman and man who made a run at her were met with an, "Eat this blade, bitch." After an explosive and violent fight, Mama claimed that, "Six people went to the hospital and I wasn't one of them." Blood was smeared everywhere and there were six men and women laying in sanguine puddles. Mama only had one scratch on her left leg. By the time the authorities had arrived, Bertha and the entourage had already slipped out the back door and made their way back to Joiner.

In time, Bertha had earned quite the reputation as a fighter. In the rural bars in Eastern Arkansas, there was cock-fighting and bare knuckle boxing. In time, Bertha was earning income from the bare-knuckle fights, too. Until her death in 1993, there was not a more avid boxing fan in the South. Bertha loved Joe Louis and often used him as an example to study hard and succeed in school. Every Saturday, when we would count our coins and wrap them, she would say, "*Learn how to count because you don't want to be fooled out of your money like poor Joe Louis.*" It was in this lesson and our weekly counting sessions that I became comfortable with math.

Because she lived through the Great Depression, Mama Green she would never let me spend coins. She would say, "*If you have at least one penny you are never broke.*" So we counted pennies, saved them religiously, and as a result, I was known by my friends for accumulating money. My favorite part of counting the money was looking at the old coins like the Mercury Head Dimes, Buffalo Nickels, Silver Dollars, Half Dollars, and the wheat pennies. Just for fun, she taught me that two bits equaled a quarter, four bits was a half dollar, three bits was $.75, and eight bit's was a dollar. "*See, if you keep adding small amounts together they become big amounts,*" she'd say. Her 1882 silver dollar, the birth year of Mama Ladd, was saved as a memory of her love for her mother.

In any case, when we watched the famous Muhammad Ali vs. Joe Frazier fight, "Rumble in the Jungle", and did so while counting coins and Mama Green cursing Joe Frazier like he as a villain in an old western. I would never laugh so hard as when she would talk to the television and say, "Oohhhhhh, that mutha fucka is hitting below the belt. Can't you see that ref. The Mutha fucka is hitting that poor man below the belt." She loved Muhammad Ali and always said to me, his real name is "Cassius Clay." Interestingly, it was during sporting events that she taught me the history of Civil Rights and issues of race. And, in Ali's case, she would say, "They treated him so bad that he threw his Olympic Gold Medal into the Ohio River."

But, I lived for the moment when she would invariably say, "Shawnee, go get me a brick, I'm going to knock a mutha fucka out." I still don't know if she believed the people were real in the television or if she just liked to make me laugh, but she did it every time we watched boxing,

Big Time Wrestling, or the Roller Derby.

During the breaks in between rounds I would routinely hear her color commentary. Typically, she would break down the fight and talk about boxing technique. "Watch baby, every time he lowers his hand, Ali punches him in the face." *"Never drop your guard in a fight."* She proclaimed that she hated Ali's "Rope-a-Dope," though. She would yell at the TV, "Oh, c'mon man, you just letting him punch you. Soon, it would typically follow with an "oh, these mutha fuckas are just dancing. Hit him, man, hit him."

Usually, during a commercial break, I would ask Mama, intentionally, how she knew so much about boxing. She said, "I used to box for money in the bars down south."

I am not sure of the number of fights Mama Green had in the bars and boxing rings, but her brother attested that she was a legend. There was a period of time where any time she entered into a bar or tavern, some male would "throw money onto the table and ask if anyone thought they could knock out Bertha." According to R.L., his wife Ruth, and her younger sister Pauline, she never lost. From what I recall, "Many a bastard tried, and many a bastard failed to beat me." Mama Green was tough and she thrived as a fighter.

There were countless times when she gave me fighting lessons. First, she would show me how to make a fist. Then, second, I was instructed where and how to punch. She would say, *"If you punch him right here (under the jaw line just under the ear), he's got to go down."* Then she would get in her boxing stance and show me how to make a short deliberate jab, as a roundhouse, in her opinion, took too long to connect, and hit through the target. Her second favorite target was an upper cut to the diaphragm, followed be a punch in the "private parts."

During the televised fights, she would typically either chew an entire bag of Red Pouch Chewing Tobacco or a box of snuff. She and her spit cup were intimate friends during such sporting events. In addition, her

41

gun, Black Beauty, was always by her side. I was not allowed to hold the gun but I was trained for battle, if needed.

In reflection, Mama was not afraid of fighting, violence, or standing up in real life. However, outside the boxing ring, her motto was simple: *"Never start a fight, but make sure you end it."* Ironically, this message was the basis of my courage to face any challenge or adversity, once confronted. Long ago, I began to use this idea when confronting obstacles; I persisted so as to avoid defeat. In time, when I had learned that I had a *"silver tongue,"* and used communication to fight and hustle to persevere. I was tiny in comparison to Mama, and wielded virtually no muscle mass, was the shortest at school, The Park, and with my athletic teams, but I was never deterred. I fought until the game was over; I withstood and persevered against any and all challenges. I was a mental fighter. I refused to lose at anything; the desire to win always drove me.

A Letter to Mama

Dear Mama,

I know that your young life was met with challenge and pain but it was not in vain. Though you shared your stories comically, I am aware that they hurt and I wish that you did not have to endure such hardship. I promise, however, that your experiences were not wasted.

I wish that I could have changed the violence that you experienced, as it hurts me knowing that you had to endure such torment. Your life, however, gave me a chance to shine and clearly shaped me in ways that are difficult to explain and fully understand. I do miss your stories but, wow, you continue to be my pillar of wisdom and the source of my undying strength. I would do anything to have one more meal with you and to hear your voice.

Fortunately, your experience made life on the Hill colorful and taught me the value of tolerance. Though I can only imagine your excitement and trepidation when you and Daddy rode the train from Memphis to Toledo, I am so happy that you did. The courage and love that you two shared is inspirational and, in the most spiritual sense, my life's saving Grace.

Mama, thank you for absorbing the pain and venom that allowed me to learn about life from inside your Temple of Pain. It has shaped me and given me a gift of courage. I have faced, and continue to face many obstacles, but I continue to hear your voice whispering in my ear. The south may have treated you poorly but it gave me a chance to live, and I can say little more than thank you.

I love you, Mama.

Your "little white boy,"

Shawn

SECTION TWO: LIFE ON "THE HILL"

Chapter 10.   Angels Lifting Angels

Mama Green worked with my mother to teach her the value of endearment. The core struggle for my mom was that she was never taught how to care. Caring for others was alien in the Schwaner home. Mama Green, however, believed in hugging and kissing. No one was allowed to leave the home without a hearty hug and a kiss on the cheek. Mama's soft, hard, and round stomach was a mound of tenderness.

When I was young and playing in the storage cupboard making flour fireworks and hiding in my secret place, the loud clang of pots and pans disturbed the kitchen's quiet. When my mom or Erma Jean tried to explode at my disobedience, Mama always said, "Let the boy play. He's exploring." After everyone else had left, Mama worked to build my esteem by saying, *"Baby, you have a million dollar personality, never let anyone tell you different. You will go far someday."* My feeble long-term imagination never realized how much of a saving grace those words would be. The future struggles and mountains of adversity and challenge, could never undermine Mama's sagacity. It was those subtle moments of wisdom that saved my life. My internal battle fluctuated between the polarity of being confident in my abilities against the specter of fraud, self-love against self-loathing, and worthiness against deserved punishment. Without the daily affirmations of love and justice I would have long lost the battle of drive and determination. Mama's kitchen was more than a nourishment center, sports arena, or a bingo hall, it was the Temple of Hope offsetting the internal self-talk within my own Temple of Pain. Hate was not permitted there and my temple was purified daily. The kitchen was the bastion of possibility, creativity, and expression.

My spiritual self was born there, though my body was born at St.

44

Vincent's hospital. Prior to my birth, on a cold spring day, the coal warmed house absorbed my mother's burning tears. My mom was standing in her typical position on the heating vent between the sink and dishwasher making a life decision. Poor, pregnant, alone, and living in a foreign city, she trembled. Erma Jean consoled her on the best options for her unwanted child.

She and Erma Jean debated abortion against adoption. My mother desperately wanted to keep her "baby" but battled the demons of her childhood abuse, poverty, a new career, and profound issues of abandonment. Though the monumental Roe V. Wade Supreme Court decision was still a few years in the future, their medical connections to doctors at Maumee Valley Hospital made for a legitimate illegitimate option.

Then, up from the basement dungeon, came Bertha. She looked at Erma with a perplexed glare of loving contempt. As the story goes, the conversation began with:

"What's wrong with her?" as Mama pointed her index finger at my sobbing mother.

"She's pregnant, Mama, and doesn't know what to do with her baby. She can't decide between having an abortion or adopting the baby out. She's scared and alone and has no money," Erma proclaimed.

At that time, my mother had moved from the motel where she had "allegedly" created me with my musical savant father and was residing in the storage room of a pizza parlor across the street from Maumee Valley Hospital. Her mother, my grandmother, was under siege from a prescription pill addiction wrapped with the gentle caress of alcoholism; my grandfather was fighting for the union and had a Supreme Court case being considered in the nation's capital. Mom's extended family had long, though not completely, isolated "little Susie" from their existence. Erma Jean was her best friend and "sister."

With the thought of abortion or adoption, Mama walked over to "Susie," hugged her, and graced her forehead with a kiss of tenderness. Mama stood beside my mother and told the story that gave me life. In Mama's words, she simply said:

"Susie, if a female dog has a litter of puppies with no place to live, she will go find a home for she and her puppies. Once she finds that place, she will return and pick up each puppy by the scruff of their neck, one by one, and carry them to safety until all of the puppies are safe at home. Susie," she said, "If you turn your back on that baby, you will be lower than a dog." My mother exploded with a waterfall of tears that Mama followed with:

"Susie, I will raise your baby. You won't need to pay me. All you need to know is that we love you."

My mother fell onto Mama's extended arms and cried the tears of someone who had never been loved, until that moment. "Susie," Mama said, "Leo and I will help you get an apartment, get your electricity turned on, and give you food." And with that proclamation, I live.

I have often considered that story and it has provided me with the deepest background of tolerance, understanding, and love. I know that Mama always told me that story so I could understand the idea of unconditional love; extending one's home to those in need, and to ***"never let anyone leave your home hungry."*** My mother arrived hungry but left full. I exist because Mama opened the doors to her Temple of Pain to a woman drowning in her own. My existence, career, and ability to reach students was shaped by one serendipitous moment in a shack on a hill.

I understand why Sir Isaac Newton said:

"I have seen further because I have stood on the shoulders of giants."

It is because Mama lifted me onto her giant shoulders that I was able to peer at an untamed and unique world. Her courage and bravery to extend her hand, in that beat up kitchen, breathed life into two souls that day. Funny how Mama Green, a cook at Waite High School, was actually a Socratic Sage of hope and goodness.

In reflection, Mama opened the doors to her "Temple of Pain" so my mother's "caged bird could sing." Life, I surmise, is composed of mythical moments that define fate. I exist, simply, because of love.

Chapter 11. A Mother's Love

Mama's kitchen was a mecca.

From the moment I could walk and support myself, I looked out the front kitchen window at 3:30 PM, every day. Sometimes I would stay for an hour or two waiting for my mom to drive by. With age, I would count the number of cars that would pass before my mother would passed on her way home from work – soon, I categorized the cars by color and type. Each day she took the same path. She would turn off of Miami Street by the grain elevators onto Oakdale Street, travel to the top of the hill and continue to Pool Street where we lived for a couple of years. After mom purchased the house on Utah Street, in 1968, she traveled the same path but turned at the top of the hill where the East-West running railroad tracks laid.

Sadly, my mom never stopped to say, "Hello." Nevertheless, I would always wave to her as she passed by. I vividly remember the feeling of being unloved and unwanted. Those two feelings, even when untrue, haunt me in every waking moment.

My little heart could never fully understand why my mother didn't want me.

After mom's car turned on to Utah Street, Mama would take her soft hands and place them on the center of my back and say, "Your mother loves you." We would hug and I would head off into the living room to lament as only a little boy could. In my heart, I knew my mother didn't love me. She didn't care. Not at that time, anyways.

When I was 2, my mother bought a new used maroon Buick Special. Daddy Green had long been a Buick fan and that's all that anyone drove, except for Guy who was given a purple Ford Mustang for his 18th birthday. For her, my mom's car was a chariot of the gods that was reliable, sturdy, and handled well in the often brutal Toledo winters.

The first car when she owned when she arrived in Toledo was a gray jalopy. It was missing a floor board and the road was visible from the passenger seat. Legend has it that, after she went back to work at Maumee Valley Hospital three weeks after my birth, that I would ride in the front seat with her hand as a seat belt. Any sudden stop would have caused me to plunge to the ground beneath and caused certain injury or death.

With the inherent risk to my safety, Mama Green and Daddy Green gave my mom the money for a down payment on a new car and introduced her to a dealer that was friends with Daddy. Leo Green was a truck driver with a penchant for fixing cars and driving with a surgeon's precision. Cars were his hobby and he loved to crawl under them with his sliding table and overalls. So, they convinced her to purchase the Buick and she did.

Daddy Green was mild, calm, and unflappable. He was my "daddy" and he showed me the essence of love. Every day before bedtime, he would sit me on his knee and break off pieces of longhorn cheese and Zesta Saltine crackers for us to share. The thoughts of the curved orange delicacy conjures a strong and vivid memory. Mama would typically join us as we would watch the 11' black and white TV that rested on the never used dishwasher resting three feet away from the sink. Eating cheese and laughing at the cross-dressing Geraldine on the Flip Wilson Show was a favorite activity.

That TV was centerpiece for other shows. Saturday nights were the worst, starting with The Lawrence Welk Show at 7:00 ,followed by Hee Haw at 8:00. These bored me terribly. Though I tried to fight it, I couldn't. And then came Mama and Daddy Green's favorite show, Adam-12. For me it was like watching a snail crawl through the forest; for them, it was policing heroism.

By 1972, Friday nights changed for the better. Sanford and Son hit the airwaves and was followed by Freddie Prinze and Scatman Crothers in

Chico and the Man. Erma Jean used to love Thursday nights at home when she would watch Maude, All in the Family and its later spinoff, The Jeffersons. But, at Mama's House, show time was Friday.

As I watched Sanford and Son, it had an eerie resemblance to my life on the "Hill." Mama was a combination of Aunt Ester and Fred Sanford. Though she did not believe in lying, like Fred, she had the *"Don't let your left hand know what your right and is doing"* down to an art. Mama worked with magic. On one hand she might tell a person that she was light (short on money) and after the person would leave, lift up a broken part of the linoleum flooring and pull out five or six hundred dollars. Bertha was 21 when the Great Depression hit and redefined her relationship with money. She stopped trusting banks and learned to hide money in "secret spots" throughout the house.

Roller Derby and Big Time Wrestling provided sports entertainment. On good nights, once Hee Haw ended, it was time for Roller Derby and wrestling; often these came on in the afternoon as well. These sporting events were incredibly violent, even if, only for show. Bobo Brazil was famous for the Coco (head) Butt and was the house idol; we loved him. The Sheik was his arch enemy as was Abdulla the Butcher. Pom Para Ferpo was Bobo Brazil's tag team partner and, according to Mama, "Could bust a basketball by placing it in his arms and squeezing it." Haystack Calhoon was the overweight country buffoon and Andre the Giant was a circus show with his height. There were others.

But, man oh, man, the Sheik would make Mama Green angry. Whenever he wrestled Bobo Brazil in an open match, cage match, or tag team match we would wait for "the bone." Inevitably, The Sheik would be losing and would pull a sharpened animal bone out of his trunks and jab Brazil in the eyes and draw blood (Abdullah the Butcher had the exact same modus operandi). No matter when the bone came out, Mama responded the same way, "Oh, look out man, that Mutha Fucka is getting the bone. He's behind you. Someone get me a brick, bring me something because this mutha fucka is going to kill him."

Of course, I would giggle the whole time, my eyes sometimes swelling with tears. Guy and Daddy would typically join me and start laughing. Before the end of the bout Daddy Green would always say, "Baby it's not real. They're just acting." She would turn with a fury and say, "Leo, *you don't know your ass from a hole in the ground.*" And he would simply laugh, shake his head and say, "Okay, baby. Okay."

After Daddy Green had died, Mama's "boyfriend," Mr. Johnny, would take us to the Toledo Sports Arena to watch wrestling when it came to town. The cage match was always the best. However, Mama had such a hate for the Sheik and Abdullah the Butcher that she would take her purse to the match and fill it with two bricks. I would say "Mama, why are you taking bricks to the match?"

She would reply with one of her storied quotes, *"You can never trust a snaggle-tooth bastard.* If they get out of the ring and come near me, someone is g*oing to the hospital and it won't be me."* Though I typically knew the forthcoming response, I would bait her to get her fired up. Her quotations always made me laugh.

In other ways, that same kitchen had stories of its own to tell. It was a shrine for food, stories, and, at times, violent expression. Once, during a light argument with Daddy at a dinner party, a guest said, "Leo, be a man. You're letting 'your woman' walk all over you."

Bertha looked at the man, curled her top lip, and stared him down. Gently nodding in his direction, she said, "I'll be right back." When she re-emerged from the bedroom she had Black Beauty in her hand. "Mutha Fucka, are you crazy?"

She waved the gun and pointed it at the man as he scrambled to his feet and fled out the kitchen door leaving a path of fear ablaze in the entry way. Daddy jumped to the ground, Guy, Ray, Ardelia, and I dove into the side bedroom and hid behind the dresser. All we could hear was, "What the fuck?" When the man crashed through the front door bullets rang into the air. "Don't you ever show your face in this house again, mother fucker."

Stunned, everyone came back to the kitchen and the party returned to normal.

Typically, though, it was in this kitchen that I learned that love superseded race and social class based inequality. But for me, 3:30 PM was my consistent moment of sadness. It was guaranteed.

Three weeks and one day after my birth, when my mother had returned to work, Mama Green proclaimed that, "I became her baby". There were periods of three and four weeks in which I did not see my mother except while she was driving her car. In many ways, that quotation was the strongest bond between me and Mama Green; it was our relationship marker. I heard it daily as did all of Mama's friends.

Sadly, as I would find out in time, my mother was ill equipped to be a parent. If I could provide a title to my mother's biography it would be "Tragedy and Triumph: The Story of Little Susie." As a child, my mother had experienced the most ruthless abuse possible, without experiencing death itself. My mother's life was defined by the abandonment by my grandfather when she was 2 and the drug addiction of my grandmother. Absent an indoor toilet, my mother used an outhouse for 18 years of her life.

She had been tortured by my grandmother. She was forced to eat only peaches during her fifth grade summer and was not permitted to eat at other's homes. In addition, because of the severe malnutrition and isolation from her Aunt Barb and Aunt Vera, she never grew taller than 4'10."

Like Mama, my mother was the product of poverty and abuse beyond the common day. Bertha had taught her how to love a child, care, and even nurture. It is not that my mom didn't want something different, she didn't know how to express it.

My mother was born in 1939, just prior to the American entry into World War II, in Mansfield, Ohio. Though her mother, Evelyn Kasner, was born into wealth she was abandoned when she fell in love with my grandfather, Phil Schwaner. Evelyn was a direct descendent of Great Great Great uncle Ulysses S. Grant, President of the United States. Unfortunately, my grandfather's womanizing personality turned the off access to the Kasners.

Known as a young, virile, and dashing playboy, my grandfather long had a reputation as a lady's man. In Mansfield, he was unmistakably regarded as a "rolling stone." He had girl friends in all corners of the region, but it did not matter to Evelyn. She loved his wit, charm, and dashing good looks. She tried to love him so much that he would love her back, but it didn't work.

Two short years after my mother was born and her brother Butch was in the womb, my grandfather abandoned them. He left his wife (Grandma Evelyn), to seek his own independence. The only time that he came to visit was when grandma needed additional discipline of the kids. He never provided money and my mother was despised in her youth by other kids. She was bullied mercilessly for her poverty and minute size. In addition, my grandfather, who is alleged to have been involved in espionage in World War II against Germany due to his ability to speak fluent German, was run out of town during the McCarthy Red Scare era. It was believed that he was a Communist and Nazi sympathizer.

Paradoxically, Grandma Evelyn was a warm, funny, and scholarly woman. She wrote poetry of the Emily Dickinson variety and was well versed in the use and control of language. Missed punctuation at school, for my mother, was blessed with a belt whipping. As is common with so many intelligent men and women, they are unable to manage

53

the groundswell of thoughts that permeate their mind. And, when they love someone that does not return their amorous attention, they implode.

My grandmother's poverty was not money, though that was certainly the case, it was her need to eliminate her pain. With a penchant for crude humor, her clamor to quell the pain devastated her soul. Alcohol became her daddy, prescription pills her father, and predatory sex her lover. My mother was beaten with hangers, belts, and shoes on a daily basis. She bled often and was not allowed to play in gym class due to the bruises on her back from the severity of the beatings.

Once, after watching her mother eat leftovers, she asked for some scraps. My intoxicated grandmother said that she "should appreciate what God has given you and not beg." Though I cannot remember if it was an electric iron or one that heated on the stove, my grandmother picked the molten hot instrument and attacked. She slammed my mother's face down into the kitchen table and held her down. Butch, who was younger at the time, laid in his feces filled diaper on the couch and watched. My grandmother ironed my mother's back and slung her to the floor demanding that she clean the "fucking house or get some more." The iron print later disappeared after a barbecue pit exploded on her and burned 75% of her body.

In 1954 when she was 15, my mother attended a cookout with her cousin Shirley. While celebrating Memorial Day, my mother was asked to put hot dogs on the grill. As my mother accomplished her goal, her cousin threw gasoline on the blaze. The fire exploded and my mother was the direct recipient of Hell. She nearly died that day but hung in with her will to survive. She was burned severely.

Mom spent six months in the hospital enduring surgery after surgery and accepting skin grafts for her disfigurement. The perfect rectangular scars that remained on her legs for life always reminded me of her pains. She had been blinded in the accident, too. The incident, according to my mom and grandfather's recollections, should have killed her but, instead, drew her to God.

While in the hospital, the Eberly Brother's song, "**Wake up, Little Susie**" had been released. Mom always told me that the group had actually heard of her near death experience and recorded the song just for her. Though I could never verify the veracity of her claims, it made sense. Also, while in the hospital, Cleveland Indians great, pitcher Bob Feller, came to visit and left behind an autographed baseball. Though she couldn't see him, his visit was the highlight of her childhood.

She laid at home for six months, blind, until, as she told the story, an Angel sat on the foot of her bed and willed her sight to return. Though the scars from the skin grafts forevermore destroyed her confidence in appearance, she fought to emerge victorious from Hell, from the beatings, and to win the game of life. When she regained her sight and saw the angel, she sat up in her bed and said, "Thank you, God."

My mother beat her brother Uncle Butch, as well. Fearful of the repercussions of a dirty home, they continuously cleaned each day. My mom would punch Butch in the mouth to get him to help. He was too slow and methodical for my young mother. So, to get him to move faster she would pummel him, even after he grew to be bigger. Nevertheless, when grandma arrived home, high and drunk, they were beaten anyhow.

In the winter, grandma would take my mother and uncle to the restaurant where she worked. They were forced to stay in the basement, remain quiet for the whole shift. Their duty was to sit in a cardboard box.

In those days, coal burning furnaces kept retail establishments and homes warm. The family-owned restaurant was no different. So, my grandmother, to enforce her rule of silence, would take Butch's head, then my mothers, and force it into the fire of a coal burning furnace.

After holding them there for 10-15 seconds, she would let them out with a finger poke to the face, "Do you understand what I mean by quiet? If not, I will put your whole body in there and burn you alive."

They never made a noise and stoically absorbed the pain to avoid more beatings. On the bad nights, she would hear other men in the house and the moans of sex as she tried to sleep. On horrid nights, she would hear grandma force Butch into fellatio, cunnilingus, and intercourse. My uncle was forced to be a concubine for my addicted grandmother. His only salvation were the nights in which another man came home with grandma. It was in those nights, that the "angels," as grandma referred them to others, were allowed to eat real meals.

Sadly, they were one of the poorest families in Mansfield. My mother and Mama Green both shared a similar abusive background. Neither had more than one or two dresses and both had cheap and makeshift shoes. The lack of clothes, the shame of poverty, and abuse gave them a special bond and understanding. It is amazing how shared pain is a vehicle for tattered souls to build enduring relationships.

School for my mother was a dismal experience and even worse for Uncle Butch. Both were blessed with genius IQs, but the lack of nutrition and the control of the dictator made learning secondary at best. So my mother suffered from hunger and never had the ability to grow. If they did ask for food, Grandma would come to school and smack them and drag them home. She was a broken woman whose heart was annihilated when my grandfather left. Her love turned to private hate and it was passed to her children. My mother fared much better than my uncle though both were considerably damaged. But, given the totality of it all, my mother overcame death defying odds to give me a life; Mama Green was, in fact, a savior.

Unfortunately, the chronic abuse doused my mother's own internal flame and left pain, hate, depression, and anger in its wake. As a parent, my mother had learned the scripts of abuse and used them on

56

me. Though she had the support and buffer of Mama Green, she wavered between strength and depression. And, with the influence of alcoholism, her anger often exploded under the search light of the next drink.

There were times when I paid for my mother's torture and grandma's addiction. On one particular morning in Mama Green's Holy kitchen, my mom had stopped to visit, if only for a moment. As Mama Green told it, when I walked up to my mom to express my love (at the framed window that I had stood countless times waiting for her to pass by after work), I tugged on her dress to say, "Mom, I love you." At that moment she yelled at me, "Get out of my goddamned face you little bastard," and took her left hand and slapped me so hard across the face that I flew into and through the air. When I landed some 12 feet away, my head narrowly missed hitting the exposed pipe under the sink and rammed squarely into the wall. I had been knocked unconscious. It was my first, but not my last, visit to the hospital for a concussion. My mother, that day, smacked the love out of my heart and produced a void that lingered and provoked a silent battle for the ages.

My mother's anger was deep seeded, historical, and her personal demon.

When I was conceived, my mother had been living in Toledo for a short time. She had come from Cleveland Nursing School with a brain like a steel trap and a survival mentality of a tiger in the jungle. She initially lived in a motel next door to the High Level Bridge (the Anthony Wayne Street Bridge). It was here that mom was forced into prostitution to survive.

Once, at the end of a brutal argument, as Erma Jean was leaving the kitchen, she proclaimed that I was a bastard child of a trick. I thought to myself that I was created for $25. For years, that story shaped my sense of self. It's one thing to be a bastard, it's another to be a bastard trick. In the writing of this story of woe and survival, I found a set of

57

pictures which confirmed that my mother lived in the basement of a pizza parlor's storage area as told by Mama Green.

Ironically, my mother was a true survivor and inspirational leader in my life. Yes, it is true that we had a lot of distance between us, but it is safe to say that we loved each other dearly. When she died in 2014, we shared a day in that was purely a mother and her only son enjoying one another. The false pretenses were gone, her hurt was vanquished, and mine was suspended. In a soft and aged voice, she reminisced with me for hours and appreciated the friendship of Mama Green.

Because of their grotesque experiences with abuse, Mama and my mother were very friendly and bonded closely. They loved to drink homebrew, homemade wine, moonshine, beer, and share stories. Both were strong, both were warriors, but Mama had learned to display love and affection through hugging and touching, but my mother grew emotionally cold.

In reflection, it is true that my mother was excellent at socializing, kind to others, and a gregarious woman. Ready to fight or argue in a heartbeat or to preserve the integrity of her brother, love was a difficult script for her to read. Mama was one of the few people who could connect with and coach my mother. For years after I was born, my mom learned that warmth was good and loving a child a gift. Erma Jean was, at the time, a great friend to my mother. She was funny, self-conscious about her weight, but loving toward her friends. Jean had a streak in her, however, that was ornery as she liked her friends to get drunk and act foolishly. But she also tried to look out and guide my mother in sanding the rough edges of her public self. Together, Mama and Erma combined to elevate and cultivate my mother's social ability.

My mom needed Mama to buffer her from her childhood torments and saved both of our lives while giving us a chance, over time, to be mother and son.

Chapter 12. The Death of a King

I was playing Match Box cars perched in the kitchen at Jerry Berry's house when Neil Armstrong walked on the moon. Playing in the kitchen with Jerry was pure joy as Buster, Jo (Jerry's father and mother), my mom, and Erma Jean drank beer. Just as the rocket descended upon the fictitious Swiss cheese surface, Buster said, "Come here, Knucklehead, they're about to land on the moon." "OK."

Jerry Berry and I left the cars on the floor and we sat on Buster's lap. "Guys," he said, "you are about to witness history. Man is going to walk on the moon." We watched intently and once the boring moment was over, we went back to the cars. Erma, mom, and Joe laughed as Jerry and I carelessly played in the dungeon of our neighbors home on Utah Street.

One year earlier, on April 4, I can recount my first memory. While playing in the kitchen the news broke on the radio. Martin Luther King had been shot in Memphis. Though I was two years old, I can vividly recall Erma Jean, all 350 pounds of love, fall to her knees in front of the refrigerator. She rolled and cried a pauper's hungered pain.

"Why, Jesus, why?" She yelled. Too heavy for me to pick up, and confused by the sight before me, I stared. What could bring such a mountain to her knees? How can such a woman of strength be reduced to such putty? I didn't get it and I stood there scared.

My mom picked me up and hugged me to shelter me from the confusion. She held me as a mother should. "Mom, what happened? Why is Jean so sad? I'm scared Mommy, I'm scared."

Some twenty minutes passed and Jean made her way to the kitchen chair to sit. She continued to cry and I walked over to her and wrapped my arms around her tummy. She picked me up, hugged me, and kissed me on the cheek. "A great man died today and it hit hurts me to my

59

heart." I didn't know what it all meant but I could feel the pain seeping from her eyes and I just simply laid on her stomach. I looked back at mom, and she extended her hands and simply said, "Come on, Shawnee."

Mom drove me the half mile to Mama's house where Daddy and Guy sat soulfully at the kitchen table. Mama poured my mom something to drink and I took my seat. "Mrs. Bertha," mom said, "Shawn is scared and doesn't understand what has happened. Can you help explain it to him?"

So Mama extended her hand, gently, took my baby's paw, and led me into her bedroom. She turned me slowly to the picture on the wall and simply said, "Somebody killed that man in the picture," as she pointed at the Dr. Martin Luther King calendar that hung on the wall, lonely and isolated on a barren gray canvas.

Mom entered the room as Mama was tearing up in the corners of her eyes. She looked at me and simply said, *"Never hate."* "That man was killed because of the color of his skin. He was a great man and helped many people have an opportunity in their life. It is because of him that you and your mother can be a part of our family. He made it possible."

Mom picked me up, looked at Bertha and said, "Thank you."

She carried me back into the kitchen and placed me at my spot at the table. Mama came out and mom left and went back to Utah Street. I didn't see Erma Jean for a while but the next time I did, she was back to normal. She hugged me, as she loved to do, and said, "Are you okay? I didn't mean to scare you." I was fine.

The Vietnam War blazed nightly across television screens nationwide; riots and protests were erupting throughout the country, and the music of solidarity enshrouded daily life. Guy played Rare Earth's song, "I Just Want to Celebrate," and Sly Stone's "Everyday People", in celebration of

60

peaceful protest. News stories of people thinking they were Superman while high on Angel Dust predominated. Murder in the Motor City and orange military bullets zipping across the screen were commonplace. There was nothing like the end of the 1960s and 1970s.

Mama's background, rife with violence, set the stage for her fortress like existence. An army of vicious dogs walked the perimeter of her yard, guns were nestled in every room of the house, and she never left home unarmed. Daddy Green had a shotgun and it rested in the corner of my bedroom after he died; Mama had Black Beauty; Guy had a gun; I had a pearl handled Colt .45, but my mom didn't have a gun. However, given the violence in the 43605 zip code, AKA the "'05", Erma Jean soon bought one.

When I was older, though, I was instructed to shoot to kill if someone broke into my bedroom. I never felt safe with guns around. In the back of my mind, angry people and guns were a bad mix. I was always concerned that someone would get drunk, engage in an argument, and shoot a loved one. Though intruders were of concern, my greatest fear were those who were there to protect me.

Back on Utah Street, when I did stay at home, I had to sleep in the same bed as my mother since Jean lived in my room. Erma was great. She washed clothes, cooked, and managed the daily affairs of the home. It wasn't until I was in my teens that my neighborhood friends learned that she wasn't a maid but a nurse. Erma, though, used her income to make sure that I had the clothes needed to attend Maumee Valley Day School. She was determined that I would not be regarded as a second class citizen and she assured that all of my clothes would be name brands, cleaned, and pressed.

Erma Jean, though, was cut from the same tough mold as Mama Green, but could also be bossy and controlling. Though she was typically humorous and loving, her angry side was demonic. So, whenever she demanded that I pick weeds out of the cement in the patio out back, I

61

did; whenever it was time to wash dishes, I did; when it was time to run the vacuum cleaner and dust, I did. At times, she was so demanding that I wished she would sleep upstairs in her own apartment.

On one particular night, I went to bed angry. She and mom had been arguing a ferocious battle over my shoes. For some reason that I cannot recount, Guy had stayed the night before to watch me. In any case, he had left his gun in my mom's bedroom. The entire night of the argument, I kept dreaming that I could see a face of an old woman in the plug board on the wall. A spooky creak from the closet door persisted and I was scared the entire night. I saw the gun on the night stand, picked it up, and put it under my pillow. Having been surrounded with guns my whole life, I knew what they were for. After finally sleeping, I woke up and mom was sitting on the edge of the bed. I took the gun, playfully put it to her head, and pulled the trigger while saying, "Bang." Guy had put on the safety lock; my mom ran as a gazelle being chased by a lioness. "Oh My God, Shawnee."

In reflection, I often, and sadly, think about that morning. I always wonder what would life had been like had the safety switch been unlocked. Although the Second Amendment guarantees the right to bear arms, guns are dangerous, and, contrary to popular opinion, used for destructive purposes. By five, I had seen war on TV, guns in the house, the death of a King, and nearly killed my mother in an accidental shooting. Though I do not oppose people owning arms, to deny their danger is ludicrous. That day, I saw with my own eyes that life, itself, was indeed fragile and that as Mama said, *Tomorrow is never promised to anyone."*

Chapter 13. Scratch Your Ass and Get Glad

Summer days on "The Hill" were made for childhood adventure.

Mama's house at 140 Oakdale was peculiarly situated and really made little sense except that it was home. The shack itself was green and infected with peeling paint. From the street it was shielded, somewhat, by a couple of huge oaks and a myriad of fruit trees. The stone driveway ran about 100 yards south off of Oakdale and made a sharp right in front of an emaciated but wildly productive peach tree. The driveway ended at the foot of a dilapidated garage.

I could never fully understand where the yard started or ended. The dandelion filled yard ran About 20 yards to the front of the house; the war with the summer weeds started there. From the street and to the left of the driveway stood her mailbox, about 15 yards from the road, and ten feet past that was a barbed wire fence that circled an aging and rarely used factory. The fence ran about 40 yards beyond the back of Mama's house where the fence made an abrupt right had turn and ran into the back section of the weed covered, "Field of Mystery."

Just in front of the aged garage laid a steel dog house that was surrounded by a dirt patch, worn down by the warriors that watched the yard by night. The supreme leader, and most vicious, yet loving dog, was Toji. He stayed on a chain except for the rare days in which Mama would let him roam free; this happened when she sensed threat from a pending break-in or other unwelcome guests. To the left of the house, and running along the weed line to the Field of Mystery, was the side yard. Though I rarely played there, it was a special place. Every Fourth of July Mama and I would sit in her sticky rubber laced lawn chairs and eat watermelon and watch the meager Toledo Firework display that rained over the nearby Maumee River.

Beyond the Field of Mystery was the largest railroad turntable in

Northwest Ohio. About a half mile along the tracks stood a neighborhood that felt like it was located in another country. There was only one red brick house located in the middle of several other houses. Mama never liked the people who lived there because they had either shot, poisoned, or otherwise attempted to kill her dogs with vile maliciousness. One dog, Smut, died when someone had put screws and nails into his dog food. To this day, I cannot imagine how anyone was capable of surpassing her army of intimidating, and if need be, vicious dogs. Further, starting at around three or four in the morning, Mama would march through her house with Black Beauty drawn, loaded, and ready for battle. It was wise, especially after Daddy Green had died in 1974, given the ongoing threat of burglars.

The red house was the home of a "Snaggle Toothed Bastard." Evidently, on one occasion on of her prized dogs, Bojack, had come home bleeding from having been shot in the side. When he arrived and laid in a pool of blood on the front porch, Mama used a homemade salve and treated the wound for infection. I think she mixed Castor Oil with Rubbing Alcohol to treat it. Having some Cherokee Indian in her lineage, she followed the trail of Bojack's blood through the "Field of Mystery" to the red house.

Later in the day, she told me to hop into the car because we were going for a ride. As we turned right onto Oakdale and then Tracy Road we passed the Hofman's Convenience Store and turned right again. She stopped in front of the red house, and I noticed as she exited the car, she had brought her black purse filled with hundreds of bullets that laid next to Black Beauty. As she hopped out, I cried "Mama, don't shoot nobody." She looked back and said, "Just stay in the car. I need to take care of some business."

Armed with her purse in her right hand and her switchblade, "Bladey Mae", in her left, she closed the door. With a calm and collected stare, she said, "I'll be right back." Mama was ready for combat. No one could harm one of her family members, or dogs, without significant consequences. Ever since I was born she would tell everyone, **"There ain't nothing in the drug store that will kill you faster than me over that boy there!"**

She knocked on the door and an overweight man with a tank top t-shirt appeared. His wife stood beside him as two kids peeked through the curtains. Though I could not hear the conversation, I saw the action. With a flip of her wrist, the blade slung explosively out of the handle and her purse dropped to the ground while she balled up her fist (the Big-African-Soup-Bone). "Oh shit," is all I could think.

I watched with fear laden trepidation. I was so worried that the broken-chicken leg story was going to return home to roost. I didn't want to lose Mama to prison or a vengeful death. I sat in "Old Betsy," frozen, and scared as my heart pounded.

Words were quickly exchanged and, in an instant, the wife fell, crying, to her knees. The kids slammed the curtains closed as I watched them run. Mama and the man exchanged words as she raised up the blade and put it to his face. When he raised his hand in retreat, Mama simply pointed at him. He closed the door and she routinely picked up her purse and walked away.

She returned to the car and said, "I told you so, **you can never trust a snaggle-toothed bastard.** He said that they were mad because the dogs entered his yard. I told him that **If you're mad, then scratch your ass and get glad.** Talk to me first and don't hurt my dogs, asshole." And, just like a kid watching Saturday morning cartoons, I chuckled out loud.

On the way home she stopped at the store, picked up some Schlitz Malt Liquor beer and we shared a "taste" that afternoon. This silent fear of intruders and threats to our stability on the hill was an unreported war, it was our experience; it was our life.

Chapter 14.   Leo, Cut the Grass

Guy was hilarious. Standing at 5'8" and weighing around 250, he was loaded with the ability to perform imitations of cartoon characters and horror movie actors, such as Bela Legosi as Count Dracula.   His renditions of Popeye the Sailor Man were of show worthy quality. His timing, pitch, and humorous delivery was a gift.   Before he was old enough to drive, we would watch Saturday cartoons on the Zenith television set in the living room and would perform for me. Once, he and I played a makeshift guitar and created our song entitled, "Cornbread and Greens."

Our favorite show was the Three Stooges. Every Saturday, we would try to tune into Channel 50 out of Detroit. On a good day the snow on the screen would make Larry, Curly, and Moe visible; on bad days we had to listen to their voices. No matter, the slapstick comedy of the Three Stooges made way for our greatest fun. Guy's favorite scene was Curly telling his fish story to Moe.

In this clip, Curly would start while standing face to face with Moe and said," I once caught a fish that was this big." His hand would be about a foot apart. Then he would say, "And then I caught a fish that was this big." He would extend is hands to about three feet apart. Finally, he would say, "And then I caught a fish that was this big," with his arms fully extended and Moe watching with intensity, and he would follow with "and his tail went like this." Then he would slap Moe in the face three times and we would laugh hysterically.

His other favorite scene was the one in which Moe would try to use two fingers to poke Curly in the eyes. Though we were never true fans of Curly Joe or Shemp, Curly was hilarious, with his Curly Shuffle and his befuddled "nyuck, nyuck, nyuck." At the point in which Moe attempts to poke Curly in the Eyes, Curly puts his hand up to his nose, in a perpendicular salute, to block the poke. When Moe inevitably failed, Curly launched his famous "nyuck, nyuck, nyuck." Then Moe would respond with a poking Curly with both of his index fingers at the same time. Curly would respond with, "Oh, a wise guy," in a voice that only he could do.

Larry was typically the balance between the Moe and Curly drama. Typically, either Guy or I had to hold the antennae to assure better reception of the show. Though our viewing was hindered we would spend hours imitating the Three Stooges antics. We would slap each other in the face and do "Coco Butts." At the time, I was only four and guy was sixteen years old.

The Coco (head) Butts always hurt my head though. When Guy would hit me in the head I would literally see stars. But, being a boy, I was always taught that, **"Boys don't cry,"** and I didn't. I was dizzy often, however. Then we would hit the top of the others hand and the hand would do a full circle motion and a fist would smash the top of the other person's head. Clearly, the comedy was violent and its imitation hurt. Nonetheless, Guy loved me; he was my brother; but he didn't mind hurting me either.

The interior of Mama's house was humble at best and in hindsight, ragged. Guy had a bedroom that sat off to the West side of the house just behind the dishwasher with the black and white TV. He had an accordion sliding door with a dresser and a single bed with no room for anything else except for a purple statue of Buddha sitting with an extended middle finger. His window opened to a huge apple tree in the side yard and another window to a closet where Mama Green and Daddy Green stored their clothes as they did not have a closet of their own.

My roll out bed was stored there, too. It was smaller than a single bed and rolled out as a cot. Its little mattress sat atop springs that gouged me in the night. Each evening around 7:00, Mama Green would roll the bed out of the closet and set it in the dining room between the side board and the dining room table. My head laid near the kitchen entry way.

I slept like an angel.

Guy's room was bare but he had an etch-a-sketch and a toy binocular set that showed scenes of wild animals in 3-d. He would allow me to look at those pictures for hours. In the corner rested his trumpet.

Guy had a magical ability to play "the horn," as Bertha called it. He was a professional and earned scholarships in band at Mary Mance College, long closed down, and the University of Toledo, among others. I remember the day when he came running into the house through the front door yelling out, "Mama, I got another scholarship, in history". It was Guy's greatest moment. Guy had a brilliant mind, but life has a way of changing destiny's path.

Along the way, he fell in love with a high school classmate named Gloria and soon had a son, Jason. After only two years in college, he stopped attending. Mama and Daddy were devastated by his choice and never recovered from his choice to quit school. In many ways, marrying Gloria ruined his relationships with Mama and Daddy.

I fondly remember him playing in the band, though. On Thanksgiving and Christmas, the Waite High School Marching Band played in the parade. Mama, Daddy, and I would sit in the bleachers at the area where Portside would be built, on Summit Street. Though it was cold, we waited for the parade processional. And then, finally, he came around the corner, and I jumped and cheered for my brother Guy. He winked at me as he turned the corner and our bond was solidified again. Mama cheered and Daddy simply waved.

Unfortunately, after the Three Stooges ended it was time for the Notre Dame Football Replay and then the Woody Hayes Show for the Ohio

State Buckeyes. Even as a small child, I loved football. Though I was too young to really understand the game fully, I loved the fast running backs, like John Brockington and Archie Griffin, and later Cornelius Green at quarterback. Guy, however, couldn't stand football, so he wanted to watch shows like Batman and Superman. If he tried to watch his shows, being a little brat-like, I would start to cry and whine to Mama, "Guy won't let me watch football." And, as the script played out, she would force him to change the channel. Under his breath he would always say, "I'm going to get you for this." Typically, Mama would snap him with a dish towel for his refusing to change the channel.

One day, he disobeyed. Playfully, Mama said, "What did you say, Leo?" Before he could respond, she had spun him to the ground, rolled him to his stomach, jumped on his back, and put him in the Sheik's "Camel Hold." He was locked immobile and had to beg for her to stop. I ran into the kitchen, slid on the floor, and did a referee count, "One, two, three, and the winner is, "Mama!" We all laughed.

Guy could never intentionally hurt me. Any such attempt would result in his certain demise. So instead, he would wake me up to play "Big Time Wrestling." Before I could get out of bed we were in full combat. I tried to take him to town and would jump on his head and hold on for dear life. He would twist and turn until I fell. We played for hours, or so it seemed. The match always ended with a Coco Butt to the head and me seeing stars.

When he was done and I laid there laughing hysterically, he would put me in the "sleeper hold." He would wrap his arms around my neck with his hand wrapped around the top of my head and forehead. In duty, I would act as if going limp and fall "asleep." Then the nastiness ensued. If Mama Green wasn't looking, he would stick his finger into his butt, take it out, and force me to smell his finger. As hard as I would writhe and twist I couldn't break his high school grip. The smell of "shit" was nauseating and, oddly, we would laugh hysterically. His strength

69

compared to mine was obvious, and without Mama there, I think, he could have really hurt me.

He was always jealous that I never got into trouble with Mama. The underlying anger always created slight levels of fear for me but I knew I was safe as long as Mama Green was around.

Mama Green had been abusive, at times, to Guy and Jean. According to older living relatives, Mama controlled the house with force. Everyone fell in line to her commands. If she said to wash the dishes, you washed them. Guy refused once. When he did, Mama said, "Okay, boy, don't do the dishes." She walked outside to the plum tree, pulled off a switch, and came back in. The branch was thin and pliable so as to create a greater "whip" effect. Guy, who was sitting in his chair at the end of the table closest to the TV, was frozen when she snapped the switch to the ground. The crack sounded like thunder falling behind a lightning strike.

He jumped up from his seat in an attempt to run. His socks caused him to slip and she was "on his ass" like a cheetah in the Sahara. Smack, smack, smack. The welts on his legs protruded and he cried out in pain. "Leo, wash the dishes. Disobey again, and *I'll **knock the cow walking piss out of your mouth.**"*

On another occasion, I learned of Mama Green's raw strength. One beautiful spring day, Guy and I were shooting basketball in the yard. The rim was nailed to the tree and was without a backboard. It was a makeshift court with tree root emanating in the place where a basketball key would be painted on a court. If the ball came down and hit the ground it would assuredly hit the root and bounce in who knows what direction.

Daddy Green was working on the car in the driveway. As we played basketball, Mama asked Guy to cut the grass with the mower that was stored in a secret place underneath the back porch. That storage room fascinated me; it was small, dark, and odd. I always wanted to go in the room but was too afraid of ghosts and thought a nasty spirit lived in there. Guy said, "I'll cut it in a few minutes."

A few minutes passed and we continued to shoot around. Mama came out a second time, "Leo cut the grass." "Ok, Mama, just a few more minutes." A half hour passed and on the third time, she came out and said, "Leo, it's going to be dark soon, cut the grass." "Okay, Mama, just a few more minutes."

Her response was one of bottled fury. "Leo, I should never have to ask my son three times to do anything." Just then, the ball hit the root and bounced into the middle of the yard. As I went to retrieve it, I looked back and saw her grab Guy by the shirt, swing him in a full circle as his feet lifted off the ground. Like a wrestler on television, she lifted him into the air. I stood frozen. The moment he landed on the cusp of the grass and stones in the driveway, she pounced. In an act of strength that was dumbfounding, she picked Guy up over her head and body slammed him to the hood of the car. He bounced like a rubber ball onto the stones on the driveway. Before he was fully nestled on the ground, she pounced again. She picked him up, pinned him to the car with her hands clutching his shirt, immobilizing him. She pressed him to the car door and barricaded him with the weight of her full 250 pounds and said, "I am not going to ask you again. Cut the goddamned grass."

Just then, Daddy Green rolled out from under the car, and said, "Is everything okay, baby?" She simply replied, "Yeah."

Guy cut the grass.

His bloody nose poured but it was really his pride that was hurt. Here he was, 16 years old, and the recipient of a beat down at the hands of his mother. He cursed her under his breath but I did not tattle; I wanted to play with him more and had to assure that he was still alive at the end of the day.

Chapter 15.   Lisa Beans and a Pencil in my Eye

Toddler's Nursery School was a simple two story house that sat on Euclid Street near Front and Main. Attendance there marked a season of new beginnings. Though I had been receiving a remarkable home based education on Godzilla, Vincent Price, Boris Karloff, and the Three Stooges, I had no idea that the stories and socialization on the "Hill" had sunk in.

The years of permission to play creatively with pots and pans, flour in the storage cabinet, and listen to music had granted me a sense of learning as exploration. At Mama's, I was always hugged, held, and praised. Even as a little boy I was treated as an angel; as someone who was above ordinary pain and circumstance. I had a thirst for perfection from the days of building blocks.   Mom and Erma Jean distinctly remember a day in which I was playing blocks in Mama's dining room and the blocks fell and I went into a rage by throwing them all over the room. Rather than getting angry, Mama told my mother to watch what happens - I would crawl and gather the blocks and try again until they would stand as a house. If they fell, rage; if they stood, pride. Mama permitted me to explore my infantile emotions without repercussion. In time, and with practice, she would get on the floor with me and help me develop patience.

As I started to walk, I developed a silly streak. On one occasion, as the poop fell from my diaper, I turned and looked toward the kitchen from the corner of my eye and started throwing the doo-doo balls, while laughing. I climbed on everyone as a mountaineer seeking gold in the 1850s Gold Rush. Everyone allowed it.

Similarly, I never really ate baby food. Mama would cook collard greens and cornbread, chew it as a mother bird, and say, "Come here baby and get a little food." Then she would take it out of her mouth and feed me. According to Erma Jean, I was so fat as a baby that I couldn't walk. I would rub Daddy Green's unshaven cheeks because of the bristly feeling. Then, when he went to the bathroom to shave, he would take out is straight edge razor blade, sharpen in against a special belt, and allow me to put the brush into the shaving cream and dabble it on his face while Mama held me. Sometimes she would shave her groom's whiskers with love and sometimes he did so on his own.

When my teeth finally grew in I brushed them with a mixture of baking soda and salt instead of toothpaste; it wasn't until years later that toothpaste became a regular staple in my routine. On some mornings, I took a bath in the claw foot bathtub and made tidal waves. I loved to watch how the little boats moved in the water and studied their path. My secret passion was to fart in the tub, look up at Daddy, and laugh. Sometimes, as a joke, Mama would fart and cough at the same time and say "what was that sound? Did anyone see any geese walk through here?" Then the three of us would laugh and Daddy would simply shake his head and keep shaving.

Once in a while, Mama would burp out the alphabet or unload a huge belch. Humorously, Mama could burp on cue and she would say, "Listen up, here comes a buuuuurrrrrpppppp." Then I would giggle while miniature waves in the tub crashed up against my stomach and she'd say, "Look at that beautiful smile, Mr. Personality."

We used Prell shampoo and Mama would say, "Baby, you have such beautiful black hair." Years later, I realized that I was learning self-esteem, the value of creativity and exploration, and that humor was a great salve to daily life. To laugh, learn, and explore was a pretty good lesson to inculcate as a child. Mama was preparing me for the world and her "Little White Baby" had no idea, except that he was loved.

Each morning before nursery school I bathed and brushed my teeth. My mom had blessed Daddy Green with the permission to drive me to Toddler's Nursery School after he dropped Mama off at Waite High School. Each day, he waited in the parking lot until she walked into the

73

side entrance, looked back, and blew a kiss. She was mountain of strength, but love filled her heart.

Then, Daddy took me to school.

I only remember a few things about Toddler's Nursery School, but the experience was fun. Our teacher's name was Mrs. Bunny and when we arrived we were congregated in the left side bedroom, watched Romper Room, Patches and Pockets, and Sesame Street on the television. When all of the students had arrived for school we would sit side by side with one person directly across from us. Billy Marston sat across from me and Lisa Beans, who lived on Utah Street and had a father that owned and operated the Mr. Frosty Ice Cream Truck, sat next to me. Mrs. Bunny sat at the front of the room watching us color.

During breaks we played on the playground equipment in the back yard. Our favorite was the slide where we would go down backwards, without our hands, or with our feet in the air. One of the parents had complained of the danger of permitting such practices and we were ordered not to slide that way. When I got to the top of the slide I mimicked all of the tricks that were prohibited. Then, I slid correctly to the bottom and Mrs. Bunny angrily said, "What were you doing up there?" I said, "I was following the rules and practicing what not to do." She said, "You're lying," and she took me into the bathroom where she proceeded to wash my mouth out with soap. It was bitter, stinging, and made me gag. When mom picked me up, she said, "Follow the rules, Shawnee." I was disappointed when she didn't go in and raise a commotion as I had seen her do with bill collectors and Erma Jean.

Nonetheless, my experience at Toddler's was built around play. Once, Billy and Lisa Beans got into a sword fight with pencils and I pleaded for them to stop since they were swinging wildly. Just then, Lisa's pencil was jammed into the white of my left eye. The black dot of lead is still visible 45 years later. Oddly, no one got in trouble or got their mouth washed out with soap which left me with a sense of injustice. I couldn't understand how they were exonerated while I was punished when I followed the rules and they didn't. It didn't feel right but I couldn't explain it. Mama simply stated when I got home, *"Life's not always fair but that doesn't mean you should do wrong."* She'd say, *"Two wrongs don't make a right."*

On the last day school, we put on a cowboys and Indians play. When my mother walked upstairs to see the play, I saw her and couldn't help but to beam with pride; every time I came around in the circle on the stage I waved and she waved back. It was one of my greatest childhood memories; proof, finally, that mom loved me. To her credit, she never missed my special events unless she was at work.

Once the play was over, as was customary, Mrs. Bunny announced which school each graduate was going to attend in the fall. When she announced that I was going to Maumee Valley and not Franklin, Navarre, Birmingham, or Good Shepherd, I was confused. However, I had remembered a day when mom had taken me to Maumee Valley to take a test and talk to one of the teachers. Years later, I learned that the IQ test I had taken was below average, but my speaking skills and creativity were exceptional. Mrs. Coffin had recommended me for admission, in spite of the standardized scores, and told my mom that she thought I was very articulate for my age. I attributed this blessing to the fact that my family always spoke to me as an adult, read Bible stories, and allowed me avenues to express my thoughts.

As the summer on the hill came and went I arrived at Maumee Valley Country Day School. Founded in 1884 as an all-girls school, it was regarded as one of the best, if not the best, schools in Northwest Ohio. In hindsight, it was incredible how my mom, Mama, and Jean pooled together their resources to assure my success. Erma Jean, a single woman with no kids, bought and washed my clothes; mom paid my tuition; Daddy took me to the bus stop; Mama built my confidence and communication skills; Guy played the role of brother. As I look back, I learned the important lesson that resources for survival were built into our social networks and those provide us with the capital to survive and provide access into the world.

Mama helped me navigate the difficult process of trying to fit in. On one hand, I developed friendships quickly and easily. Six of my close friends stayed together until we graduated high school: Matt Bretz, Bill Stewart, Jamey Katzner, Stephen Foster, and Brian Rothman. It was amazing that we spent 13 years together and actually were more like brothers than students.

On the other hand, there were people who I wanted to befriend but couldn't. Richie Tavetigan, Kevin Cornell, and Glenda Washington wouldn't budge. As a matter of fact, in the early fall I had asked the three of them to let me play in the Kindergarten tool box with them and they refused. When I said, "these tools are meant for everyone to play with," Glenda picked up a steel saw, turned, and slammed it down the middle of my head. It stuck and made a "boinnnnnnggggg" sound that reminded me of the washboard player in the television show Hee Haw. Mrs. Coffin came running into the room as I was crying, and saw blood running from the top of my head. After she stopped the bleeding, it was determined that I did not need stitches, so I hopped on the yellow school bus and went home.

Aside from the saw incident, kindergarten was a great experience. Halfway through the school year we were moved from the old Smead Building and into the new school lined with carpet and a huge open space for grades 1-8. The kindergarten room was through the double doors, near the music room at the intersection heading to the restrooms, water fountain, and science room. Mrs. Lewis' secretarial office was across from the kindergarten room.

It was in Kindergarten that gendered differences became real. First, I found out that Andy Abernathy, my best friend at the time, looked like a boy but was a girl. Second, Bill Connelly pulled the head off of Amy

Coolidge's Barbie Doll and all of the boys started playing football with it. We took off the legs and arms and Amy cried as we played. I felt terribly for her and wanted to comfort her but had to stay with the boys. Thirdly, I was beginning to notice that I was not as smart as the other kids, as they were moving through our math book faster than me and I wanted to be the first to finish our yellow trove of knowledge. When Mrs. Coffin graded my work she called me aside the next day and said, "Shawn, you didn't get any questions right in this entire book, why? I said, "Well, everyone is so smart that I just wanted to catch up and not feel stupid, so I guessed."

Mrs. Coffin put the book down and gave me a huge hug. "Shawn, you are smart and don't need to cheat. If you have questions, just ask."

In reflection, though I appreciated the gesture, and never forgot it, I spent 13 years feeling inferior. At home, Mama constantly reiterated that I was full of *"more brains than I'll ever have….,"* and I had *"a million-dollar personality [and] a beautiful smile and hair."* For my entire school career, however, I felt torn between being regarded as smart but feeling stupid; being told I'm handsome, but feeling ugly. I suppose part of it was tied to the battles that I witnessed between Erma Jean and my mom and the countervailing force of being built up like a mountain of strength by Mama, Daddy, and, at times, Guy and beaten as a worthless bastard by my mom. These internal dichotomies and sources of confusion played with my self-image that both kept me humble and grounded while fueling a drive to succeed with my every breath. For certain, my socialization and early school experience shaped my life; that much is certain.

Chapter 16.   Roller Derby and Psychosocial Myths

It sucked that Guy was 12 years older than me. He was my brother and played with me, whenever he was home and not hanging out with his friends, especially Jerry. In the winter months our favorite adventure was playing Roller Derby in the kitchen in our socks. As was shown on television, we would elbow each other, bang each other into the table, freezer, window sill, dishwasher, the stove, and even the refrigerator. Once in a while, Mama would skate a couple laps with us but not usually. In any case, the goal was to knock the opponent to the ground; I rarely won unless Guy let me win, but God knows that I tried.

Sometimes Guy's best friend Jerry would come over to the house and play. Jerry was exceptionally frail both physically and psychologically. Their favorite game was to play "shoot the man" with guns that fired ping pong balls. Though Guy wouldn't let me play, if I said, "Mama......" he would quickly say, "Here, take this," and hand over his gun. Aside from his future wife, Gloria, I never met many of Guy's friends.

Jerry was a good man but his presence saddened me with his distraught and troubled face. As a child, his mother was negligent and incestuous. She was a *"fast ass hoe"* that Mama despised. Instead of feeding her son, she used the money to go to the bars on Oak Street and in nearby Northwood on Tracy Street. Sadly, even if it were sub-zero weather, she would leave Jerry in the car, alone, and sometimes, if he were lucky, with a blanket; in the hot summer he sat alone throughout the night. It was nothing for her to have engage in oral sex with him sleeping in the back.

Mama hated this scene in Jerry's movie and when she had learned of it, quickly and decidedly intervened. Six years before I as born, she would bring Jerry to the house, feed him, and allow him to stay the night. Eventually, she confronted his mother (and there were some changes), but it was too late. Jerry had become an emaciated ghost of a man; as an adult he could not maintain employment, a home, or any friendships beyond the one with Guy. In 1976, he spent Christmas with my family; by 1979, Jerry had died of suicide by hanging. Guy was devastated and Mama was saddened for months over the loss of one of her "children." I suppose it reminded her of the death of her brother Earl, who died at five from pneumonia, and the miscarriage she had in between Erma Jean and Guy's births. Erma Jean always believed that her tenderness and sacrifice for me was a psychological buffer for the self-blame of her unborn baby's death. Perhaps, that is why she was so adamant about caring for others who couldn't do so for themselves; I'm not sure.

Though Jerry died a broken man, his gentle nature was warm. He and Guy reluctantly let me shoot arrows in the side yard, fly a kite in the "Fields of Mystery," and play army in the spring garden. I had always felt like a little brother and was treated as such.

Unfortunately, when I was in second grade, during Show and Tell, I mentioned that my brother and I played Roller Derby in the kitchen and Big Time Wrestling in the dining room. On one particular day, I even told the class how my brother had painted two local factories (which he did as a summer job) gray. When I discussed his first trip to New York with the Waite High School Marching Band, and provided some Popeye and Three Stooges imitations, they laughed. My teacher's didn't laugh. And because of the war zone that I lived in at home, I also regularly got up and walked out of the classroom and into the library without recollection – I had the tendency to go blank and disappear as a detachment mechanism. Due to those incidents, my discussing Guy as my brother and the detail to which I described he and my "black family," my teachers developed grave concerns about my psychological stability.

In those days, a private school could discipline and test students best for their "well-being." Knowing that I had only tested at 104 in the IQ test, the wonderful teachers worried and had me tested for a plethora of psychological abnormalities. Once the battery of tests was completed, it was discovered that I was (though I cannot remember what my mother told me precisely) delusional and/or schizophrenic as I had created an entire fantasy world of people with great accuracy and detail. After calling my mother in for a parent-teacher conference, they shared their results and to my mother's delight, she laughed out loud. She told the administrators that "all of those people are real. Shawn thinks they are his family and Leo is his brother. The Greens are helping me raise him since I work the night shift at Maumee Valley Hospital." So, the mystery of the "black family" was clarified. However, the walking out of the classroom unannounced and sitting in the library alone was not absolved. All I can recall is that Mama Green had told me that, "Your mother had a nervous breakdown" because of the embarrassment.

I can remember that soon after the parent-teacher conference, I received one of the worst beatings of my life. When we had arrived home I was hit with Mom's tirade of "We are broke because you go to that private school. How dare you embarrass me by walking out of the classroom." At that point, all I can remember is a short and intense flurry of pain. It started with her taking off my belt and whipping me mercilessly. Though I screamed in agony, my cries weren't enough. My mother picked me up and body slammed me onto the kitchen stove. And though I fought and tried to push her away with my legs, she kept smacking me in the face and pounding my head into the stove top. As if in a trance, she swung me like a baseball bat, face first, into the refrigerator. I was knocked unconscious.

I can only remember the story that Mama Green had told me after that perilous slam. I was told that I ended up in the hospital and she and Daddy picked me up when I was discharged. Though I do not know any of the details of my mother's condition at home, or what happened to her, three months passed before I saw her again. And, like earlier, I would watch her drive by the "Hill" every day. Erma Jean's apartment on the second floor was not refinished and so she stayed in my room, perhaps to care for me, too. All I know is that in this period of time, Guy spent considerable time playing with me.

We flew kites in the early spring before the weeds grew in the "Field of Mystery." We explored the woods behind the factories, went to the bathhouse across the street looking for lost coins, and climbed and ate from the various fruit trees. We loved the plums, peaches, apples, and assorted berries that grew in front and around the house. The juice would run onto our chins with each bite. Once in a while, we would bite into an apple that had the trail of surreptitious work in its core; we didn't eat the apples with worms.

Guy and I used his battery operated tank to fire ballistics off the porch at tin can targets. We threw clods of dirt in the garden and tried to destroy imaginary forts during our wartime fantasies. He taught me how to hit a target with a bow and arrow and finally to fire a bb gun. We were master marksmen and even shot ravens and crows. Mama Green, however, would not permit us to shoot morning doves; she would always say, **"Never shoot a morning dove, they are birds of peace. It was a dove that carried the olive branch to the Ark."**

One day, while Guy was off with his girlfriend Gloria, I shot a dove. It sat atop a telephone pole above the "Doghouse of Doom" beside the frail garage. Taking into account the curve of the bb trajectory I aimed slight left of the target not thinking that I would actually hit it. The bullet curved and hit the dove straight in the heart and it fell to the dog pen below. Fearing for my life, I plotted my way out of the situation. Though I never feared Mama, as she was so very gentle and protective of me, she did not like it when someone disobeyed; Mama had only spanked me once with a plum tree branch for not listening when she told me not to run with a cup in my hand and I dropped it, shattering it. So, I picked up the dove and took it out to the railroad tracks and dropped it into a ditch near the trains. Then, as guilt set in for disobeying Mama and killing a bird of peace, I re-considered. "What would be a fair punishment for killing the dove?" I meditated. Finally, I decided that I had to shoot myself, "but where?"

I thought about shooting myself in the chest as I had done the dove but thought it would kill me too. I didn't want to die. Not my face. Not my leg or arm. So, smartly, I chose to shoot my big toe on my right foot. I pumped the bb into the chamber, put the opening from the barrel of the gun on my toe, and fired. "Goddammit, oh God, what a stupid ass fucker" is all I could say to myself. I limped around the side yard right by the covered well and bounced on one leg for what felt like hours. The pain was wretched. After it wore off, I collected myself. When it was time to go inside and eat the homemade Salisbury steak and mashed potatoes, I had purged my body of its sins. Luckily, Mama Green never knew that I shot the dove and then it dawned on me; had I disposed of the feathery victim and should have simply vowed not to shoot one again, it would have been over. "Dumb ass," I thought to myself.

If reflection, my young life was complicated and confusing. The ongoing threat of violence at home mixed with tenderness, provided for a true ying/yang existence. Bleeding out was a precursor to a life of adaptation and ongoing social psychological debate. The nature of my love for Mama Greed buffered me from a life, I believe, of mental illness.

Simultaneously, I was fully enveloped in the ethics of a caring moral system. I was instructed to respect others, respect peace, and appreciate life. The line between peace and war was narrow but I learned to identify the difference. Most importantly, Mama's edifying my goodness protected me from the message of motherly disdain.

Chapter 17.   Hate, Race, and Pancake Tolerance

On a few occasions, I tried to find reasons to separate from other people. It wasn't in my heart but I wanted to express it. Though I was typically affable, significantly introspective, and intense in my desire for perfection, I was human. Once, after having started school at Maumee Valley Country Day School, I marched around the perimeter of the kitchen table as we feasted on Mama's transcendent pancakes, playing a new version of Duck Duck Goose.

My pancakes were covered in homemade elderberry jelly cut to the specifications of a prince. No one could either cook, or cut, pancakes like my culinary maestro, Mama. Guy sat with his back to the freezer, Mama's back was to the master bedroom, daddy's back was to the front windows and the roaster as my back stood in front of the heater and black and white television. Suddenly, and without warning, I stood and stepped to Daddy Green and tapped him on the head saying, "Black." Then, I giggled.

I touched Mama Green on her head and said, "Pink."

I walked over to Guy as everyone stared at me, giggled, and said, "Black."

I sat in my chair, proudly pointed at my own head and said, "White." I was honored to have let it be known that I could identify race and color. In my proudest moment I dug into my pancakes and beamed in delight as I overlooked my kitchen kingdom. No one laughed. Instead everyone gazed, perplexed, at the, self-proclaimed "genius."

Gently, Mama Green said, "Where did you learn that?"

"School. The kids talk about it all the time," I responded.

"Umm hmm," she said. "I see. Can I ask you something?"

"Yes."

"Does daddy love you?"

"Yes."

"Does Guy love you?"

"Yes."

"Does Jean love you?"

"Yes."

"Do I love you?"

"Yes."

Then she asked me, "Do you love us?"

"Yes, I do."

Then Mama said, "Baby, the color of people's skin is not important. Love matters most. If you love someone, or they love you, the color of their skin does not make a difference. And, we love you. Do you understand?"

"Yes, I do." After sinking into my seat I simply said, "I'm sorry."

"Baby, there's no need to be sorry. Just remember that people use race to hate each other for no reason. So, rather than hate others, try to understand them. After all, *you should not judge another man unless you have walked in their shoes. Do not judge them and never hate. They may save your life someday.*"

She went on to say, "Should you feel the need to hate, *Keep your tongue.* Give people a chance."

She would continue with, "If you are not sure if they are trustworthy,

84

"plant a seed and see if it comes back to you." If it does, then let them go, they can't be trusted. Don't hate them, just understand that they have other concerns. If the seed doesn't return, then they can be trusted and you can be a friend. But always remember, don't talk about others in a negative way either, because it will come back. So, remember that *"A still tongue makes for a wise head"* and people will always respect you."

In retrospect, it is safe to say that moments change the course of time and destiny as the pancake experience impacted my life forever and is etched as stone in my memory. That breakfast created a sociologist and a man of tolerance. My greatest gift was granted on that fateful day in 1971 or 1972 with lessons of race that were fortified and cannot be shaken. Love, I learned, transcends race and always will.

Chapter 18. God Loves the Ants

Though I was learning to love and respect diversity, I had a real problem with ants.

At one point in 1972, ants had invaded the kitchen. Guy and I were sent on a mission to locate and end the military operation of our six legged combatants. As we combed the yard, we found a series of monster ant hills between the broken down fence, woodpile, and the back of the house. There were three mounds and each was at least two to three feet in diameter. Mama Green believed in the slash and burn method of farming as had been practiced in her childhood. And though she had unsuccessfully burned the entire yard that approached the house, she wanted Guy to solve the ant problem with fire. He took the gasoline used for the lawnmower to the battlefield (a new Toro that replaced the manual straight blade cutter).

He carefully poured gasoline on the mounds and lit a match. The height of the fire was only a couple of feet but I stared with great intrigue. After burning for a few minutes, we put the fire out with a garden hose. Though ants continued to exist in the yard and found their way to the house, the huge fortress had been destroyed. In addition, other bugs resided in the house; flies were common as we didn't have air conditioning and given food was always out and being prepared. I remember the never ending ambush of tse tse flies and the maggots emerging from the old and rotted meat. I never knew their origin but they grossed me out considerably.

On summer days, we used to take turns swatting the flies in the windows. For me, Mama, and Guy, it was a game. Eventually, and thanks to my uncommon reflexes from practicing baseball, I began to catch the flies in mid-air and crush them on the window sill. I know that much of the violence toward the flies was due to my anger from the War Zone at 1315 Utah Street. Though I was gentle to lightning bugs, dogs, and stuffed animals, my Bozo the clown doll was not so lucky. One spring day, Jerry Berry and I had operated on my Bozo the Clown doll and tried to sew him back together. I told my mom and Jean that I was trying to be a doctor just like them and they laughed. Though mom was sporadically upset about trite issues, she was also brilliant, humorous, and loving, for the most part.

Ant's and bees, however, were not my friends. Once while holding a large black ant, it bit me. Though I had no intention of harming it, after the bite, and I sought revenge. Having witnessed Guy burn the ants alive, I decided that nothing was going to hurt me without me paying the "price." I crushed the ant and smeared it all over the sidewalk. From then on, I began to seek revenge by finding big black ants, pluck off one leg at a time, and watch its three part body seek salvation. As my anger towards ants intensified, I began to dismember the parts of the body and watched them suffer. Within a couple of weeks, I was decapitating flies as well. Soon, bees were suitable targets. Daddy long legs freaked me out and, therefore, lost their legs.

Fortunately, Mama Green once observed me torturing ants as she peered from the hallway octagonal window that oversaw the yard. She came out and asked, "What are you doing, baby?"

I replied by saying, "Oh, nothing."

She then told me, simply and effectively, *"**God loves all creatures**, even the ants."*

Her magnificently simple statement brought my violence toward the insect kingdom to an end. I ceased to kill bugs As a reward, I suppose, Mama sent Daddy Green outside to spend time with me. When he came out, and in an attempt to cover any wrongdoing towards ants, I said, "Watch this daddy, I can tie my shoes."

I created a big and ridiculous knot. Within the next ten minutes, he

87

showed me how to tie my shoes.

Afterwards, Daddy said, "Shawn, do you want to share some watermelon with me?" We stood up together, hand in hand, walked toward the front door while I admired my double-knotted shoe strings. When we walked in the door, Mama saw my shoe strings, came over and hugged me. "You did it, baby! You did it! Now, who can tie his shoes?" Their love defined me.

Given the stress internalized from the violence on Utah Street and the ongoing violent crime in the neighborhood, I am happy to have been caught torturing ants. The long term outcome of such emotional detachment to the pain of others was potentially problematic. Given my blackouts and sleep walking tendencies, rather than detaching pain from consciousness, I remained a human capable of emotion. Happily, empathy for others became a core trait of mine as I have always loved people; the detachment process eventually stopped.

Chapter 19.   The Detroit Tigers, Hammerin' Hank, and Home Brew

Mama's real passions were cooking and baseball.

In the mid-1920's, it was noted that she had played professional baseball for a woman's team. Though I have never confirmed the truth of this, when I was older, Mama proved to be a fantastic fielder and had remarkable eye hand coordination. She would typically play catch with me and teach me how to hit the ball. I distinctly, and fondly, remember the day my mother bought me a wiffle ball set, it was like a magic spell had been cast. On my first swing, I hit the ball over my mother's head and it landed in the "Strock's" yard next door; soon t eafter, I developed a best friendship with Chris Strock. His dad, Wayne (Butch, Whitey) had played in the minor league with the Detroit Tigers, I believe.

So it was, I spent my days with Mama shooting baskets on a broken down rim on a tree and hitting a wiffle ball in the yard. Daddy Green was usually working on a car but when he was done he always took me to go and get an ice cream cone. Mama loved lemon chiffon from the little ice cream place next to the railroad tracks on the corner of Fassett and Miami streets. Daddy Green and I had chocolate and vanilla swirl. This was a fair treat after a long day of practice.

Once it was obvious that I loved playing baseball as much as listening to Tiger games on the radio, Mama's baseball lessons started.

The foundation of the house "on the hill" was made out of brick that was rugged and irregular. I was given a hard rubber ball that was similar to a baseball, and Guy's baseball mitt. Being a trumpet player, Guy had little interest in playing sports, so I was allowed to use his glove. It was old and had been purchased in the early 1960's. It was a deep brown mitt with wide fingers and a pocket held together by shoe laces. I used it until I was 9 and mom could afford to buy me a real "Wilson."

89

A sidewalk separated the house from the grass and was about three feet wide. Mama would always tell me that I was a good baseball player but with practice, I could be the best. So, on one spring day in 1971, she had me stand 8-10 feet away from the wall and throw the ball up against the bricks. Given its irregular contours, it was impossible to know where the ball would bounce. Sometimes it went left, right, straight, resembled a line drive, and once in a while, it hit the wall just right and become a soft blooper over my head. Mama said that the goal was to field 100 balls in a row without an error, and it was a near impossible task given the jagged layout of the yard and cracked sidewalk.

There were days when it would take 4, 5, or 6 hours to accomplish the goal. Sometimes, I would feel the pressure when I would get into the 90's and I didn't want to make a mistake and start again. At times, it felt like self-inflicted punishment, but little did I know that practicing this skill of patience, persistence, and perseverance would eternally shape my life. If nothing else, this lesson gave me the confidence to face up to challenges, never give up, and develop confidence. It was my favorite game.

After I had learned the "ball off the wall game," she showed me how her first husband, (professional Negro league player Freddie Bennett) Erma Jean's father, learned how to hit. He was known to have hit a home run off of the legendary Satchel Paige in a barnstorming match, and was regarded as one of the best power hitters in his league. According to Mama, he was so good that the fans would say," Hit a home run and get some of this money, Freddie." They would put the money on the dugout down the left field line and when he hit a home run, he collected the money while running to home plate and would pass it to Bertha, who securely locked it in her "bosom."

Just like Hank Aaron, Freddie would practice by taking a broom handle, throw stones into the air and hit them. Mama lined me up at the front edge of the driveway, by the porch, and faced me toward Oakdale Street. Then, my job was to toss the stone into the air and hit ten in a row into the Field of Mystery.

When the sun blazed, this summertime game would get exceedingly hot. I never sweat much as a kid, but I felt the heat. Daddy Green used to sit on the steel chair on the front porch and no matter how long I took, he would eat watermelon. Once in a while, I would connect with a stone and send it into orbit. The routine created an incredible sense of eye-hand coordination. When the task was completed, Daddy and I would play the "Spit the Watermelon Seeds Across the Driveway" game. He had an incredible ability to put the seed on his tongue and fire it like a projectile; I was lucky to get the seed off the porch.

In one post practice sitting, he also allowed me to lie as only a five-year-old could. I remember speaking "Chinese" to him. When I spoke so he would ask, "What does that mean?"

Humorously and quick wittedly, I said, "It means that a plane crashed in a field in China."

"Wow," he would respond, "You are so smart."

"Thank you, Daddy."

When I tried the same line with Mama Green, she laughed and responded with, "Baby, *I'm too old a cat to get scratched in the ass by a kitten."* Daddy and I laughed, shook our heads, and we went into the house.

When I was big enough, I started to hit with a genuine Willie Horton bat that was held together with a couple of nails and had a rotted tip. The bat was a heavy 36" one but I swung it anyways. At some point, I had learned to connect and hit the rocks with the real bat, too. On Utah Street, Whitey would permit me and Chris to use a tennis ball and play baseball games in his back yard. The fence pole behind the tree was

91

first base, the swing seat was second base, the bush was third, and the crack in the patio was home. No matter how long it took, Whitey would allow me and Chris to finish our games with scores like 75-68.

Whenever I finished the watermelon spitting contests with Daddy Green, we went into the house to get ready for dinner. While waiting, I would play baseball with a marble and pencil on the couch. The objective was to hit the marble over the "green monster" with one flick of the wrist but no arm motion. Once, I broke a piece of glass with the marble and he came into the living room and kindly said, "Be careful when you play marble baseball." And that simple request was the only, and strongest, punishment ever given to me by Daddy Green.

On some rare evenings, Mama, Daddy, and I would watch a baseball game on television. Most of the time Daddy and I listened to the Tigers on transistor radio. The radio was central in our lives as we would listen to the radio show "The Shadow," WOHO radio in Toledo, WSPD in the morning, and CKLW out of Detroit for the games. The beauty of radio sports was that it forced imagination and a thorough understanding of the game. With each pitch, he and Mama Green would set the strategy and paint a picture of what the game looked like; they would call out pitches and tell me where the players should stand. Sometimes they even arranged my baseball cards so as to provide a visual overview of the game. It sharpened my knowledge considerably.

In addition, Mama and Daddy Green had many Tiger-loving friends. Mr. Bill, for example, was a gray-haired man who was an overweight but funny man who loved to drink cold tap water in the yard. He had once spent time in the Jackson Correctional facility for an unknown crime, after a short career with the Tigers. It was always odd to me, but he would ask for a huge 32 oz. green glass of water and sit in the yard and listen to the games. I liked showing him how good I was at shooting baskets, arrows, and playing the "Off the Wall" game. He would laugh, watch, and coach. All the while, Mr. Bill would listen to the Tigers. And man, just like hundreds of other of Mama and Daddy's friends, Mr. Bill loved to drink home brew and homemade wine that Mama made with berries picked from the yard. She and Daddy ran a cottage industry of spirit distribution and earned a nice sum additional income. By time I was 3, I was sampling brews, wines and moonshine, and loving it.

The holidays were always the best. People flocked from Detroit, Chicago, Cincinnati, and all the way from Memphis to come up for Mama's secret rib sauce, barbecue chicken, and a plethora of other festive treats. Her famous "shimmy" sauce marinated for days; her fried chicken was legendary and after her death I refused to eat any other fried chicken for years. Typically, she would make sweet potato pies, pineapple upside down cakes, apple pie, and her favorite, coconut cake; Erma Jean mastered the mouth-watering lemon glaze pound cake. Her crowd pleaser was moonshine, however.

Typically, anywhere from 25-75 people would show up. Her half-brother Buddy (he may have been daddy's half-brother) often showed up, and Erma Jean's uncle, cousin Lucky, was always present. Her dad, Freddie Bennett, had long since passed away and I don't think Erma Jean ever recovered. Erma's best friend, Jimmy Mays, his brother Sonny Mays, their wives, and a character named Chuck-A-Luck also joined in. Typically, Jimmy Mays would show up to the house, always intoxicated, and wipe out on his motorcycle coming up the hill. Chuck-A-Luck was never to be outdone. Whenever he entered a party he would say his cryptic mantra, "The gun, the gun, the only gun gun, gun the gun gun gun, gun shotgun." Though I never knew what it meant, it was the funniest damned entrance that I ever witnessed. Then he would go on to perform magic, including card tricks and eating fire. He was a true showman and Jimmy was a tall mashed potato dancing, Crown Royal drinking friend. I must confess, as a side note, that Erma would have Jimmy give me baths when I was pre-school, and though it was embarrassing, he was never inappropriate. Holidays at Mama's brought out all of the characters.

Though Erma always had a streak of jealousy with Guy and a whole lot of hatred for Daddy Green, no matter his kindness, she loved the parties. Memorial Day, The Fourth of July, and Labor Day were crowd favorites and, man, did the liquor run free.

People would come up and buy "shit" and sauce by the loads. By 4:00 - 5:00pm people were drunk and listening to music on her huge wooden stereo in the living room that moved everyone. "I'll Take you There", "Let's Stay Together" (Mama's long-time favorite song), "Green Onions" (Daddy's favorite song), "Midnight Train to Georgia" (Mama and Daddy's favorite song as a couple) were favorites. People danced, played Pokeno (a variation of Bingo) as well as poker for money. Fortunately, I was permitted to play Pokeno and won often. In Pokeno, I had the "two cards of doom" that left everyone in my wake.

Having grown up in the Depression and not trusting anyone, Mama hid her money everywhere. She had money stuffed in the holes of the mattress, under flooring, in plastic baggies placed in her canned vegetables, in the pages of school books stored in the basement, and in frozen meats in her three freezers. Money was everywhere and only one person knew it's whereabouts. Mama would map out the house for me, swear me to secrecy, and we would count. I never shared her secrets nor did I ever steal a penny. She always told me, *"Never steal from another human being, they had to earn it and you don't want to take their work. How would you like to work and have someone steal your efforts?"*

My neighbors on Utah Street, Buster and Joe (parents to my long-time friend Jerry Berry) were also welcomed to the festivities. Buster was a frail man with a scruffy beard and looked like the Deputy Marshal on the television show The Rifleman. Joe was very nice but suicidal. Jerry Berry was exceptionally quiet but gifted with intelligence. My "Knucklehead" nickname was coined by Buster for my stubborn, youthful, long-winded, and never shy conversational style. With precision, Buster would start me on a day of riches. By 4:00 or 5:00 he would let me have a sip of his homebrew and then he would pay me a nickel, dime, or quarter. Soon, and without pause, the Kitchen Mecca became my piggy bank Mecca. The more I sipped "like a bird" the more I was paid. The drinking rule set forth by my mother, Erma Jean, and Mama was that me and Guy could drink as long as it was in the house and in their view.

Years before, Chuckie and Timmy (also known as Smiley for his everlasting smile), Mama Green's grand-nephew and son to R.L.s daughter Wizette, had taught me to dance to songs by the Jackson Five. My favorite move was to kick my right foot up behind my left leg, touch my foot with my left hand, spin, and do the robot. Whenever I hit that move in the kitchen, the money rolled. All of Mama's African-American friends would say, "Bertha your little white boy can dance." Money rained; people laughed; the party roared.

Soon, Mama would have someone put on James Brown, Stevie Wonder, or Chaka Khan and she and I would do the Camel Walk dance through the kitchen. Everyone laughed and celebrate with tears. Though she and I would sometimes break into the Apple Jack, by 1972 they absolutely loved when I would imitate Fred G. Sanford from the television show, Sanford and Son. Fred was famous for his painful-looking arthritic gait and make-believe heart attacks. So, after everyone was juiced and the party was in full flow I would hear, "do the Fred G., Shawn." "Come on, boy, do the Fred G." On cue, I would walk in from the dining room and into the kitchen. Then, depending on the beat, I would keep my left foot on the ground, slowly take one step forward, one step back, the two steps forward, with one step back until I had done a full circle. The entire time my right hand was on my heart. Then, after a full circle was completed, I would fall back and fake a heart attack and say, in my deepest voice, "Oh Elizabeth, I'm coming to join you, Honey." And man did the crowd laugh. I can remember Erma Jean and my mom laughing so hard that she literally cried. Then, if, and when, Guy joined me, the house would erupt.

When I was fully intoxicated, I would go lay on the green carpet in the living room in front of the stereo, cross my legs, play "Higher Ground" by Stevie Wonder for an hour, and would sing as if no one heard me. Then, when it was time to get up I'd go back and perform or play Pokeno. The feeling of being on stage was always exhilarating. I told jokes, conversed, danced, and even shared stories of my ventures in the side yard, as if it mattered. Later in life, it was clear that I had to be social, teach, or perform in front of others. Even more, I loved earning that money – my dream was to be a millionaire by the time I was 40, but I failed. The next day, and without fail, Mama and me would wrap coins and count our earnings.

In reflection, I miss those days where community was shared and bread was broken. Mama's house was a place where differences produced tolerance, struggles were met with community, and race was rendered irrelevant. The combination of food, spirits, and love made the house a home; I didn't even know we were poor, and I didn't recognize that I was white. Race and social class were unimportant to me.

It was always amazing how such diverse personalities could mesh together in unity. Though much of the interaction was lubricated with food and alcohol and music acting as the backdrop, personal issues were absorbed by the group. Kids were ingratiated into the events as full participants and hate was not allowed. As a matter of fact, the kitchen celebration of life demonstrated the power of love and respect that swelled my heart with joy. And, by the end of the evening, the entire show was built around Mama's storytelling; linking participants to the past brought a sense of peace to the present. Parties on the "Hill" were ostensibly great lessons of building peace; life on the "Hill" was fantastic.

In reflection, the house served as counterpoint to the socially contrived meaning of race, and replaced it with unconditional love. Though

96

sports were important, the nature and direction of relationships and intimacy are irreplaceable. The value of male love, as a young man, is uncontested and the loss of Daddy affected me immeasurably. His gentle nature redefined the typical and stereotypical notions of what it is to be a man and confirmed that being "soft" and "loving" is a valued expression as well.

Chapter 20.   The Swarm

A major disadvantage with attending Maumee Valley was that there were very few families from East Toledo. Cindy Warren attended for a year in second grade and Randy Rossler was there for a couple of years, too. Kenny Brown went to MV for three years as his mother, Ruth, was friendly with my mom and she actually took me to the Detroit Lions VS. The Green Bay Packers football game to watch Ohio State star, John Brockington, play in the sloshy mud pit at Tiger stadium. Aside from John Lagger (who attended from Kindergarten through 12th grade, and was one year behind me), Becky Raisner, John Norieka, and Alicia Beard were the only other students that I remember from the "other side of the tracks."

Though it was not a shock to me, I hated when kids would say, "Hey, Shawn, we heard that someone was killed in East Toledo last night." Once, that pronouncement explained why I had to step through blood outside of Chardee's Bar on my way to the bus stop. East Toledo was violent and was enmeshed in a deep drug and gang culture. My childhood best friend's mother (or maybe it was her father) from Walbridge, Bobbie, was shot and killed in the kitchen during a domestic dispute. Violence was seemingly everywhere.

Even more, the driving distance from East Toledo to MV, in conjunction with few riders made it a financial liability to provide yellow school bus services to the East Side. After my mother waged a small war to get bussing, they only came to the border of Rossford at the Hospitality Inn, lying at the foot of I-75. John Lagger and I were the first to get on the bus in the morning and the last to get off in the evening. We had immense fun playing rocket ship, PIG, cards, and the occasional football game until the day he threw my ball out the window on the Maumee Bridge and into the cascading river below.

Early in the fall of 1974, John and I had to wait for Kathy Richards, our student teacher and carpool driver, to take us home. She had to stay late at school to attend a faculty meeting with Mr. Wickes (also known as "The Claw"), Mrs. Priebus and Mrs. Leader.

The meeting was held in a new building designed around a 60's ideal of "open learning", as the school was nestled in 104 acres of land mostly surrounded by "The Woods." It was common for classes to learn about science and Native American Indians culture, with trips to the wooded refuge. We collected leaves there for art projects, too. Roughly fifty yards west of the main building was "Vine Valley." It was a place that overlooked a tall hill and was used as a natural swing set where us kids would swing and jump and fly as far as possible down the hill. On the South side of the woods rested our "football field" where Mr. Wickes was renowned for his underhand forward pass. Jamey Katzner and I had learned to emulate the long bomb threat of Cincinnati Bengals Kenny Anderson to Isaac Curtis. We had mastered the "go to the right and cut behind the thorn tree and the ball will be waiting" play that he threw and I caught with mechanical precision. Just west of the football field was a monster hill used for sled riding, the first cousin of the more dangerous, and often avoided, "Dead Man's Hill."

In the winter, the kids were permitted to sled ride with impunity. Sneaking off to Dead Man's Hill was not permitted, yet Bill Stewart and I did it regularly. Starting just behind the original old white "Smead" building, the hill was bumpy and fast. After taking my turn, I returned the rubber roll up sled to Bill who ran and dove onto it. He hit the first hill and all I can remember is him saying, "my back, my back, I can't get up." I ran to Mr. Wickes who aided Bill until he could get up and walk back to the school. We were shocked that Mr. Wickes didn't use the "Claw" and pick us up by the shoulders, airborne, and carry us to the Headmaster's Office. Instead, he said, "Please, don't sled ride down Dead Man's Hill, again. It's too dangerous and I don't want anyone get hurt. Will you stay with the group next time?" Of course we agreed.

In that preceding fall, however, knowing the woods as "Mohawk Chiefs," John and I set out for adventure during the teacher conference. We walked by vine valley, stayed on the main trails, crossed the creek twice heading north, and stumbled upon the serenity of an isolated location. Choosing the ideal spot was paramount for our pending "boat race" of leaves. When we discovered our perfect spot, I led the trek down the 8' hill to the creek.

The creek was serene that day as crawdad homes invaded the muddy edge. While I waited to see one peek its head out from the miniature volcano shaped home, I heard John yelp.

He yelled something that was indiscernible. From the back of the woods, two boys were approaching dressed as cowboys and wearing red bandannas over their mouths; they were some 100 feet away and carrying little cap guns. John yelped, again.

"Shawn, I'm getting stung," he said in a panic.

Unable to hear him, I said, "what did you say, John." I couldn't hear him through the soft buzzing din that had captured my hearing.

When he capped his hands around his mouth for an intensified effect, he uttered again, "I'm getting stung."

"Damn," I thought to myself. "What in the hell is he saying?"

Just then, I felt a thorn prick me on top of my head. When I looked up, I did not see a tree. Then, a thorn hit me in the left hand and then my right. There was no thorn tree. I looked up at John who was flailing his arms in a swimming motions, "Help, I'm getting stung."

Then a wasp stung me on the face and I realized that one of us had stepped on and angered a wasp nest. We were under attack. As I looked up the hill, there was a wall of bees; when I looked to the creek, there was another wall of bees. Frightfully, I had to choose to either jump over the creek and climb a hill to run in a direction that I had never explored or turnaround and run through the "Wall of Death."

As I decided to confront the "Wall of Death," I yelled, "Run back to school, John. Run." Just then a bee flew into my mouth and stung my tongue.

John ran and I covered my eyes to charge up the hill.

As I ran up the hill, I slipped on the loose dirt and was immediately swarmed. In fear and undeniable pain, I forced my legs to keep moving (as Donnie Shepherd had told us so many times while playing football in the yard) and pulled on roots of trees and shimmied to the top of the hill. I wasn't ready to die. When I pulled myself to the top of the hill I saw horror. The "cowboys" were looking at Hell and their face petrified. When I screamed "Help! Help! I need help." They dropped their cap guns and ran home. I followed exasperated and in need of humanity.

They ran into their house, the second one on the cul-du-sac from the woods. I banged on the door and rang the bell. All I could hear on the other side was, "don't open the door mom he's covered in bees. The mother peeked out and said, "I can't open the door. I can't open the door." The cowboy and his mother, I thought to myself were "Scared ass fucking punks...how could they turn their back to someone in agony?"

When I looked back to head toward the school, all I could see were bees. They had already engulfed my shirt; my hair and its thick blackness were a nesting haven for the attack. My only path to safety was through the defending army, and I was the invader. Like a jet propelled apparition haunting a castle's corridors, I ran. My adrenaline kicked in and I ran like a "bat out of hell." Over the first hill I thought to myself, "Dive into the creek" but I knew the bees would be awaiting my reappearance.

So, I hurdled the creek and sprinted up another hill. I could see wasps about 75 yards behind me and they were swirling. I knocked a thick swath of bees off my shirt and continued forward. As I peeled through the woods, I passed John some fifty feet to his left.

"Help me, help me," he screamed.

"You gotta help yourself. I'm getting stung, too. Go through the third grade door, John, it's the only one that's unlocked." I screamed.

Some thirty or forty seconds later I ran into and through the cubby room (where I had hit David Kutcher (aka "The Big Fat Butcher", for calling my mother a bitch in math class), and a ran into the master open space. Horrified, Mr. Wickes jumped up with fear in his eyes and said, "Run around the square hallway and come back."

When I returned, crying in agony and deathly pain, Ms. Coffin took her thick blue down coat, and began to beat me in order to kill the bees. All of the other teachers were killing any bee that they could find. Ms. Coffin's second grade son, Brad, watching in disbelief, was stung in the throat. As she was swinging and killing bees her coat zipper kept hitting me in the face. "Ouch, ouch, your zipper is hitting me in the face!" I said.

When they had gotten the bees off of my body, Mrs. Lewis, the Lower School secretary, dropped to her knees and starting pulling them out of my hair. Some had eaten through the fabric of my shirt and were biting me through the holes. My legs were covered but the Wrangler brand denim jeans prevented further penetration. Even when she thought she had pulled all of the bees out of my hair, I kept repeating, "There's more in my hair! Get them." I felt faint and dizzy.

Mr. Wickes ran over and said, "I'll drive him to the hospital."

"No, Mr. Wickes, there's another victim outside. John Lagger was with me," I said. Just then, Mrs. Lundholm said, "There's another one, Ned."

102

John, who was able to walk, followed Mr. Wickes as I was carried to his car. The doctors estimated that I had been stung between 200-300 times and John was roughly 50-100. As we approached the car, in an attempt not to cry, I turned to the Claw and said, "We can't ride in your car."

He responded with a puzzled look and said, "Why?"

I said, "Because you are driving a Hornet." Though I tried to make a joke to divert my mind from my agony, he did laugh. "That's pretty funny, Shawn," he said.

John looked out the window and laughed, too.

When we arrived at St. Luke's Hospital, the nurses took our information. Earlier that morning, I had memorized John's address and phone number and filled in his paper work. Then, though I was trembling from the poison in the stingers, I had to fill out my paperwork as well. The nurses stripped us down and submerged us into cold ice baths in a steel athlete's tub. I couldn't tell if the stings or the ice were worse. Then I looked at John and said, "Are you okay?"

He said, "Yeah. Are you?"

I replied with, "It hurts, John. God, am I dying?"

Soon thereafter, Mr. Lagger walked in with his pipe hanging from his mouth and said, "Thanks for saving, John, Shawn." "I didn't," I replied.

"You told him how to get back to school and had the teachers wait for him, and you filled in his paperwork so he could get help," he said. "Thank you."

Within a half hour, my mother entered the room with tears rolling down her cheeks. She was mortified by the welts as the nurses were still pulling stingers out from my skin. She hugged me and said, "I love you,

Shawnee. I'm going to take care of you." My old mother would have berated me and perhaps slapped me; my improving mom was trying to show me love and succeeded. It was the first time that I felt her care. Though there were anger, tensions, and troubles still to come, she was real and cared. That's all I knew. I thought to myself, "My mom cares for me after all."

Until her death, my mother believed that I should have remained in the hospital for observation. The poison in my body made it shake and tremble on the couch for two days. When Mama and Daddy Green arrived to the house shortly thereafter, Mama fell to her knees, clasped her hands together and starting screaming,

"Why lord, did you do this to my baby? Why? It should have been me." She cried like an uncontrollable baby and I was scared. I had never seen tears fall to her face; her vulnerability made me try to turn my head and look at her. Finally, I saw the pillar of strength muted powerless; she was human. Daddy Green, with the touch of a sanctified saint, tears rolling down his face, took his hand and swept mamas hair.

"It's going to be okay, baby."

They said, "Here, we brought you some chocolate pudding and apples."

They called and visited for the next two days and I never moved. I laid and trembled in pain. I had seen that my mother was changing. Mama was soft, and daddy became the caretaker. Pain from a near death experience and calamity had brought out new mirrors and windows into the souls of others. Erma, sitting in disbelief, prayed for "her baby" and gently patted my hair as Mama had gotten up to rub my arms with her medicinal hands.

In reflection, although the swarm was the most physically scary and important event of my young life, it also opened a window into the notion of *turning points*. Within a person's journey, there are two dominant forces that change an individual's path: turning points and crossroads. A turning point occurs when external forces shape and redefine our journey. It is akin to Otto's notion of the numinous experience; crossroads occur when people have to make a decision that will shape the long term trajectory of their life. In either case, people change.

Agony trembled through my curdling veins. Pain dominated my existence and dizziness confused my soul, as the swarm redefined the lives of my angels, demons, and gods alike. In fear of blame and a beating, I received instead, love and understanding. Rather than Mama standing as an oak in a storm, she fell to the ground in unconditional love, tormented by circumstance. The meek and mild Daddy held everyone on his 150 pound shoulders; Erma maintained the balance and operations of the home. The attack had reversed the roles and direction of my caretakers. I felt love and the recuperation was a reprise from the daily Civil War. Though I taunted death, I rested with peace.

At Maumee Valley, rules changed. When I returned to school humming the song *Fly Robin Fly,* I was, received with community love there, too. Mrs. Lewis waved from her office, Ms. Coffin and Mrs. Lundholm waved as I flew past the first and second grade space, and I was greeted with the biggest and warmest hug from "the Claw," who welcomed me back as a human and not a teacher.

My friends rallied. John Lagger told me, "Thank you". Jamey, Matt, Steven, Brian, Bill, Seksom, Ronnie, Jeep, Jody, Pratik, Angie Anagnos, George, Doug, David, Heller, Maria, and Kevin (all from the third grade), Jonathon, Lee, Zack, Sarah, Abby, Joe, Debbie L. (the girl whom I had a monster crush on at the time), Wendy, Debbie G., Michael, Scott, Mrs. Priebus, and of course, Kathy Richards, all welcomed me back as a soldier returning from war. I was hugged, regarded, and loved as a member of a community that superseded my social class, unique family background, or neighborhood of origin. The horrid event was the first true confirmation of an outside world loving me and valuing my personhood. I had value and it was confirmed; my life changed in perpetuity. This is why, *"Love conquers all."*

Chapter 21.   One Mighty Storm, One Mighty Swing

Mama was a master sky reader. Every spring during my childhood we had "sky reading" training. The routine was always the same. She would teach me how to read the sky. If the sky were red the night before, storms were coming. However, during the day she always waited for a calm still in the air. When the air was dry and hot and there was an unnatural stillness, she would begin to get nervous.

"Hey baby, do you feel that stillness?" She would say. Then she would look at the leaves on the ground and trees, watch the grass, and stare at the sky. If there were light streaky clouds above, a storm was coming. She always prayed for a slight breeze when she saw the streaks because, in her opinion, the power of the storm was diffusing. However, if the leaves levitated off the ground subtly without an upper air breeze, it was a certain tornadic condition.

Whenever stillness occurred she took her post. She was just like a general leading the Marines into battle. She would travel to all corners of the yard looking at the clouds. Were they high or low? Low clouds signified danger. Were the clouds rolling or sliding? Rolling clouds meant that there was rotation in the air and that a tornado was possible? Was there an underlying subtle coolness or was the air hot? Cool air meant that dangerous air masses were forming. She never missed.

All too often, Mama believed that God had taken care of her from the ongoing and devastating impact of the threat and existence of tornadoes. It has been said, such as in the book Black Elk Speaks, that Native American Indians could read stories in cloud formations including the threat of cyclones, as she called them, in the Plains states. Given the ongoing threat of severe weather, and, as she claimed, her Cherokee background, she could read the clouds.

She and I spent numerous days learning how to read weather patterns. Being a child, I was unable to understand the veracity of her weather acumen. In the 1970's, and preceding the devastating tornado outbreak of 1974, weather warning systems were in their infancy in effectiveness and Mama did not trust bureaucratic solutions to everyday problems. The fall of the banks during the Great Depression had instilled in her a distrust of the financial system and any agency that espoused truth on the one hand but acted in a different capacity on the other.

We practiced how to avoid harm during a tornado. We would practice making our way from the house and down the labyrinth like basement stairs to find our way into the coal storage bin beneath the master bedroom. I was always taught that if we could not get into the basement to either get into the claw foot bathtub (we didn't have a shower) and cover our head with towels or get into the southwest corner of the house away from windows.

She was adamant, and as I learned later, correct, about avoiding taking a bath during lightning storms as the electric current could pass through the copper pipes and into the water; she avoided sitting in front of a television during a storm for the same reason, and sat in the middle of the house and away from windows. When the conditions for a storm were ripe, she became a cat sneaking around the house and surveying the signs of danger outside.

Practicing tornado drills was a common experience at Mama's House. She would always say, "Stay away from the windows. Go to the basement." "Put your head between your knees and get into the southwest corner." "If you don't have a basement get into a claw foot bathtub or a southwest corner of a closet."

These skills came in handy twice in my young life. First, in 1969 there was the Memorial Day storm and the historical 1974 outbreak that destroyed the city of Xenia, Ohio; Toledo was not spared that day. True to form, when the tornadoes rolled in and around Toledo, we were in

108

the basement sheltered and safe. The cover of the Toledo Blade had a face-on view of the Xenia tornado that destroyed the small city not far from Cincinnati. As always, Mama knew what to do.

The next day, Henry Aaron made history in Cincinnati. He had tied Babe Ruth's home run record at 714. Nothing in the sports world was more sacred the monumental legend protected by Babe Ruth, the King. By the time midnight rolled around, Aaron was tied for the most significant of all sports records.

On April 8, the Braves and Dodgers game in Atlanta was televised live. I had my 1973 Hank Aaron baseball card handy (it had been destroyed as I wrote the home run countdown on it to chart Aaron's monumental record). Then, Al Downing threw a pitch down the middle of the plate which permitted Aaron to rotate his hips and wrists with the power of a lumberjack and the ball found the bull pen in left center field. As Aaron turned from second and was heading toward third base, two men in their late teens or early twenties ran from right field onto the diamond to congratulate Hammerin' Hank on his accomplishment.

I jumped in the air with excitement. Aaron and Joe Morgan were my two favorite players at the time and the Babe's record had fallen. As was customary in those days, when a great and historical play took place, I would run through the house like a madman. This was no exception. I ran to the front door in the kitchen yelling, "Hank Aaron hit 715, Hank Aaron hit 715. He's the greatest ever."

In a Socratic twist, Mama Green, who was equally happy about the home run, stopped me for a moment and asked me a simple, yet complicated, question. "Baby, why do you think Hank Aaron is the greatest player ever?"

With a spontaneous and joyful response, I said, "Because he just broke Babe Ruth's all-time home run record." Then I kissed the card, wrote the number 715 on it, and shook my fist in the air.

Mama, calmly, said to me, "That's not why he's the greatest baseball player ever."

I said, "What? What do you mean? He just hit number 715. That makes him the greatest."

"No baby, that's not it," She said. "He's the greatest player ever because he has been receiving death threats ever since he passed Willie Mays. There are a lot of white people who have threatened his life because they are not ready to see a black man be better than a white man, not even in baseball. In spite of the fear of death, Hank Aaron kept playing using bravery and courage. He is the greatest player because he faced the adversity of death but kept working hard and doing his job. He showed the value of perseverance and dedication."

I sat on the footstool dumbfounded. I wasn't sure what to make of the moment but I knew it was bigger than baseball. I was being introduced into some deep thoughts and perspectives that would change my life forever.

She continued saying, "When Hank Aaron first started playing baseball he wasn't even allowed to play pro ball with whites. You see, in the 1950s, Jim Crow laws prevented Negros from playing in the major leagues. My first husband, Freddie Bennett, Erma Jean's dad, was a great Negro league home run hitter but was never allowed to play baseball with whites. There were a lot of great players who were not allowed to play pro ball because of their race. That's why Hank Aaron is a great player, he overcame race and was determined to be the best. He has courage, strength, and is able to persist against anything."

She continued, "There are a lot of people who hate others over race without even knowing the person. The man who is on the calendar in the bedroom [Martin Luther King] fought so that everyone could be equal. In those days, blacks had to ride in the back of the bus and weren't even allowed to eat in white restaurants. Blacks had their own

110

bathrooms, swimming pools, and even schools. "You see," she said, "when people hate it keeps people apart from one another. And who knows, maybe those people could have been best friends." She finished with her simplest and most powerful quotation, "***Baby, never hate another person. You can dislike them, but don't hate them. You have never walked in their shoes.***"

She finished by saying, "Always ***do onto others as you would have them do on to you.*** If you do that, someday we may live in a more peaceful world." She finished with her most powerful idea, "***God doesn't like ugly.***"

And in that moment, I learned lessons that were beyond baseball. Yes, I was happy that Hank Aaron had hit the home run, however, the life lesson on kindness, respect, tolerance, and strength in the face of adversity became the cornerstones of my entire existence. When I grewto an adult, anger never became hate. Even during periods of challenge, including the threat of death, I remained strong. My life would no longer be the same. To handle my sadness of knowing that Mama Green was hated because of her skin color and that the world divided people due to race, I took a sip of home brew to settle my nerves.

The night continued as I asked many questions about the Negro leagues, racism, hate, baseball, and how she overcame all of it. For those who have always wondered about my de-racialized self you can rest, knowing that the mighty blast by Hammerin' Hank was one moments with my life that taught me tolerance of differences, strength in the face of adversity, and that history shapes the present. One moment in time created life.

Chapter 22.   A Fucking Coat

Leo Green, Sr., was a gentleman, a kind-hearted spirit, and had a soul of gold. When Mama Green arrived in Toledo by train they moved directly to the "House on the Hill" that Mama Ladd purchased on on Girard Street, near Oakdale School.

It is true that Mama often bullied Daddy Green. Once at breakfast, as Daddy, Guy, and I ate pancakes, something happened to anger her, and she took the butcher knife to Daddy's throat saying," Don't you ever say that again, Leo, because I will kill you." As he leaned back in his chair and raised his hands in retreat, he simply said, "I won't baby." Guy and I watched in fear and shock and when it was over and continued eating as if nothing had happened.   I was rattled and confused but Daddy's calm response reassured me that everything was alright in the world.

Before Mama moved north to meet up with Daddy Green in Toledo, she worked as a cook at the school that Erma Jean (and Pauline) attended in Memphis. It was during this period of caring for her mother, brother, sister, and daughter that she became a master cook for which she was remembered by all with whom she came in contact with. Her fried chicken, collard greens, fried okra, pigs in the blanket, Salisbury steaks, macaroni and cheese, fish, candied sweet potatoes, fried bread, tea cake breads, homemade vegetable soup, bread pudding, peach cobbler, cakes, and especially her pancakes were made of legend. She could cook anything and even her grandson, Jason, would call her for advice as he attended Johnson and Wales Culinary School in Providence, Rhode Island. He later confessed that the chefs could cook but they "couldn't touch Bertha Green."

I remember seeing a pile of paycheck stubs for Daddy after the butcher knife incident. Mama and Daddy had stored all of their personal documents in the basement. Every so often, especially when they would bottle the home brew, I would rummage through the papers and ask questions. Daddy earned $3.30 every week and he saved every penny while living in boarding houses to bring his family to Toledo; they used World War II food rationing stamps to purchase groceries.

In the year following Mama and Erma Jean's arrival in Toledo, Mama Green had a miscarriage. The loss devastated both Mama and Daddy, and the secret was kept from Erma Jean. By 1954, though, they had produced Leo, Jr., my beloved Guy. Daddy Green was the type of man that I wanted to model as a father, friend, and person. He was family-centered, hard-working, mild-mannered, and kind. Though he loved Detroit Tiger baseball and feeding me cheese, his health was always compromised.

During one particular evening, while eating cheese and bananas, I asked if he had ever had a heart attack. While sitting on his knee (probably around 1972 when Fred G. Sanford had faked "the big one" on the television show Sanford and Son), he said, "Yes, Shawnee, I have had three."

Mortified and saddened, I asked him what it was like. He told me that, "I could feel a sharp pain shoot down through my elbows like getting hit by lightning. It was first in the right arm and then the left and then I fainted."

I asked, "Did it hurt?"

And he gently responded, "Yes, it hurt a lot. But, I'm okay now."

When I started to attend Toddler's Nursery School on Euclid Street near the Maumee River, and later Maumee Valley, he drove me to school and the bus stop. Usually, we would drop Mama Green off at Waite High School, where she worked as a cook, and then traveled to Toddler's Nursery School. After Kindergarten, we did the same thing, except I was dropped off at the Hospitality Inn, on Miami Street at the exit off I-75, where we would wait for the bus to arrive.

Daddy and I listened to the radio, talked about Mama's stories, Guy, and just loved each other. Then, in the fall of 1974, he dropped me off at the bus stop before he went to his annual physical check-up at St. Luke's hospital. Just after he was given a clean bill of health and while putting his shirt back on, he had a massive stroke. He slipped into a coma from which he would never awaken.

Though I continued to stay at Mama's house, we arranged for me to get picked up by John Lagger's father, a police detective, who lived on the border of East Toledo and Rossford on Linwood Avenue. The nights were miserable as Mama Green moped about incessantly. She spent days and nights by Daddy's side. Every day after school I was taken to the waiting room at the hospital and sat with Gloria as Guy and Mama would visit. I always had the hope that he would "wake up." And, each day, Mama would come back with just a little more of her soul decayed. On some nights, she stayed at the hospital and Guy spent the night with me. On the weekends, I went home.

For three weeks I begged to see Daddy Green as I had heard he was showing signs of improvement. Everyone worried about me seeing him with the "tubes in his nose" and hooked up to life saving devices. Every day I begged to see "my Daddy" and every day I was denied. Eventually, as I waited for Daddy to get better, I began to draw horse's heads and sell them in the waiting room for a nickel each to others waiting at the hospital. Soon, the nurses who had grown fond of me and began buying them too. Gloria fed me caramels from the machine and pushed my wares.

By early November, Daddy Green continued his battle. Mama had started sending him messages from me and she said that he would try to open his eyes. I believed that if I could talk to him he would wake up. My mother knew how my heart ached and the she tried to comfort me, all the while refusing my visit.

Finally, on Friday, November 3, the hospital administrators finally granted me permission to go see Daddy. But my mom said that. "He needs a coat. I won't let him go back without a new coat." No matter how much I begged, the stupid fucking coat became the excuse that prevented me from seeing him.

Then, on Saturday, my first school friend to play at my home, Bill Stewart, came to my house on Utah Street to play. That morning, mom said she would get me the coat so I could go visit on Monday after school. When Bill arrived, we played soccer and football in my backyard. Chris Strock, my five year old neighbor and friend and Jerry Berry played, too. After we were done, while mom prepared lunch, the phone hissed a quiet roar.

I answered.

Mama Green had called from St. Luke's Hospital and simply said, "Daddy is dead. I sent him your message that you loved him and were coming to visit on Monday. He tried to open eyes but couldn't. He died, and now, it's just you and me." And, at that moment, Mama Green cried like a child. The giant temple of strength was reduced to a mound of human love.

Immediately following the news, I dropped my head on the back of the dining room chair, without tears, but was broken like a shattered window. I just kept shaking my head, "It can't be, I was coming to see him on Monday." I didn't feel self-blame but I always felt that if I could have gotten there, he would have snapped out of it. Bill put his hand on my back and rubbed my shoulders as a dear friend embraces a fallen soldier in war. I told my mom the news as she replied "I'm so sorry, Shawnee." She hugged me and all I could think about, to myself, was "a fucking coat." I couldn't see him because I didn't have a "fucking coat."

I shook my head one last time, looked at Bill, and ate my bacon, lettuce, and tomato sandwich.

115

When I saw Mama Green on the Hill that night, she cried, and I held her as she had done for me over the years. I was now her "Mama" and we were forced into a life of perpetual togetherness. The loss of daddy tore at us emotionally but made us into one soul. After his death, Toji (Daddy's big, vicious, and lovable dog), whined of heartbreak. Mama, for once, let him into the house in search of his Master and he left brokenhearted as his tail ducked beneath his massive body in the long march to his dog house.

At the funeral she cried endlessly, and kept looking at me, head tilted, saying, "It's just you and me, now, Baby." It's just you and me." I was scared because I couldn't fully understand the magnitude of the loss but climbed up on Mama and hugged her with all of my 60 pound life.

Life has always had a void for me since he died and I have never been quite the same.

For me, sociologically, the traditions of race and gender were challenged and provided the basis for a life of compassion. The lessons learned from Daddy Green's death have set the script for me as a father. Eat cheese with them on your knees, spit watermelon seeds, run in the rain, and laugh. Play, love, and hug your children in every possible moment. Death can strike quickly and steal away unforeseen precious moments; "love your children," I thought to myself.

Empathy was a gift freely granted by Daddy at 140 Oakdale Street, my rundown palace on the "Hill."

Chapter 23.   Government Cheese, Butter, and the Underground

I quit drinking when I was 12.

When I was young, I had been accustomed to "sipping" homebrew and homemade wine.   Mama Green and daddy would spend weeks preparing,   cooking,   fermenting,   and   bottling   their   intoxicating refreshments.   Mama had two huge pots that sat on the oven cooking the fruits, sugar, and yeast.   After cooking and fermenting for days, the three of us would carefully place the brew into the bottles, strategically place the caps, and mash down on the antique capper.

All along, Mama and I would test the brew for flavor. Though it was a delicious past-time, I had no idea that the behavior was illegal. Drinking alcohol was normalized at home and I knew no different.   Everyone drank, relaxed, and socialized.   To me, the use of home brew built a sense of community.

The distribution of the homemade drink was, also, illegal.   For us, however, it was a necessary source of additional income.   After a childhood of hunger and surviving by hiding cheese and crackers in the hay, Mama and Daddy vowed that their kids would never be hungry. So, the majority of their money was used to fill their three large freezers with meat, vegetables, and store canned goods behind the curtain on the side porch.   For us, the extra money was used to assure that everyone had clothes and access to emergency money. We didn't have much, but we were always prepared for the unexpected.   As such, I never really thought of bootlegging as a problem.   It was used to bring friends together on holidays, break bread during times of remorse, and share during times of need and celebration.

And, it was fun. Having a couple of drinks was a seductive way to enhance the music we played, encourage adaptation to stress, and to laugh. As far as I knew, Mama and Daddy had a little cottage industry that helped offset her free babysitting charges and helped my mother furnish her house, turn on her utilities, and purchase a reliable car. It all seemed so normal and the change in consciousness was exhilarating.

Without liquor sales, it is unlikely that I would have met Jimmy Mays, Chuck-A-Luck, Uncle Lucky, Uncle Buddy, or a whole host of other bigger-than-life characters. Those colorful personalities permitted me to learn the value of diversity and tolerance at an early age. In combination with a deeply accepting and inquisitive nature, I learned how to place individual foibles into a neat little box and look at that which was good in people. In this vein, for us, drunks, offenders, and the broken were still family.

The attainment of food and resources was a constant need for Mama, my mom, and family. Because of the manner in which resources are distributed among the poor extended families, including non-blood family members, it was always known that, *"If I have a dime you have a nickel."* I learned early on that sharing without holding people liable and in debt was an effective way to survive. Calamities happen and sometimes individuals are not prepared for the devastation. However, within an extended resource distribution system, the mantra held true that if, *"I have money you never have to want."* This sentiment, when carried without keeping score, ensures survival.

Mama was gloriously remembered as the provider of life, the one who fed the poor and hungry within our network. In the winter she would bring the "hobos" to the house from the railroad tracks so that they could eat a hot meal. When government cheese became a staple of the church and community center locations, Mama was the first in line. Even though families were only permitted one pound of cheese and one pound of butter per distribution period, Mama managed to get five pounds of each. Interestingly, though the cheese was awful to eat on its own, when placed on a hamburger, grilled cheese, or in macaroni and cheese, it was as if Julia Child herself had created a masterpiece. The butter would cook to a golden brown glow and the cheese would ooze out from the bread and gently brown in the buttered skillet beneath. Government cheese was superb.

After Daddy had died, whenever Mama picked up her "widow's" cheese, as she qualified for special welfare programs, she refused other government handouts of a monetary type. The cheese, however, was a bartering item. With it, she fed hungry kids as they visited the house, she gave it out to non-eligible friends and families that struggled financially. Her distribution of government cheese was applauded and met with in-kind benefits. Sharing the cheese and butter earned her free car, lawn, and painting services. Once I started playing organized baseball and couldn't always cut the grass any longer, the cheese (and home brew) got the job done. I learned that we never felt poor because we never **wanted for anything.** We did, however, trade resources.

In exchange for homebrew, Coach George would give Mama Green four or five cases of McDonald's Quarter Pounders. The value of the 400 patties was well over $250. And, as always, Mama would use her salt, pepper, and other spices to marinate the burgers and use the government cheese as a topping. Honestly, McDonald's never tasted better than the Bertha Green's version. Friends and family, alike, filled up on the burgers as we had enough to last for a year or two.

For example, though Erma Jean never cooked grilled cheese sandwiches for adults, she was really kind at making BLTs and "crunchy potatoes" when my friends came over to the house. Though I was never allowed to eat anywhere else, I was allowed to play there without questions, as long as I made it home by dinner. Erma Jean, though, was also very giving when it came to making Tanqueray Gin or Crown Royal. Every Christmas she would purchase and give the mailman, the milkman (when we had one), Cyril the grass cutter, Jim the garbage collector, The Cat Lady, the police, and Mrs. Keister (the Avon Lady) a bottle of Johnny Walker. Jean was very giving but she also received many in-kind benefits as well. Between Mama and Jean, we were running our own micro-economy.

For example, Jim, who never learned to read, would find merchandise of value on his garbage truck collection routes. He furnished his entire modest home with items he found along the routes and shared his treasures with my mom and Erma Jean. We had paintings, chairs, and many "knickknacks" that he had found.

Our neighbor, G-Ray, was a handyman that provided electrical work, painting, and other services in exchange for a drink. Ms. Keister would bring free samples to the house of make-up, nail polish, and jewelry. The Cat Lady told amazingly funny and zany stories of wrestlers, and Whitey, who worked for Servicemaster Carpet Cleaning, regularly cleaned our carpets. In hindsight, though many of these shared services were "underground," they kept us afloat. As a matter of fact, the informal economy which was built around cheese, butter, homebrew and liquor, was significant.

The same learned behaviors existed among us kids. Those who had dope, shared it. Those who had beer, passed the bottle. One of my best friends was renowned for hopping on the trains behind his house on Utah Street and "borrowed" clothes and shoes. From third grade through fifth, all of my tennis shoes were obtained through this methodology. Though we bought our clothes, since the supply of stolen property was never guaranteed, it was a nice additional benefit when the merchandise arrived. I remember one time during a particularly difficult financial year, I had to wear tennis shoes that were two sizes too big. So, each day when I went to school, I would find notebook paper, ball it up, and jam it into the toes of my shoe. One of my friends noticed that my shoes were far too big and called me a clown. In an imitation of Arthur "The Fonz" Fonzerelli of the television show, Happy Days, I grabbed his shirt with my left hand, balled up a fist with my right, and threatened to punch him in the face and said, "I have big feet and don't you ever forget it." I was too ashamed to say that we were poor and couldn't afford the same shoes as he.

Prostitution and drug trafficking were a common means of earning an extra living in our neighborhood. We had a few teenage girls and boys who sold their bodies for money. Though much of it was rumored, no one was ever surprised when such stories emerged. Each of the girls and the boy came from households that were poor and the extra money was much needed. Further, sexual assault and abuse was so widespread, that it almost seemed like the "thing to do." When rumors emerged of a rape or sexual assault, it was almost as if it were expected. One of my dearest friends was exonerated on a gang rape charge when he was 11, and it paved the way for him to have a great career. The others were sentenced and spent time in juvenile detention at the Training Institute of Central Ohio.

Sadly, the vast majority of the perpetrators knew their victims. That was no truer than what was found under John Wayne Gacy's house in the 1970's, which represented the greatest fear of all parents. Aside from such celebrated cases, I learned early on that it was not strangers that posed the greatest criminal threat of assault and crime, it was the actual people that lived in our homes, or were allowed entry, that caused the greatest damage. Many of the perpetrators, by the way, had themselves been assaulted in their youth, thereby setting the stage for a cycle of violence that was beyond reprehensible.

One of my friends was raped routinely by his older brother. The brother raped many others, too. For my buddy, it was so common that he had to develop escape routes out of his house to avoid attack. As a matter of fact, he trained himself to flee through his bedroom window, down the eaves, and into the yard where he could run away. In time, the brother invited his friend from down the street to engage in the same rapist behavior. Though these stories were buried and concealed for years, it provided each of us with a script to understand one another, even if we didn't know the facts and specific events.

The rapists' brother spent time in prison for rape, and later for burglary and robbery. Interestingly, his predatory prowess followed him into the prison system where he became the master of the underground potato chip distribution system. He would sell chips as contraband to monetize its value so that he could buy drugs from a nurse he befriended as his lover. After having an affair with her (though he was married to his underage cousin from Kentucky) she sold him drugs that he, in turn, distributed to other inmates. His underground activity in the neighborhood provided him with skills to run a strong business in prison, as well.

Recently, however, his prowess came to an end when a fellow inmate bashed his skull in with the claw of a hammer while on the prison unit. None of his victims felt a sense of remorse. As a matter of fact, for my friend, it relieved his fear that his brother would be released and rape his daughters - he's still haunted by dreams of his brother's ghost. Sexual abuse destroys.

For me, the underground economy was omnipresent and provided a viable opportunity for survival as any other legitimate mechanism. As a matter of fact, as a child, it was nearly impossible to distinguish right from wrong given that everyone bartered and Mama sold moonshine to make ends meet. Interestingly, those who mingled in the underground were also fully ingratiated with the above ground. Criminals were friends and associates with non-criminals and often the lines were very blurry. During one period of time, while "stuff" took place at the park, Boonie and I served as lookouts watching for the police. I watched the Utah Street side while he watched Felt Street side. When the "funny stuff" was done, we went back to playing sports.

Though the lines were unclear at times, Mama had worked hard, along with my mom and Erma Jean, to know where the lines were drawn and how to avoid stepping over into the darker side. Though I experienced several significant bouts of physical abuse, I was also instilled with a great sense of self-worth. Mama edified my confidence and belief in my ability; Erma Jean constantly compared my education to other kids in the neighborhood to build a sense of advantage; Mom always assured me that with hard work, anything was possible. In other words, the three dominant and strong women in my life dedicated their lives, and love, to assure me worthiness.

Fortunately, the confidence to stand up to threat and temptation were issues that I could handle. Thus, when one of my Oak Street buddies ran into me at the big yellow house on the corner of Hathaway, he offered me my first job. Having been known as socially gifted, he offered me a job to sell marijuana. He noted that my ability to get along with others would assure me an income level that I had never before imagined. He offered me a $50 bill and a partnership in selling dope. Given my need and desire for money, I was tempted and seriously considered accepting the job. But, when I reflected on the fact that I had always turned down smoking marijuana from the big guys and they respected that, and given that I believed that I had a bright future due to sports and school, I said "No." There is something to be said about decision making for those with a deferred gratification perspective versus a present orientation.

Those who build their self-concept around survival and living in the moment found their path to be one of treachery. Many sold drugs, even more used drugs, and a few of my friends found their way into and out of prison. For me, the decision to walk the other way wasn't tied to a campaign of "just say no," it was tied to being deeply embedded in a family and friendship system of love and respect in which I was allowed to be myself, believe in myself, and understood as being different. My lifelong dance in the underground was one that taught me lessons of understanding criminal offenders, the seductions of crime, and the value of an underground economy so deeply valued within resource deprived communities.

Being surrounded by such lines of opportunities and survival mechanisms has been the foundation of my career as a sociologist and criminologist. I survived because of elements of the underground and learned, oxymoronically, how to avoid felonious elements of the same underground. Saying "no to drugs" was the one time in which I avoided the life lesson that, *"Bought sense is the best sense."*

Government cheese and butter were tasty crime control staples. Who could have imagined such collateral worth?

Chapter 24. I Don't Care if He's the "Juice," a Gallon of Milk, or Kool Aid

The kitchen "on the Hill" was a Mecca.

After Daddy Green had died, Mama and I became inseparable. Our relationship was built around storytelling, school, sports, and food with the kitchen as our universe's center. It was a place of celebration.

Though Mama went to the grocery store regularly, she had three freezers in the house, one huge storage area on the front porch snuggly hidden behind a draping blanket, a cabinet, and a slow roaster oven. She would watch for sales at Foodtown and buy meat, canned vegetables, and paper products in bulk. We bought cheap and dented cans of food at "the salvage" downtown near the recycling center. Her belief, developed during the Great Depression, was that there would never be hunger in her home. Two freezers were jammed with burgers, ribs, steak, pork chops, pig's feet, chitterlings, rabbit, pheasant, and chicken.

Her storage on the porch was filled with vegetables that she had grown in the garden. Typically, she grew corn, lima beans, string beans, potatoes, corn, cabbage, lettuce, tomatoes, peanuts, watermelon, squash, and other staples. We spent the spring using a hoe to break up the dirt and compose rows for planting. She had a plow that broke the ground and she told me that as a kid she had a mule to create the rows.

Once the dirt was broken, she taught me how to plant seeds at roughly 6 inches apart but a finger length deep. Each hole had three or four seeds planted in it. However, before she planted the first seed she read the clouds to "sense" the weather best for planting. In addition, the moon had to be in the "right" part of the sky and when all of the signs lined up, we planted. The garden was thirty yards wide and fifteen yards deep and had a fence at the back end blocking it from a gray

125

factory that Guy had once painted.

Once the seeds were planted I was permitted to play "army man" in the garden until the sprouts showed.

In the fall we cultivated the food, snapped beans, cleaned greens, peeled corn, and canned for weeks. She had an army of "Ball" jars that lined her storage area with enough produce to last for nine months. We never ran out of food.

There was nothing better than fresh vegetables from the garden or her homemade vegetable soup.

Everyday Mama would wake up and start cooking at 4:30 or 5:00 in the morning. At about 7:30, especially on Sundays, I would wake up to the smell of thick cut bacon, fried bread, or pancakes. Her pancakes were always homemade because she refused to use box products for any food item; they were thick with a golden brown crust lightly cooked in oil until the tender inside was matched by a flawless exterior – she would warm the oil in the cast iron skillet until a "drop of water danced on its surface." Her pancakes were a crowd favorite for me and all of my visiting friends.

Sundays were most special.

Usually, I ate 9-12 pancakes in the morning. She believed that Log Cabin syrup was too thin so we used either Karo Syrup, Sorghum, or some a homemade jelly like elderberry, cherry, grape, raspberry, peach marmalade, or apple as made from fruit picked in the yard. Her fried bread, also known as hoe cake bread as made by slaves in the field and cooked on the tip of the hoe, was skillet sized. I ate it all by dipping pieces into syrup mixed with butter. She always said that if, *"You have flour, baking powder, and water, you can make fried bread; you will never go hungry."*

Typically, she would baste her fried chicken in salt and pepper early in the morning to allow it to "seep" into the meat. As she cooked, I was invited over to learn her techniques, she would say, "Baby, *don't be afraid of your spices."* When she came home from church at 2:00 the chicken was ready to fry. Often, she made macaroni and cheese, collard or wild greens that we picked at the railroad tracks on Utah Street, as well as peach cobbler. The sugary delight had a golden and flakey crust with a light drizzle of goop that braced the edges.

All the time that she cooked, I used her food timer to pretend that I was engaged in a full-court basketball game. The Nerf basketball was 6" in width with a 9" rim and backboard that hung about the kitchen door entering into the dining room. I would practice my Julius Erving dunks from the free throw line and finger rolls over imaginary centers. All the while, as the timer was going, I had a piece of notebook paper and kept score of imaginary games. My goal was to score as many points as possible before the timer expired. Then I would tell Mama the score and she would always say, "What a great game, baby. Play it again." When I would start doing trick dunks to show her how high I could jump, or do trick shots off the ceiling or off the freezer to the wall and into the hoop; she would say "Wow, that's great baby." Sometimes, I would run from the back hallway and try to change directions in the air to work on my Dr. J flying antics; I was learning creativity and how to be confident, even if my style was different and unique when compared to my friends and contemporaries.

When she was done cooking and the accolades were shared, I made my way to the living room to watch both the Notre Dame and Ohio State replays from the day before. When Guy was still living in the house, prior to moving out to live with his future wife, Gloria, I would get him in trouble when he wanted to watch the Three Stooges or anything else. If, however, Godzilla was on TV, I relented and we watched the pre-historic Japanese movie creation.

Otherwise, I'd say, "Ma, Guy won't let me watch Ohio State." Then he would thump me on the head and grunt epithets under his breath. He would say, "I'm going to get you for this."

And every Sunday, it was the same thing. On one occasion, he spoke too loudly and Mama heard him. She said, "Come here, Leo." When he came into the kitchen she snapped him, playfully, with the dish towel hanging from the kitchen sink. She spun behind him, took him to the floor, and put him into the "Sheik's" Big Time Wrestling Camel Hold and he cried, in playful pain, when she put him into the scissor hold and rendered him incapable of motion. Though it was a joke, she was clearly showing her 17 year old son her speed, dexterity, and strength.

After Daddy had died and Guy moved out, Mama would leave me alone to my own devices as she attended church. After she had made her tea cakes and had her food cooked, she started to get dressed for church. Her hair irons rested on the fire on the stove waiting to curl or straighten her auburn red hair.

Mama was very competitive and always wanted to be the best dressed at Shiloh Baptist Church and have the most stylish hats. My favorite was her blue hat with the three foot long peacock feather. People knew her hats too; wherever we went, people who saw her would routinely say, "where did you get that hat, girl, I want one like that."

Typically, the congregation had fellowship afterwards where the neighborhood members ate and celebrated together. Whenever Mama returned home she was, as she called it, "sanctified." For the rest of the day she tried to avoid using the *"Lord's Name in vain."* Though Guy and I were not allowed to curse, she usually broke her own rule by 2:00. For Guy and I, speaking to others had rules, as we couldn't *"Speak to adults unless spoken to."* Childhood, at Mama's house on the "Hill," was all about respecting elders.

128

While she was gone, the early NFL games started at 1:00. I loved Mack Herron of the Patriots as he was the shortest in the league but rushed for a 1000 yards; Greg Pruitt for the Browns was similar and electric in his ability, and my favorite running back, at the time, was O.J. Simpson for the Buffalo Bills.

O.J. was a smooth upright runner who had the grace and stride of a gazelle. However, if the defensive line got into the backfield they could generally overpower OJ and take him to the ground. By the end of the first quarter I would have eaten a sleeve of Zesta Crackers with peanut butter, with Black Beauty laying by my side. When OJ came on, I would take my orange Nerf football and set up the furniture as if they were defenders. Then I would work on my head fakes and breakaway moves on the furniture. Mama would come home, usually midway through the second quarter, sanctified. After she changed clothes, she'd finish dinner and bring it in for us to eat lunch in front of the television. She would say, **"Clean your plate because you never know if it is going to be your last meal since tomorrow is not promised to anyone."** So I ate, and in all honesty, should have weighed 300 pounds. Instead, my never ending sports play in the kitchen and the yard burned calories at a bionic rate.

As much as she tried to like football, she hated it. She would watch and on every tackle she would complain and close her eyes saying, "Why do they have to be so rough on that one man?"

Then I would giggle and say, "Ma, those are the rules."

Gang tackles would magnify her upset. Sometimes, if OJ had four or five guys tackle him at once, she would get a little more boisterous, "Oh lawd have mercy, Jesus. Why are all of those mother fuckers jumping on that one man?" By the end of the game, she would be swearing and cursing on each play praying for the back not to carry the ball. If he got the ball she would yell, "Run Negro, run." I would shake my head and say, "Ma, that's not nice to say." And she would respond with, "but he's

129

got to get away from those mother fuckers." And I would giggle.

By the time the 1:00 game ended and the 4:00 game started, she would have had enough. She would leave me alone and go to the kitchen to "piddle around." She'd say, "I can't take this shit anymore."

Even then, however, she would sneak back in and join me. Usually, she would bring a deck of cards and we would play a card game of Coon-Can. Simply, in the game, 7s, 8s, and 9s were removed from the deck and each player was dealt ten cards. On a turn, a player could pull from the top of the deck. The goal was to either group cards into four or run a straight flush with as many cards as possible. After each pull the player either used the card and disband another one or placed the drawn card on the disband pile. The person who was first to have 11 cards won. We played for hours.

Bertha often went to play BINGO at night and left me home alone. She had a penchant for winning and often returned home with amounts ranging from $50 to $200, and would share with me. "Like I always say, *if I have a dime, you have a nickel.*" We would spend hours discussing her winning and her style of play. Simply stated, anything and everything was a source of entertainment for us. We watched television in the evenings, played games, listened to music, danced, and she told me stories all the while. Sometimes we traded stories; she loved learning about my Maumee Valley and "The Park."

In reflection, our days alone on the "hill" were private lessons of growing older. I learned how to manage my mother's growth and occasional abusive outbursts; it was during this period that I received 24 hour a day tutoring. This four-year period where Mama and I lived together on "The Hill" was the greatest period of my youth and it shaped the nature and direction of my philosophy, my college major, and career. I became the walking and talking embodiment of Bertha Lee Green; I wasn't a "poor black child," any longer; I was becoming a C. Wright Mills theorist mastering the sociological imagination. I was learning how to appreciate, accept, and see the good in people. Those Sundays defined my life and entire existence.

Sundays were a day of peace and Mama's house was my safe place.

Chapter 25.   Cheeseburger Truth at Woolworth's

Mama was convinced that everyone had a guardian angel and this was her truth.

Guy, while attending school, had a friend who had died far too early for his age. He was a young white boy who had befriended Guy when he started kindergarten at Oakdale. Inseparable, the boy died quickly and abruptly in his youth. Though Guy was devastated by his death, Mama believed that the boy became Guy's guardian angel. Here is why she believed this.

Mama and I had a wonderful monthly tradition where we would travel downtown for lunch at Woolworths Department Store where I was encouraged to eat anything I wanted. Typically, we both ordered cheeseburgers, French fries, and had a chocolate shake. Though the food never matched Mama's culinary homemade artistry, we reveled in our Woolworths visits. I was never keen on pickles so she would trade those for her fries.

Each time we dined, we sat on the red stools at the curved end of the table with our back facing the wall. We always looked over the restaurant for potential violent threats of persons seeking to rob the diner or pull a gun on the patrons. We were always on alert and made sure that we were safe.

At this time, Woolworths was a thriving business located downtown near the Toledo Blade Newspaper building. It was here that she reconfirmed her teachings of the Civil Rights Movement. I learned that Mama Green was separated from dominant society by a line based upon color; and that she had to drink from a "blacks only" water fountain and step off the sidewalk when whites approached. These arbitrary distinctions bothered me and sometimes I couldn't eat. In fact, I was nauseated by these images. The notion of hate hurt me to my soul. In response, she would rub my back and say, "It's okay, baby, we overcame."

As we discussed the Civil Rights Movement and the student sit-ins, I was always amazed that people would risk their lives over a cheeseburger in a fight for peace and equal rights. It was deeply ingrained in me that the separation of water fountains, dining establishments, and bathrooms were created over the innocuous and irrelevant nature of race. People were, and are, more similar than different, I was taught. While we ate I learned that love and respect should define relationships and not skin color. She taught me that people adapt to their circumstances based up their needs. If a person is hungry, they eat. If they are in love, they marry. If people are broke, they work. If people have, they share. If a person is in need, extend a hand. Feeding, loving, and sharing are elements of the human condition and not a matter of race. Mama proclaimed that **"A hungry white man seeks food just like a hungry black man."** These ideas had a direct and powerful impact on my thinking about humanity in general and race in particular.

Racial disparity and hate never made sense to me; people and respect of each other's humanity matter. Why hate when we, ourselves, are imperfect. She taught me that it is healthier to see the good in others than the bad, after all, *"We are all a little crazy." "People,"* she said, *"are more similar than they are different. Be good to people because honey attracts more bees than vinegar."*

After eating our cheeseburgers, we would walk to the Lion's Store, a few blocks away. The store had two lion statues that guarded the front door. Upon entry we made our way the second floor to pay her credit bill, which is where she bought clothes for me, herself, and Guy. My favorite part of the trip was to ride on the elevators that were opened to the walls and only separated by a golden gate that was manually operated. I rode in fear of losing a limb but was less fearful of that than the terrifying escalators. I had a secret fear that my shoestring would get eaten by the teeth at the top of the climb and shred me to pieces. Sensing my trepidation, Mama always held my hand in comfort.

Following the Lion's Store, we would cross the street and stand at the foot of the "Top of the Tower," the tallest skyscraper in Toledo. As we peered back at the Lion's Store, Mama pointed to a black haired boy across the street who looked at us and waved. She said, "Do you see that boy?"

"Yeah, Mama," I said.

She replied with, "That's Leo's guardian angel. He's the boy who died when Leo was younger. I see him whenever I stand here and look at the store." "Do you see him now?"

"No, Mama, he's gone." I replied.

"That's right, baby. He simply checks in on us and when he sees that everything is okay, then he disappears."

I could never prove or disprove her theory but being incapable of explaining otherwise, I reserved the right to believe that we all have guardian angels.

From there we would proceed and walk to the Nut House. They served all sorts of peanuts and we would purchase a pound of hot Spanish nuts. I was always permitted to eat a handful before arrived home. After dinner, typically fried chicken, mashed potatoes, greens, and crackling cornbread, I was permitted to finish the whole bag. It took hours as it was my custom to bite them in the center half to create a motor boat, where the seed rested, and its companion part. Though Mama would typically work in the kitchen preparing food for the next day, on occasion she would indulge me and play the boat game and let out a healthy "burp." Then I would have her burp the alphabet which she did

134

with laughter in her heart. At times, Mama, for fun, would say, "Listen closely," and "riiiiiiipppppppp," she'd burp again. That silly game always made me laugh, especially when I was down.

Sadly, the street corner between the Lion's Store and the Top of the Tower was the site of my most prolific and consistent nightmare. Periodically, I would dream that I was crossing the High Level Bridge from the East Side and heading to the Nut House. I would see Guy on my way to the location as he would head back to Mama's on Oakdale. As he waved goodbye, I would turn right onto Superior Street in the prodigious rain. When I looked down into the sewer pipe, I saw a high school teen who had slipped into the drainage grate and died when his neck snapped as his body sought the flow below. Each time I tried to run he would open his eyes, rolled back in his head, and say, "Tell Leo, I said Hello."

The night terror would prevent me from moving but I could scream. Mama would run into the room and wait for me to awaken. "Wake up, baby, it's just a dream." Each time I repeated the dream she would just hold me and say, "It's okay, baby. Everything is going to be alright, it's just a dream"

Similarly, my childhood friend, Tommy Thanasu (the boy I beat the hell out of in 1971 for hitting me in the nose with a roof tile as I rode my tricycle) and I both had a habit of sleep walking. Though he would often exit his home and walk down the middle of the street, I was more urine oriented. That is, I would walk over to Mama's flip top kitchen trash can concealed to the left by the oven, flip up the lid with my foot, and urinate into its opening. By the time I would wake up, thinking that I was at my mother's house on Utah Street, the can was filled. Embarrassed, I would close it quickly and sprint back to my bedroom, slip my hand under the pillow to feel the gun, double check the shotgun in the corner, and fall asleep.

Mama never once made an issue of my puddled mess in the garbage.

135

In reflection, I did experience peace and tranquility living in a threatening environment and a home of perpetual threat from outside intruders. I learned how to live in peace; all I had to do was call Mama. She provided me with an education that I did not learn at school but allowed me to see the value of love. Eating nuts, going downtown, and dining at Woolworth's Department Store was a great experience in valuing history, diversity, and education. And, I was taught that guardian angels exist, even if it is only through the spirit of memories.

Aside from the ongoing fear of never-ending threat, I always knew that I was safe. I yearn for that place today, still.

Chapter 26.   Mr. Johnny and Calls from the Grave

After Daddy died, Mr. Johnny soon entered the picture and started to date Mama. I always wondered to myself, where did this little round man, with a cigar permanently perched to his lips, come from? Did Daddy Green know him? Didn't Mama love Daddy Green? I was jealous and angry, especially when I saw her kiss him on the front porch by the canned vegetables. She assured me, though, that Mr. Johnny was a good and hard-working man and I, unconditionally, accepted her proclamation.

Mr. Johnny was always kind to me. Like Daddy, he was a truck driver and was quiet, kind, and funny. He was a jovial man, though he was not Daddy. He drove a Lincoln jalopy and lived in a shack off of Manhattan Blvd., on the west end. His yard was unkempt and his indoor living space was disheveled beyond belief. I never saw any rats there but their entrails encrusted the outside of his fake Persian carpet. But, man, oh man, he loved Mama Green. Often he would bring food, usually buffalo carp, and she would cook it. No matter the meal, somehow, she always began telling stories and we would sit and listen. Though the cigar smoke from Mr. Johnny would burn my eyes, we all laughed nonetheless.

At times, Mr. Johnny would say that he was late for whatever reason and she would reply, "John White, *you're as full of shit as a fat dog is fleas.*" I would laugh and he would roar with this unreal bellow that rattled as, "Ooohhhhhhh hoooooooo hooooooo hooooooooo hooooooo, Bertha you're just so ridiculous." Then she would quickly reply with, "*You think you're so high [soriety]? Well you're not.*" That was their running joke. Whenever Mama dressed well for church he would say, "Bertha, you're so high soriety." When he came over wearing a tie she would say, "John White, you think you're so high soriety." I would just giggle and laugh as "high soriety" echoed in my head.

After Mama's death many others rallied to her side. Iris, a light skinned and overweight friend, with a big mole on the inside right side of her nose, would call her on the phone. She tended to talk too much and get on Mama's nerves. It got to the point where I had to screen messages to avoid Iris. Somehow, though, when she visited, Iris always got Mama to drink homebrew and perform the Camel Walk and the Apple Jack to James Brown's, "I Feel Good." The songs and dancing would last late into the night.

But, in time, though, Mama developed a phone code for whenever I called which consisted of, "Let it ring twice, hang up, and call again." Mama would answer on the second call and, typically, it was to let her know I was on my way to her house. She wanted to know my whereabouts so she could watch out the window to make sure I was safe.

Once, though, while walking the railroad tracks, I had crossed under the railroad to a barrage of rocks flying from above. A bunch of boys were hitting me in the head and taunting my mother with, "Your mother is a bitch. Your mother is a bitch." I yelled up at them, "You better run punks because I'm coming back to shoot you in your ass."

I stormed into Mama Green's house as Guy was visiting with his first son, Jason, and I walked straight to the purse holding "Black Beauty" and pulled it out. As I spun toward the front door with the gun in hand, Mama said, petrified, said "No baby, put the gun down. Leo stop him." I said, "Mama, some kids were talking about my mother and calling her names. I am going to kill them." Inside, I just wanted to be tough like Mama; I wanted to prove that I was strong and not a weakling. I wanted my mother to be proud that I stood up for her.

So, Guy backed away when I pointed the gun at him and said, "Move out of the way, Guy," as fire lurched in my eyes. All of the pent up abuse was seething through my pores and I felt that if I shot these bullies, my mother would be proud of me for having courage.

138

I crashed through the front door and yelled for Mama's Army of dogs to stand in line and follow me off to war. "Tweety, Bojack, Smut, Toji, let's go." In my head, I knew someone was going to die as me and my army marched down the stone covered driveway to Oakdale Street. In single file, we crossed the street, ran to the side of the railroad tracks, and marched to the overpass. Prepared to pull the trigger, I looked up for the boys and said, "I hope you are ready to die mother fuckers because I'm back." No one was there and I thanked God that I didn't have to shoot anyone.

As I walked back to the house, I realized that it was all a blur. The world that I had known had gone white, and I had blacked out. As I walked into the house Guy stared at me, and I put the gun back in the purse. "Mama," I said, "Do you have any peach cobbler, I'm hungry."

She never said a word about it and Guy buried the event as well (until we talked about it after dropping Jason off at Johnson and Wales, 20 years later).

Other people called Mama on the phone as well. Mr. and Mrs. Prater called often; R.L. and bald-headed Ruth visited; Dottie and Wizette and their kids, Coco, Lisa, Tammy, Sonya, Timmy, Tyrone, and Tony spent much of the summer with us in 1975. Their kids and I were "cousins" and inseparable. Sonya and I were the youngest and she was probably my best friend. She was so fair, quiet, and sweet that we bonded immediately. She grew up to be so beautiful and actually went to see Beverly Hills Cop with me and Mama in 1984; it was the last, and only, movie that Mama and I ever saw together at a theatre.

As cousins, us kids simply enjoyed each other. Coco was affectionately known as Grandma. Each evening she wore a long gown that skirted the floor and Mama said she looked like her grandmother. Tammy was the eldest and was the leader, except when Tony or Tyrone were around. Timmy was known as "Smiley" since he always had a grin on his face. Lisa was the toughest of them all and full of life and humor.

139

Sonya, was my buddy. We joked together, told stories together, and she even allowed me to show her how I played "war" in the garden by launching dirt clumps at mini-soldiers. My cousins and I loved each other unconditionally as only kids can.

One evening, Mama had allowed all of us to walk over to the Hoffman's Convenient Store on Tracy Road. It wasn't a far walk but it was one where we had to pay close attention to traffic. At the end of Mama's driveway, we had to turn right and travel without a sidewalk along the outskirts of the factory fence. Cars raced by as we held hands. The dogs were obedient to me, and all I had to say at the "Field of Mystery" was, "Stay here guys;" and they would sit and watch us walk. They never moved until we returned.

Hoffman's had six aisles and a meat counter in the back. Mama had given us $2.00 each to purchase whatever "your little hearts desired." I bought Cane's Potato Chips, Timmy bought the new Nacho Cheese flavored Doritos, and all of the girls bought a candy bar. Our little excursion was one that built a friendship bond that lasted for decades. As a matter of fact, I wanted to marry Sonya badly but I just didn't know exactly what that meant. I just knew she was special and made my little heart patter whenever she was near.

At night, Timmy and I slept in Mama Green's bed. Though my bedroom was Guy's old room, if it were too cold (and I usually had 5-6 blankets) I slept with Mama. She would wrap her huge feet around mine to keep me warm. And, as always, I slept with a pistol under my pillow; in Guy's bedroom, I had an antique shotgun in the corner. Given the frequency of break-in attempts, I was instructed to fire if anyone entered my room; happily, the guns never flashed their deadly flame.

At night, I would take strings and ropes and construct "booby" traps. They were designed to knock the clock off of the dresser to awaken me; another string was tied to my big toe. I was always prepared for intruders. On that summer night, when Timmy saw me put the gun

140

under my pillow, he said, "What is that for?"

I simply said, "To shoot someone if they break in." Mama used to always tell me, *"Shoot to kill because they can always come back to get revenge."* When I told Timmy my intentions he humorously said, "Oh, okay," nodded in agreement, and off to sleep we went.

One morning we were all playing in the front room listening to Sly Stone, the Jackson Five, and a series of Stevie Wonder songs. Tony, who was old enough to drive, had come over to check on everyone to make sure things were running smoothly. When he arrived, Mama told me, as she often would, *"Don't go to a party and be a wallflower, dance."* So she put on ABC by the Jackson Five and told Tony to teach me how to dance. The first move he taught me was to raise my right foot behind my back up to my left hand, drop it to the ground, spin to my left, and slide my feet to the left, while imitating a robot with my hands and head. Though the girls laughed, Mama made us all dance. Dancing became my greatest lifelong hobby that afternoon.

As we partied in the living room, Mama would put a huge wad of Red Man Chewing Tobacco into her gum and cheek (sometimes she would use snuff or unroll a cigar and chew it) and spit it into her cup. One day, Tammy wanted to try it and kept asking Mama Green for some chewing tobacco. Mama had told me to never smoke or use tobacco because it could rot your teeth out and, *"You always want to take care of your teeth. I don't have any teeth so I don't have a beautiful smile like you."* Bertha had started chewing at the age of ten and it had ruined her teeth and "[Gumes]," as she called them.

So, being the extrovert that I am, I said, "Mama, I want to try it too."

"Okay, all you kids, I want you to take a little out of the bag and hold it in your hand. When I count to three, I want you to put it in your mouth."

141

"One....Two....Three....chew."

"Okay, taste the juice?"

"Okay, swallow it."

Giggling as school kids do, we all put the tobacco in our mouths, chewed, and swallowed as instructed. The nasty filth burned in my throat as it went down to my stomach and exploded. I tried with all of the speed that my hands could muster to wipe the brown wretchedness from my tongue but it wouldn't leave. "Oh, my God! Oh, my God, this is awful!" I just wanted to die.

When we were done with our agony, Mama simply said, "How did you like that? Are you ever going to use tobacco again?"

We uniformly said, "Noooooooooooooooooooooooooooooooooo." Sadly, Timmy and Tony would go on to have drug addictions, that would lead them to the crack cocaine train and ultimately into prison. It's ironic, though, when I had heard of their travels to the Department of Rehabilitation and Correction, it dawned on me that not all prisoners are bad people, they just do "bad" things. Timmy and Tony were two of the funniest and most charismatic people that I had ever met; the drug demons stole their young souls, but not my friendship or love for them.

It was hard watching beautiful Sonya gag but we all laughed, nonetheless. I never chewed tobacco or smoked cigarettes after that. Erma Jean and my mom smoked 2-3 packs a day and Mama smoked cigars. But me, forget it.

I always thought it was ironic that all of the adults in our lives smoked and used tobacco products but the kids were not allowed. We could drink but we couldn't smoke. At times, especially when we were all in a car together, the tobacco was a thick cloud that embraced my body. I always wondered if I smelled like smoke when I went to school; as it was a part of my daily existence; I must have smelled awful. Thankfully, smoking was normalized behavior in the 1970's so that I really did not worry too much about stigma. When I was with my cousins, such concerns were moot.

When my cousins and I played, I always felt like a star showing them what I did for fun. Timmy shined playing baseball with me at Hathaway Park; the girls danced with me; Lisa, who went on to be a basketball sensation at Scott High School, shot hoops with me on the broken rim nailed to the tree; and Sonya and I talked. Well, she listened and laughed as I talked. I had motor mouth around her and she was, by nature, quiet.

On one particular evening, my mother had unexpectedly come to pick me up to go home. Having had a great time, I simply said, "Can I stay another night?" And it happened, the control that my mother had worked so hard to develop disappeared and a raging maniac presented herself -" What, don't you love me? You love her [Mama Green] more than you love me?" And an unexpected rage exploded.

She grabbed me by the hair and pulled me down the porch stairs to drag me across the driveway to the car. As the other kids watched out the window in horror, she began flinging me around and threw me inside the automobile. Then, she continued pulling my hair from the driver's seat and punching me. She said, "If you don't want me as a mother, you little bastard, you can just stay here forever."

I protested, "I love you mom and I want to be with you."

Mama ran to the car and stood at the window pleading for "Susie" to "stop!" "He can stay with me; he can stay with me. Don't hurt him."

"Mom," I said, "I want to be with you." My tears looked at Mama as she extended her hand toward me. "You can stay with me."

My mother peeled out of the driveway as Mama looked on in tears. From the corner of my eyes, I could see her standing by the woodpile

143

next to the stones lining the driveway. "No, Susie. No, Susie." I was beat mercilessly when we arrived home. I was body slammed onto the stove, punched, and swung face first into the refrigerator as I blacked out from the pain; my body went into shock; I awoke in the hospital but cannot, to this day, remember much of it. The next thing I knew, I was being released from the hospital. Mama Green was taking me home to be with my cousins. Shame permeated my soul and my cousins simply hugged me and said, independently, "I love you; you are family."

Mama held me and declared that it would never happen again. She used her old adage that, *"There is nothing the drugstore that will kill you faster than me over you."* My torments rose, however; my spirit was detaching from my body as anticipatory terror filled my veins. I was petrified of my mother, especially if she drank alcohol. But I nestled into Mama Green's bosom so as to allow my soul to be guarded by this angel. My fear of mom and detachment of pain from body had become rooted in the core and fiber of my essence. My only salvation was the fortress "on the hill."

Though the memory is unmistakable and conjures terror in my heart, the aftermath was even more troubling. While I was staying at Mama's house, my mother received a late night phone call. At roughly three or four in the morning, as Mama told me (and my mother confirmed the story in 2012), Daddy Green had called her from the grave. According to Mama, he simply called my mother and gently said, "Do not beat that boy any more, Susie." Then he made his distinct whistle sound and faded off the phone. My mother, who was deeply enmeshed in the world of the supernatural and paranormal, sat frozen. She never told me of the call until nearly four decades had passed.

The phone call shook her to the quick. The physical violence dropped off immeasurably, though not altogether, as I always lived in terror as alcohol certainly overrode her good judgment. Sadly, there was more embarrassment in front of friends when she would come home drunk, trip over furniture, pass out on the floor or couch in front of us, or she would yell at me saying that I was the reason for our poverty. She would say, "Sending you to Maumee Valley is keeping us broke and you don't even appreciate it." I think the mental and emotional abuse hurt more than the physical but I'm not sure. Though Daddy's "call" helped curtail the physical violence, it never fully disappeared.

Two years after the driveway beating, while watching television at Mama's House, Jason looked up in the window overlooking the kitchen/dining room doorway and said:

"Who is that man up there with the angel?"

Mama and I looked and didn't see anything. Jason repeated, "Don't you see that man with the angel?" We looked at each other puzzled when suddenly we both heard Daddy Green's whistle travel from the kitchen, to the back hallway, and out the back door to the porch.

We looked at each other, stunned, and said, "Did you hear that?"

Jason said, "Did you see the man walk out the back door?"

In reflection, I have never been able to fully understand the phone call or angel events. I do, however, remember the insidious nature of anticipatory terror, humiliation, and the despair associated with alcoholism and childhood violence. Though my mother still had growing to do, I was blessed to have a social "family," a spirit, school buffers, and a woman named Mama. With age I learned of the term "shaken baby syndrome" and feel that would have been my fate had the stars not aligned and dropped the spirit of Bertha and Leo Green in my path.

I am, in my heart, a statistic that never happened; I was neither aborted nor murdered. And, for that, I owe the universe.

Section Three: LIFE AWAY FROM "THE HILL"

Chapter 27.   Baseball and the Big Guys

Prior to the fall of 1974, I had only been stung once by a bee. It was early summer and Mr. Bill and I were listening to the Tigers on the radio. Gates Brown, a renowned pinch hitter, had belted a two run shot to deep centerfield. As we were celebrating and eating well sauced spare ribs, I took a drink of cold water from my tin cup. A yellow jacket surreptitiously landed on my right middle finger and ejected his tiny but mighty stinger.

I cried like I had been shot.

Within seconds, Mama had sprinted out the door to see what had happened. Mama saw the swelling and ran in the house, grabbed some ice cubes, put them in a baggy and soothed my damaged middle finger. I crushed the fuck out of that bee.

Aside from the pesky sting, the summer of '74 was one for the record books. By this time, I was a regular sports participant at Hathaway Street Park. The old Hathaway School building that rested there had long been razed; Boonie's father, Don, had attended school there. For us kids, like Boonie and myself, the "Park" was the greatest source of amusement around. We were lucky, too. Unlike most kids our age, we were allowed to play baseball with the big guys.

Life lessons, right and wrong, were learned there. Drugs, alcohol, girls, sex, and sports were daily specials. All of the older guys, Junior and Johnny Gonzalez, David Keister and his girlfriend, Kathy Wodarski, Donnie Shephard, Squeak, the Jones brothers, Bob Dudley, Billy Brady, Louie Segura, and Richie Spencer were the core of our existence.

Boonie, Billy Mills, and I were the youngest to be allowed to play baseball, basketball, and football with the older guys. Sports were seasonal and man, did we play. During the hot summer months, it was typical for the guys to drink 40 ounce Schlitz Malt Liquor Bull, smoke marijuana, use speed, and just hang out. The guys would stand in a circle and pass around the marijuana roach. I never tried any "rope," as Spence called it, but I would taste beer once in a while. I knew that if I came home smelling like marijuana, a severe beating awaited.

When we were 7, Boonie and I were usually used as "artificial" runners. Jackie Thanaseu, who had a learning disability, was always the "official" pitcher. In sandlot baseball, unless we had enough players to maintain a first basemen we played baseball where the pitcher's mound was base. Any ball hit to shortstop, or third, could result in an out if the pitcher caught it before the runner touched first base. Right field was closed. The basketball pole was considered an obstruction and a ground rule single. Anyone who hit Chuckie's house across the street had a home run. Balls hit into the thorn trees in center or left field were automatic doubles. Refreshingly, the games played from sunrise until sunset as people came from other neighborhoods to join us; the competition was fierce.

During fielding practice, Boonie and I were allowed play shortstop, outfield, or third base. Donnie Shepherd was a phenom at third and loved Brooks Robinson; Squeak played Shortstop, and Johnny was a great centerfielder. His greatest play occurred when his brother hit a line drive to center field and Johnny jumped into the thorn tree to rob the ground rule double. However, for Boonie and me, it was great to play shortstop. Incredibly, we usually played without making errors and eventually were allowed on the field with the older guys during the "actual" games. The older girls who watched would typically say, "Oh, he's so cute," and then, they would rub the hair on my head.

Sometimes we played strikeout, which was a fast pitch game using shadow runners with player created ground rules. In strikeout, there

147

was a catcher and an umpire. Usually Junior called balls and strikes as he was regarded as the most honorable member of the Hathaway Park crew; he was the leader and his nickname was "Chewy." He was Mama Green's favorite kid at Waite High School due to his diplomatic disposition; her dream was to cut his super long hair and make a wig out of it; humorously, Mama always called him Tony.

Strikeout rules were simple but different than sandlot. The fence by Eloy's house was our backstop. A line drive that made it to the basketball court was a ground rule single; a bounce over the fence and into the merry-go-round area was a double; off the wall beyond the swings was a triple and a home run was over the fence or the huge oak tree in left center field. Strikeout was the best game in the world and the pitchers relentlessly threw fastballs, curves, and dropballs. Even for his age, Boonie was a pitching legend. I played utility positions but was an excellent hitter and fielder for my size.

There were certainly moments of danger at the park. Once in a while, my attending Maumee Valley Country Day School, a top school in the region, had me defined as a snob; having Erma Jean live in our house also had me defined as a "nigger-lover." Once, a guy at the Park confronted me as a "nigger-lover" and without hesitation I said, "Well, I love you and all of these guys. So, what does that mean about you?" It was the last time that I was called that name, at the Park, at least.

At one point, neighbors actually passed a petition around the neighborhood to have Erma Jean move out of my mom's house; the leader of the movement later turned out to be a great friend to the family.

Once, while waiting to bat in a game of strikeout, a guy named "House" pulled out a switch blade and pushed it up to my neck and proclaimed, "I could kill you right now if I wanted." I agreed and said, "Yes, you could. But, House, I'm on deck and have to bat next." He pulled the knife back and said, "You're right." Though I am positive he wasn't

148

going to kill me, it shook me and my friend Chris up quite a bit. Ironically, it was that same knife that was soon used in a most heinous animal murder that I have ever witnessed.

While resting between games, smoking dope, and drinking beer, the same House brought a box of baby pigeons to the Park. I can remember looking at the thirty or so babies and thinking about how cute they were. Then it happened, House took out his knife and decapitated a baby. He threw its head into the box and tossed the pigeon into the air. I was amazed that it flew. Some ten minutes later, there was a cardboard box filled with heads and pigeon bodies in the air, on window sills, and strewn in the grass. Several birds landed in "the Mean Old Lady's" yard next to the park and the guys celebrated such an unfortunate fate. She was horrified and never kept another one of our balls that inadvertently flew onto her property.

For us younger guys, we tolerated the drugs and pigeon torture so that we could play. Donnie Shepard was our coach and constantly taught us how to hit, field, and in football season to "Keep your legs moving" when running the ball. He used to come down to the house at 1315 and play "Smear the Queer" and "Running up the Hill." Smear the queer was a one against everyone football game where a player caught the ball as all others tried to tackle [him]. And, when one landed on the tip of the ball it forced a dislodging of air that felt like death. "Up the Hill" required one player to stand at the bottom of the 8 foot hill while everyone else stood at the top. A football was thrown down to the runner who then had to avoid being tackled and score a touchdown by reaching the top of the hill safely. All of these games socialized Boonie, Chris and Brian Strock, Billy, and I to become top-tiered athletes. We were fierce, competitive, and had the drive to win at all costs.

The games were brutal, too. There is nothing quite as painful as getting tackled on the side of a hill and thrown into the cement alley. If we experienced pain, we had to "shake it off." Donnie was our first and greatest coach until the "Accident." A couple of years after Johnny had been hit by a car on Oak Street, Donnie found himself deathly intoxicated. While crawling out a window and onto a fire escape at the Bank and Bar Tavern on the corner of Fassett and Oak Streets, he fell through the hole from the second floor. He landed on his head and rolled down a flight of stairs into the cellar but, amazingly, survived. The brain damage was significant but he was able to rehabilitate and play sports, at a lower level, again.

Poor and dirty, Donnie reshaped my life. Once while the guys were smoking weed, they asked me if I wanted to smoke and I, as always, politely responded with a "No." Then, someone asked me if I thought I was "better than them. Was I judging them?"

Remembering Mama Green's advice, *"Don't judge others as you have never walked in their shoes,"* My answer was, "No, I'm not judging you for smoking dope. Are you judging me for not smoking?" Fair enough. Some months later, Donnie and Squeak pulled me aside and said, "You do know that we really respect you a lot for not smoking with us. Though you're just a kid, you are able to say no and that says a lot."

Junior chimed in, later, while pointing his index finger at me and said, "Someday, you're going to be a doctor."

My response was simple, "No, I don't want to be a doctor, I want to replace Joe Morgan as the second basemen for the Reds." The guys laughed and said, "Yeah, right, ok." Even when Deanna had offered her love to me, playing for the Reds was my excuse to avoid any physical or intimate relationship.

When the guys got bored they figured out new ways to entertain themselves. One game was to put me and Jerry Berry, my neighbor, in a trash can and roll us around the playground to make us dizzy. They knew the story of how Jerry and I would practice rolling down the stairs at his house "just in case" we were ever pushed down the stairs. So,

150

they rolled us in a trash can, down the Utah Street steps, and into a tree. Oddly, I loved the game but Jerry wasn't such a big fan.

One day, the park was packed. People were there from all over the place, including Mama Green's nephew Timmy. Dave Gwinners, the target of the local saying, "Come on Dave," was present. Anytime someone would say something stupid, trite, or obvious, the response was the same;" Come on, Dave." The other gesture of control was to take fingertips and rub them on the bottom of a targets chin suggesting fellatio or "suck my dick." That one irritated me the most and made me feel dirty, angry, and small.

Unfortunately, once, while playing right field, I dropped a pop-up using Guy's old glove. The guys on my team tore into me until Junior made them stop. "Come on, Dave." "Loser." I cried and my anger escalated. Timmy took my place and played a magnificent game making me jealous for my demotion, but happy that my cousin fit in so well. He hugged me on the way back to Mama Green's house with a sincere and apt, "It's okay, Cuz, you'll catch the next one."

That evening, I had a "real" game playing for the Maumee Valley Country Day School Mini-Mohawks. The school bent the rules and allowed me to play though I was two years too young. My mother would not permit me to be denied; spending time with Mama Green and Erma Jean was teaching her how to love and care that had long been denied in her childhood. While playing third base that evening, a player on the other team hit a screaming line drive at my head. Instinctively, I caught the ball, whipped it to second base, and then the ball was turned to first. It was my first game and we had turned a triple play – the only one in my life. When I told the guys at the Park about the play they gave me a pass for the dropped pop-up the day before. Little did I know that Junior relished me playing baseball with the Mini-Mohawks and secretly loved the team mascot's name.

151

Mr. Sowalksy, rumored to have been a partial owner of the Cincinnati Reds, was a tremendous kid's coach at MVCDS. He would say, "When a grounder comes, put your knee down and block the ball." Though it was underhand pitch and felt a little childish compared to strikeout and sandlot at Hathaway Park, it was fun, nonetheless. Toughening practices were abysmal, however. Mr. Sowalsky had a drill where he would line us up, side by side, stand five or six feet away, and throw the baseball into our stomachs. The first time it hit me, I fell to the ground in pain with a strong and passionate desire to cry.

"Does it hurt?" he yelled.

My response was, "Yes, it kills."

Quickly and unassumingly, he would say, "No, it doesn't hurt. Shake it off. Boys don't cry."

Then he threw the ball again at my stomach and I absorbed the pain. "Now, pick it up and throw it to first," he exclaimed. After I made a Joe Morgan-like snap throw to first, he raved, "Yes, that's how it's done." And with that, my separation of pain from emotion and body was underway and my prowess as a second base all-star was set. The life lessons were secure. Mike Messner's theory of the internalization of pain through detached emotions was true; to be a man, I was learning, was to be emotionally absent. It was a true lesson of masculinity but a remarkably destructive one.

His son David was a masterful switch hitter and taught me how to bat left-handed as well.

The guys at the park were always impressed that I could bat left and right handed. As I improved at baseball, football, and basketball my draft stock rose. One of the greatest days of my life was when I wasn't chosen last on a team. Though the guys were always complimentary, though I was still only half their age. My talent in playing sports somehow even made the girls like me. One sixteen year old girl even asked me if I wanted a "Foolish Pleasure," a code name for sex, after the Kentucky Derby winner of '74.

She was stunning. Her long hair danced in the sun and her huge chest was flawless. On one lucky day, her younger brother untied her top and it fell to the ground. Yes, her bared chest sat in full view for about ten seconds as I sat transfixed, thinking about the hundreds of Playboy pictures that I had seen at Tommy's House hidden in his secret dresser drawer. "Oh, my God," I thought to myself, "those are just like the ones in the magazines." Not knowing what to do I just stared in embarrassment; she simply asked, "Do you like what you see?" Like the school child that I was, I simply said, "Uh, huh." But, when her visiting friend offered me more than a sneak peek, I was petrified and said, "I'm already doing Foolish Pleasure's with a girl at school." When she went on to say, "Well, sweetie, how do you do it at school?" I said, "The same way you do it on the mattress in the yellow shed across the street." Fortunately, the conversation ended and I ran over to an emerging game of strikeout. I was such a nervous, asexual child back then.

In addition, all I could hear in my head was Mama Green saying, *"Don't mess with no fast ass hoes."* Though Ms. Long Hair was no hoe, and was always gentle with me, her friend was enticing. Erma Jean's anti-sex confirmations demanded that I never mess with the girls because I had too much going for me while attending Maumee Valley. She would say, "Don't get a girl pregnant, and keep your penis out of their mouth." Disgusted by the thought, I simply would say, "Ok, Jeeaaaannnnn." All the while, I wondered what it would be like to be alone with a girl in the shed.

At the park, sexual encounters were discussed with tremendous bravado and the yellow shed was used to store sporting equipment, but also had a twin sized mattress on the floor. Once, when given the honor

153

of collecting the bats and balls from there, I actually saw the love nest with a monster indentation in the middle. I suppose that's where the local teenage prostitution took place, though it's not confirmed. I never saw it but heard that it was a frequent occurrence, and that knowledge scared sexuality out of my development. The thought of physical intimacy was intimidating, dirty, and distant.

Meanwhile, rumors circulated that "The Cat Lady" on the street was a prostitute for professional wrestlers. She was heavy, never wore shoes, toothless, and sported a disheveled hair style. Yet, she was a friend to my mom and Erma Jean and made regular visits to our house. It was believed, and confirmed, that she also had a couple of teenage boys who she sold into prostitution. Though these cross-currents of permissive sexual standards were really strange in hindsight, the scenario seemed quite normal at the time.

Yes, I liked girls and had many, many, many girlfriends. But, intimacy was not something I cherished. Having different men in and out of my house on Utah Street, avoiding hoes, and keeping my penis in my pants just didn't make me feel like pursuing much activity. But, for some reason women were always trying to touch my hair, ask me to kiss them, to "suck my dick," or even have sex. I was only eight, for crying out loud.

I suppose, though, that I had other experiences that muddied the confusing sexuality waters. For example, whenever I went to get milk or pop at Gladys' Variety store on Fassett Street, there was an old lady who would follow me. She was shriveled, missing most teeth, and stood around the size of my mother. The first tim, she kissed me on the top of the head I felt like it was a nice gesture. After five or six times, it bothered me. Then, on one sordid occasion, she kissed me on the lips and slipped her tongue into my mouth; "Goddammit"; I thought I would die. Mama Green, who used dentures herself, had never advised me on how to deal with an old woman French kissing young boys.

154

In reflection, the Park was a great place. Little kids like me learned about life, sex, sports, drugs, and girls there. Some of the lessons were misleading and even intimidating. However, except for a few minor fist fights and erratic acts of violation, it was a place where I felt "safe." Though I had been hurt, pushed to the ground, threatened, punched, challenged, I learned that the bigger kids were simply trying to make me tough. I learned later, and from my mom, that I had to be strong and unafraid to fight. Strength and fearlessness were prized commodities in the neighborhood and were invaluable to navigating the complex "Street" rules in East Toledo.

Remarkably, the older guys allowed us to feel safe. Boonie and I were always protected though we were tested as a rite of passage. If, and when, outsiders came to the Park and challenged us, we had our backup. Sadly, some of the lessons in toughness and male bravado were damaging as well. Namely, and in combination with the ongoing threat of beatings at home, my emotions detached from my feeling self. I had to build an exterior wall of fearlessness though I was petrified internally. My intimate relationships suffered the most as I always made it a habit to build protective walls around my identity to protect my essence. Consequently, my youthful sexuality was compromised and my diplomatic and "well-mannered" upbringing was, at times, suspended. The Park provided me with some of my fondest memories of childhood while equally damaging my emotional self. It is this same internal contradiction that persists to the current day.

Chapter 28.   Boonie, Broken Windows, and Little Crazy Joe

Boonie and I used to spend considerable time practicing baseball, football, basketball, and soccer together when no one was around. One of the favorite plays in baseball was to rob another of a home run as the ball was clearing the fence. So, Boonie and I would hit fly balls with my red, white, and blue ball and try to rob each other of home runs.

Once, while Boonie was batting and I was in right field at the fence, he hit one too high for my glove to reach. Then with a mighty crash, the ball went through the picture window at "Crazy Mary's" house. Startled, I looked back and saw Boonie sprint away from the Park with my Joe Morgan bat in hand. Instead of running, I reflected on what my mom had taught me, "If you ever break a window tell the owners what happened and let them know that I will pay for its replacement."

When I looked back at Mary's house, her father was in full sprint with a sledge hammer yelling, "You are going to die for this you little mother fucker." When I looked into the eyes of the "Schneider" look alike from the Valerie Bertinelli show, "One Day at a Time," death saw my fear. I turned, and like the DC Comic book The Flash, I started to sprint like a "bat out of hell." As he chased me down the street, he kept yelling, "I'm going to kill you, you little bastard." I learned that when one is scared, their adrenalin will kick in and I could fly.

While running toward home, I decided to cut through Tommy Thanasu's yard (so that Schneider would think that was my house) and divert his attention away from me. After cutting through all of my neighborhood shortcuts (Chris Strock and I had developed a series of escape routes through the neighborhood in case we were ever chased by a predator in order to avoid capture), I had lost him as I jumped over the fence at the Big Yellow House on the corner of Hathaway and Utah. I was safe and Boonie was comfortable at home. That was the only time someone

156

threatened me with a sledge hammer. Later, though, I was chased with a pitchfork my neighbor April's dad, the tenants who moved into Jerry Berry's old house after his family moved to Oak Street.

In spite of the fear, and with continued practice and playing one-on-one strikeout with Boonie, I was finally invited to play baseball with the big guys at Weiler Homes. Though I had watched games there before, I was never allowed to play. It was fast pitch and the games were "for real." Boonie and I were the only little kids invited to play.

I was so excited the whole entire day. Erma Jean had cooked some T-Bone steaks, reserved for those few days when we had extra money, made mashed potatoes, green beans, and collard greens. Mama even celebrated with a hearty congratulation, and said, "Sock it to 'em."

When we arrived at the field, sitting just on the other side of the railroad tracks and down the hill from the structurally failing Fassett Street Bridge, the Weiler Homes boys were waiting for us. They were really a street gang with a heavily influenced structure built from the Detroit gang model. Though the games were peaceful, it was always clear that Hathaway and Weiler were mortal combatants. We wouldn't travel there without nunchucks and knives. Me, I had no weapons.

Just before the game started, I learned that our coach, Junior, had placed me eighth in the batting lineup which hurt my feelings considerably. At Maumee Valley, I was the leadoff hitter and now I was batting at the bottom of the lineup. I was crushed until Chewy made amends. It was brilliant.

"Hey, Shawn Louis," (every time I was in trouble with mom she would yell out my middle name, the guys never learned my last name was Schwaner until I was in high school), "Do you think that the cleanup hitter is important batting position on a team?" he asked.

"Yes, Junior," I said while sulking, "It's for power hitters."

157

"Correct," he said.

"Yeah and?" I responded.

Junior simply said, "You are the second cleanup hitter on our team. You like Cesar Geronimo of the Reds, right?"

"Yes, I love him and everyone else on the team," I retorted.

"Well, he bats eighth just like you, and he's an all-star, right?" Junior said.

"Right, he is." After I thought about the comparisons and analogy, all I could do was say, "Thanks Junior for making me a cleanup hitter."

Then I nested in behind the backstop as Junior said, "You have to watch the pitcher to learn his motion and speed. It's different to hit fast pitch with a baseball rather than a rubber ball in strikeout. Plus, watch, this guy throws a submarine ball. Take a bat, put a donut on it, and get ready."

After swinging the bat a few times, I sat by the fence awaiting my turn to bat. Our team was doing well as Squeak and Spence had both gotten on base. Junior batted fourth and ripped a shot to left field. After the two runs had scored, I began to get excited about my chance to step to the plate.

As my body energized for my grand debut, I could feel someone rubbing my hair. Expecting to see a girl, I was shocked to see a guy named Little Crazy Joe. He always scared me with his thin mustache, distant bloodshot eyes, and his erratic and whimsical behavior. And true to form, he was drunk. He was drinking a 40 ounce Old English 800 and was slurring his speech with red bloodshot eyes. He had come to the Park a few times but not often.

With the quickness of a lightning strike he whipped his penis out of his pants, placed it on my head, rolled it in my hair, and began to masturbate. I was frozen because I knew he was carrying a knife; I knew he was drunk; I knew he was crazy; I believed he had an arrest history. All I could think was that, "I don't matter." "Can't any of the big guys see this shit?" I thought to myself. "Where's Junior, Keister, and Squeak? Why won't they stop him?"

I felt dirty, invisible, and was experiencing an absolute level of humiliation. As the tears swelled in my eyes, a homeboy named Louie Segura, always a protector, like Junior, ran to my aid.

"What the fuck are you doing, mother fucker?" he yelled at Little Crazy Joe.

"I'm getting off on this mother fucker! What's it to you, man?"

Then I heard a "wham" and saw the beer bottle falling to the ground and rolling in the dirt. Little Crazy Joe's jeans had flapped over his penis making it invisible. Groggy, he stood up to Louie's tirade, "Get the fuck out of here and don't come back." I praise Louie (now deceased), for protecting me from a far worse trauma, though it hurt enough.

When my time to bat came, I hit an angry line drive to center field for my first big kid single. Even the pitcher for Weiler Holmes said, "Good hit, kid." After I scored, I received high fives and an extra pat on the back from Louie, "Good hit, Shawn Louis." Soon, thereafter, the day became dark, a severe thunderstorm rolled in, and we went home, winners. My esteem, though, was defeated. I came home a victor though I came home defeated. My team had won but I lost my esteem.

In reflection, the sports served as a curious overlap of affirmation, esteem, and threat. In the moment, sports provided a sense of community and belonging. In the next moment, deviance, threat, and total destruction awaited. Overall, those days of play gave me a competitive advantage to win at any, and all, cost; simultaneously, the confusion and mixed messages on friendship and safety created fears and a fatalistic attitude wrapped pristinely in mysteries that I have yet to unravel. I am a warrior afraid of shadows; I am petrified prey ready to stiffen like a bronze soldier in war. Sports, the threat of violence, and curious sexual encounters froze this mild-mannered and well behaved kid into a curious mix of fear and fearlessness. It is curious, indeed.

Thank God I had Mama and two other strong women to navigate these messy and contradictory messages.

Chapter 28.   The Mini-Mohawks and Camp Big Silver Lewdness

My mother was a fantastic orthopedic nurse and after healing from her "nervous breakdown," I began spending more time at home. She and Erma Jean had switched from their night schedules to day which permitted me to be home more often. Yet, I still spent more time on the "Hill" to avoid the wretched kitchen battleground.

With Mama's salvation, however, my mom increasingly became a mother and workplace leader. During the 1970's as Gloria Steinem, an East Toledo descendent, was leading the women's right's movement and gathering feminist support, my mother became the President of the Ohio Nurse's Association. As a nurse, she was incomparable and a local orthopedic celebrity; as a leader, she was known throughout Ohio. She campaigned, pushed for better nurse's pay, and shined as my idol. When doctors and other nurses visited the house at 1315 Utah Street, she radiated; I was so proud of her.

It is possible that my mom learned such leadership ability from my grandfather, Philip Schwaner, who was a gruff, tattered, and brilliant tactical expert. He was a perennial union leader when he worked at Westinghouse, in California, and a personal friend of Jimmy Hoffa. In addition, he was a professional golfer who once beat J.C. Snead, the golf legend, in a head to head match at Possum Run Golf course in Mansfield, Ohio. According to my mother, he was engaged in espionage as a secret agent for the United States government during World War II given his fluency in German (though I have been unable to confirm this).

Although he and my mother were estranged for over a decade, she invited him into our lives while I was a child. Occasionally, mom ran ideas for mobilizing nursing support for the movement from him. Though I was too young to remember, my first trip to Florida in 1976, was a treat for me and a tutorial for her. The vacation helped my
161

mother heal her relationships with my grandfather and Uncle Butch – a genius of compromised self-control.

Mama Green adored my mom, uncle, and loved my grandfather. She thought he was, "Mr. Cool." Mama persuaded my mother to build that relationship, and though it was strained until his death in 2000, they reached a point of understanding, as I benefited from a wonderful relationship with "Gramps."

As a testament to the life of quiet-like warrior, at one point, he kidnapped my cousin Wendy from the squalor of a bizarre life in Fort White, Florida to give her stability away from her tyrannical and unstable father, Butch (unlike Mama and my mother, his experience with childhood abuse and incest destroyed his mental sensibilities). My grandfather saved Wendy's life.

During my mother's period of greatest personal growth, and Erma Jean's constant harassment of providing me with opportunities to prevent me from being labeled as a poor kid at Maumee Valley, I became a member at the Boys Club in East Toledo. By six years old, maybe 7, I had earned the swimming rank of shark. I played tee-ball at Oregon Coy, baseball for the Maumee Valley Country Day School Mini-Mohawks, and was even permitted to attend Camp Big Silver, under the Boys Club banner, when I was 8.

Unfortunately, sex in the 1970s was exceptionally permissive and I knew everything by listening to the older kids at the park. They talked about oral sex, various and sundry positions, and regularly fondled one another at the merry-go-round. Sex was common at night on that same round, spinning saucer. I suppose it was the era.

By the time I had arrived at Camp Big Silver, my understanding of normative sexuality was already skewed, and I swept sex into a dark and fearful corner. Prior to my departure, Mama had taught me how to fight, count and manage my money, and to avoid sexual assault. I was always warned to get and hold my own drinks because people would slip a "Mickey" into it and "take advantage of you." She always worried about me getting hurt since I was so short and skinny; she was my iron fist.

Well, I didn't listen very well about the money. While at a rest stop on the way to camp, a character named Keith found out that I had $10 for the ten day trip. He pulled me near an isolated picnic table at near the vending machines and said, "Hey man, have you heard about inflation?" I had, so my response was, "Yes."

From there, he swindled me out of $6.65. He said, "You see this quarter? Inflation makes it worth a dime so, let's trade." He was big, had bucked teeth (snaggle toothed), and tattered clothes and shoes. His agitated hair intimidated me. I knew he was wrong but I didn't have the courage to counter his thievery.

After Keith had taken my money, I knew that I had been conned but was afraid to tell anyone or ask for my money back. Though Keith would later buy me chips and Coke during rest periods, I was distracted, nevertheless. As I was heading back to the bus, and not paying attention, I stepped into on-coming traffic. A teenage boy (who had been severely burned on over 75% of his body) pulled me to the sidewalk and away from the path of a bus. He simply said, "Be careful kid." Scared and shocked, I thanked him. Whenever trouble lurked at the camp, he pulled me away. I wish I could remember his name.

When we arrived at the cabin and were told to tell Paul, our counselor, how much money we had, I said, "I have $10." He counted it and said, "Shawn, you only have $3.35." Embarrassed that I had been taken as a "sucka," and for feeling like an idiot in math, I said, "Oh yeah, that's right, $3.35." I never told Mama, Jean, or my mom about the swindled loss – It confirmed Mama's belief for me though, that *"Bought sense is the best sense."* It was decades and a marriage before I ever let anyone know of the event.

163

Our cabin was named the "Paul Bunyan Gang" and my bunk mate was a cool and quiet guy named Skeebo. He was my best friend for ten days. He said that his cousin, Loco, had been to camp for several consecutive years and knew all the "rules." There was no need to take a shower or wash clothes, "Just take your soap to the lake and clean yourself during swim time." Because of my age, I had to swim in the minnow section until we could prove ourselves worthy of being a shark. To do that, we had to swim to the island at the northeast corner of the property and then to the island at the north, then back to the dock. Though I was exhausted, I made it. The camp mates and counselors were shocked that I could do it given my puny size, but they didn't know that I had the hustle and perseverance of a marine.

Sadly, the poor camping hygiene behaviors caused some problems. First, I contracted ring worm and swimmers ear and had other parasites lodged in my nasty and filthy body that required medical attention. Second, I came home with the same Wacky Packy T-shirt, unused Crest toothpaste, shorts and socks on. My hair hadn't been washed in 10 days. When mom picked me up she, Mama, and Erma Jean (all of whom were smoking cigarettes in the enclosed car) were sickened by my sight. Shocked and in disbelief, they vowed to never let me go back to camp again, and I didn't.

The irony is that I had a blast, though I was scared the entire time. Because of my athletic hands I was chosen to play tackle football and basketball with the older kids. We played capture the flag, battleball, and dodgeball as well. We sang Kool and the Gang's "Hollywood Swinger" and "Sky Rockets in Flight" all day. One camp song, however, really defined the deviant sexual practices that occurred there.

The song went:

1 plus 1, we were having some fun

In the bedroom, last night and all through the day;

2 plus 2, we knew what to do

In the bedroom, last night and all through the day;

3 plus 3, she came with me

In the bedroom, last night and all through the day;

4 plus 4, she wanted some more

In the bedroom, last night and all through the day;

5 plus 5, this ain't no jive

In the bedroom, last night and all through the day;

6 plus 6, she sucked my dick

In the bedroom, last night and all through the day;

7 plus 7, we were in heaven

In the bedroom, last night and all through the day;

8 plus 8, it felt so great

In the bedroom, last night and all through the day;

9 plus 9, that girl was fine

In the bedroom, last night and all through the day;

10 plus 10, we did it again

In the bedroom, last night and all through the day

It was truly the Camp Big Silver anthem. Nap time, though, was demented. Some of the hyper masculine males in cabin 8 were running a repugnant racket of forcing younger kids to perform oral sex on them during the nap time breaks. They would choose a young camper, ask the counselor to let them nap in the cabin, and then force the youngster to engage in fellatio. I was petrified that I was going to be chosen but later learned that Keith had told the ringleader that I was off limits; thank God for the swindler.

Back at our cabin, Paul routinely sat nude, or wearing only a jock strap, in the counselor's chair when we returned for a nap. Usually he wore a jock strap and on some days he would have a boner. Some days he played with it. Though I was never exactly sure what he was doing with it, I knew that it was inappropriate. He never molested us, and was actually decent to me (but villainous and racist toward Skeebo), but I got tired of his penis hanging out every day. Between Paul's penis and the repugnant sexual bravado of forcing my young friends into sexual assault, sexuality became increasingly unhealthy in my mind.

Every once in a while, though, I liked to fight. Towards the end of camp, Billy Sanders and I were pitted against each other by the older kids. They told him that I had been the target of his rumors and they told him the same thing. So, as I entered the damn cow-trough of a bathroom, he sucker punched me in the eye. I chased him with my socks dangling from my feet. When I caught him and punched him back, we got busted by Paul which resulted in a visit to Mr. Schoefield's office, the camp Director, at dinner next meal.

When dinner came, Billy (who ended up becoming a really good friend of mine when he came to Toledo and attended Maumee Valley) and I were to sit on the waiting bench for Mr. Schoefield. As Billy and I were talking, Mr. Schoefield came out with a canoe panel that had holes drilled in it to produce suction when it was pounded on someone's ass so as to inflict more pain. We had heard of other campers receiving the paddle and we were petrified. Just then, Mr. Schoefield came out and smashed the paddle on the bench so loudly that it hurt my eyes.

"Were you two fighting, gentlemen?"

Before Billy could speak, I said, "No, sir."

"Are you two going to behave?"

"Yes, sir, we will behave." I said as Billy nodded his head vigorously.

"Ok then, go have some dinner."

Thank God I never saw the head sexual predator, he scared me.

Chapter 29.   Pock Face and Mr. Frosty

Fishing always bored me.

I hated to sit in the sun for hours, spear worms on a hook, and wait for the fish to eat it and gouge itself through the eye and have it pop out of its socket.   There's nothing quite as sinister, in my mind, as watching such animal torture on an innocent creature.

Mama and I only went fishing one time at Fort Meigs, a fortress built during the War of 1812.   It was always cool to travel there on school field trips where we played "Buck Buck" and rolled down the massive hill from outside the fortress to the river bed.   For years, my school bus traveled from Maumee to Perrysburg beside the war fort.   Aside from John Lagger throwing my football out the school bus window and into the river below, it was a rather uneventful bridge.

True, winter blizzards, like the ones in 1976 and 1978 made the Maumee Bridge slippery and treacherous.   The kids though, didn't really notice.   Instead, we played rocket ship in the back seats and imagined the red lights were rocket engines blasting off to fly to the moon.   Matt Bretz and I always enjoyed drawing nude pictures of women under the back seat.   Though they looked like a Picasso painting, in general, exploring girl's body parts in our secret compartment was laugh material.   We especially loved drawing circles with a black dot in the middle and a black triangle just below the belly button.   Just the words tits and pussy made us laugh in a roar – No girls, like Sarah McPeck or Abby Stranahan were allowed into the secret rocket ship – "TwinkleToes" Black was certainly not allowed, as she scared us little kids (and for no real reason other than being tall and quiet).   The rocket was for "boys only."

Because of the open view from the bridge to the fort, it was a perfect place for us to fish.   On a warm and muggy day, Mama had decided to teach me how to catch catfish. She bought a famers hat with oranges and dolphins on it, two new fishing poles at Western Auto, and all of the hooks and sinkers a team of fisherman could use. She purchased two lawn chairs made out of the rubber that stuck to our legs and made an imprint on our thighs that looked like guitar strings when we stood up.

I found it hilarious that she had taken her spit cup to the river. She would take either a huge wad or roll the round cylinder into her bottom lip. When she was out it was nothing to unroll a cigar and chew the tobacco. Mama didn't have any teeth and I always laughed when she would talk about her "gumes" and eat chips or fried chicken with them. But man, oh, man could she spit. Erma Jean, my mom, and Guy used to laugh at how she never missed the cup no matter the distance. We even joked and made the legend that she could spit around corners if she had to.

The spit cup was nasty, though. I could hardly stand looking at it. She typically put a mound of toilet paper in the bottom and cupped it within the odd shaped round cup the size of a large salad bowl. At the bottom was a lake of brown spit up tobacco. A direct glimpse was nauseating.

As she pulled up her green Dodge Polaris, better known as "Old Betsy," we were singing Chaka Khan's "Tell Me Something Good," our favorite Home Brew Anthem. Hopping out of the car we took the rods to the shore, noticed the low tide, and explored the crayfish holes. I didn't know much about crayfish but I explained their life cycle as if I did. No matter how made up the story, she would always say the same thing, *"Your brains are so big that you can do anything you want in this life."* Then she would always follow up with, *"You have a million dollar personality and no one can take that away."* Little did I know that she was instilling a sense of confidence that would carry me through life adversities that lay waiting in the future and were beyond my imagination.

Before we arrived at Fort Meigs, Mama had asked me to go to the

169

"Trails" to dig up worms. She had given me a steel bowl that was roughly 16 inches in radius to put the worms in. Towards the back of the area near Oak Street was a wooded area that was moist with fallen leaves from the fall that made for great worm hunting.

The kids always had the fondest memories of this daredevil arena. It was here that dirt bikes had carved narrow pathways for the kids to race and explore. There was a hill there in which we would race down and jump over ramps made of plywood stacked against some discarded tires. Everyone tried to emulate the legendary daredeveil, Evil Kneivel, and make the longest and highest jump. I was pretty fearless and always raced at top speed and regularly cleared six paint cans and a car tire. I missed once and tears exploded from my eyes as pain emanated from my jammed back.

The explosion was enhanced with the fear of a solid ass whipping. I laid in pain until I could stand; Chris tried to pick me up but couldn't. After what seemed to be an hour, I got up, took a shit in the woods, and wiped my ass with leaves. Unfortunately, Chris wiped his with poison ivy which marked the last Trails shitting exploration of our youth. His mother whipped his ass with a spatula and threatened me with it as well. She spanked me once for paying Chris a nickel to "moon" April when she walked by us in the alley while digging for treasure. The bribery ceased immediately.

Once a forest fire broke out while Chris and I were using sticks and string to pretend we were fishing. As we tried to catch paint cans and discarded shoes with our makeshift rods, we heard crackling and saw an orange fire about 100 yards away. We quickly raced our bikes to the nearby fire department on Oak and Hathaway and led them to the blaze. Though we never were formally blamed, Chewy and the others were in consensus that Chris and I had started the fire; we didn't. The guys laughed while watching the fire and said, "There's the culprits." We shook our heads in disagreement as the guys laughed and the firefighters pacified the raging inferno.

In any case, I found about 36 worms. Mama put them on the hook and I cast them into the river after having practiced in the yard for hours. My goal was to cast it across the river in hopes of catching a catfish for Mama to cook and eat. We had a dismal fishing day, though. We did, however, sing Rock The Boat, eat a picnic lunch, and relax under one Charlie Brown Christmas-like shade tree. As we decided to leave, we finally caught a tiny blue gill.

I kept the fish in a blue steel bowl for half a day as I wanted a fish pet. However, the more it gasped to survive, Erma Jean convinced me that God wanted the fish back home in the river. Mom took me to the train bridge by the grain elevators on Miami Street, near Navarre, and I threw it into the river from about 50 feet high (with no support railings) and was happy I didn't slip and fall to my death.

In any case, whenever I walked to Mama's house I traveled up Utah Street to the blue factory, turned right at the front entrance to the trails, and followed the tracks to her house on Oakdale. That pathway to Mama's was desolate, abandoned, and creeped me out considerably. Then, a few days after fishing, my nightmare happened.

As I walked down the street holding a rare bag of Fritos that my mom had bought for me, I approached the blue factory. I noticed three drunken high school aged students, roughly 16 years old, walking down the tracks and away from the river. The three were loud, laughing, and staggering. When they had passed Utah Street by about 20-30 yards I thought it safe to turn towards Mama's house to continue my trek. As I turned to cross the street, a beer bottle landed and shattered in front of my feet. Like a thunderous crash, the three boys had surrounded me and pushed me up against the wall of the factory.

The leader of the group had unmistakable pock marks from acne gone haywire. It was obvious he had a bad case of pimples that he picked relentlessly. Just like a prison scene, he got up in my face and began to taunt me." What are you doing here by yourself, punk?"

"Hey kid, give me your Fritos," he demanded. Petrified, but warrior-like, I refused.

The heat of his intoxicated breath smelled of fresh puke as his reddened eyes flamed toxic acid into my olfactory system. My death, I feared, was imminent. I wanted to cry. I wanted to fight. I wanted to kill. I wanted the nightmare to disappear. I held my Frito's for dear life out of the fear of an ass-whipping from my mother. I froze like a deer staring into the proverbial headlights but maintained my mental alacrity.

Pock Face said, "What the fuck are you doing?" "Are you fucking crazy?"

I replied, "If I give you these Fritos that my mother will beat me and I don't want to be beaten."

He retorted, "Like this?"

Just then, he and his boys started punching me in my 10 year old stomach. No matter, I held onto my Fritos like it was life itself. While I was staggering, one of the boys started to urinate on my left leg. The hot wetness sickened me as "Pock Face" said something to the effect, "Come and get some of this wetness." By now, he had pulled out his erect penis as the third boy tried to force my head down to "Suck [his] dick." I had never seen an erection in front of my face before but I was resolute that it wasn't going in my mouth. After a couple more punches to my stomach, I heard the Mr. Freeze Ice Cream Truck, owned by Lisa Bean's family, coming towards the factory.

All I could think to say was, "Look, it's the ice cream man." For an instant they looked. Then I threw the Fritos at Pock Face's face and ran to the truck. When I looked back the boys were gone. The driver made sure I was okay and after about five minutes allowed me to walk to

172

Mama's. When I arrived and told her what had happened, we burst out of the house with Black Beauty in hand seeking revenge.

By the time we arrived at the factory, the boys were gone. When I saw the urine dripping from my pants leg, I wished them death. Mama wrapped her massive arm around my shoulder and walked me to the car. In an attempt to calm my disrupted heart, she proclaimed, "Don't worry baby, **God doesn't like ugly.** They will get their fair due in the end."

Upon reflection, I think about Pock Face and always wonder what would have happened had Mr. Freeze not shown up. I don't know for sure but it did justify Mama Green's notion that you should, *"Never go fishing with a group of boys because you may not come back."* Though she was enraged, Mama Green regained her composure. Had Pock Face still been at the blue factory he would have died during that day, I'm certain. In my imagination, I bet he lives somewhere, today, not knowing that his life was nearly terminated some four decades ago.

When we arrived home, Mama simply said that if you live by the following, you will have peace in your life: "Please, baby, **do onto others as you would want done onto you.** Nobody would want that done to themselves so trust that he will get his in the end." With that statement, I felt at peace. I was scared but peaceful. All that I know is that Pock Face and his urinating buddies nearly died that day. For me, and in hindsight, I believe that I would have been gang raped had the Mr. Frosty Ice Cream Truck not shown up in that moment. At worst, my body would have been found, decayed, in the trash on a bike path near some paint cans and discarded shoes. To this day, I still painfully wonder...

Chapter 30.   Always Say, "Please and Thank You"

The fact that I had never met my father had little impact on me, but the Blizzards of '76 and '78 were monsters that changed the course of my familial heritage. In 1976, Maumee Valley had closed down due to a rupture in a gas line that closed the school through the spring. In its place we rented a mostly vacant hotel in Downtown Toledo, The Secor Hotel. I personally preferred the location as it was a simple jaunt across the Maumee River from the East Side and was such a relief to be dropped off by mom or Mama Green rather than riding a school bus for an hour and being the first one picked up and last dropped off each day.

Cleverly, MV had broken the fifth and sixth graders into several groups and arranged us by our academic advisor. My room was with Mr. Al Getman, and we were called "Al's Pals." Our window faced north where the "hawk" – regarded as cold air by Mama - blew in through our windows. We were forced to stay in our coats the whole time. And, during the first week of school there, WOHO Radio came to interview the kids. They came to our classroom where J.J. and I were interviewed. I got nauseous but spoke nonetheless. When asked by the interviewer what it was like, I remember nervously saying, "It's cold, there must be a draft coming through the windows." Nothing profound, but it was a great feeling to be heard and recognized for an opinion.

My class of fifth graders was saturated with some of the smartest people that I have ever met. My room was occupied by Jamey Katzner (later of William and Mary), Pratik Multani (Yale and Harvard Medical School), Seksom Suriyapa (Williams College), Insead (Stanford Law School), Larry Gordon (Stanford and Ohio State Medical School), Jeep McNichol, a musician also known as Mr. Anonymous, and many other incredible stars. Then there was me, the happy-go-lucky comedic kid, carrying the weight of a life filled with anticipatory terror; I feared violent assault daily but held my head high. Nobody knew my fears.

Our financial struggles at home coupled with the expense of Maumee Valley had a significant impact on my mother. She drank a lot and threated me with violence often, while blaming me and my education for our poverty. Living with her and Erma Jean was an exercise in viewing war with a front stage pass. My daily existence was filled with arguing, fighting, insults, defamation, and guilt. My only security came when I stayed at Mama Green's.

Mama Green rarely mentioned my father. All that Mama said was that he was a nice man. Nonetheless, the image of my father had long been deeply buried. As a matter of fact, it was because of him that I learned about reproduction.

One spring morning in 1976, while attending school at the Secor Hotel, I had a heated debate with Jamey Katzner. While playing "Buck Buck" at the local Centennial Park, he asked about my father. I told him that I didn't have one, not a biological one.

His response, though accurate, made me feel like a moron. He simply said, "Everyone has a father. You have to have a man to impregnate the mother." I knew about sex, hell, everyone at the Hathaway Street Park knew about that. But, reproduction and the idea of having a father was not even a thought to me. It was a dark mystery hidden behind a sea of illusion.

When I told my mother of the incident with Jamey, she said, "He's right. Do you want to meet your father?" All I could say was, "sure." Hell, I didn't even know that he was alive.

Mom made arrangements for us to meet at the Golden Lily Chinese Restaurant that sat diagonally across from the Secor Hotel and directly across from the Top of the Tower. Interestingly, it was situated near the Lion's Store where Guy's "guardian angel" was known to meet Mama when she paid her credit bill downtown. The restaurant location provided me with a sense of safety as it was near angels, my school, and merely a few miles away from where I lived. Not knowing what to expect, we met on a Friday evening.

In preparation, I talked to Mama about meeting my dad and expressed my confusion in thinking that Leo Green was my dad. It was at this time that she explained that there are different types of "Daddys." There is the biological father who "made you" and the daddy that "raised you." She explained that my birth father, Bryce Cole, was a kind and gentle man but had personal issues that were beyond his ability to control. He was a professional musician who had his own symphony, but he was unreliable. My mother confirmed Mama's information and added that he had left the state and went to Florida before my birth.

When Mama finished distinguishing for me the difference between blood lines and "family" lines, she re-affirmed one of her most oft used sayings and made it clear that, "When you meet your father, be polite and remember to *always say please and thank you.*" Though I was always positive that my family consisted of a unique blend of social and ethnic diversity, the forthcoming introduction of my father posed questions of childbirth, potential siblings, and the complicated nature of family.

In time, I would learn that my father, upon my birth, had severe bi-polar disorder and was a heavy drinker. He had a wife and seven children that had never been mentioned to me. Once in a conversation, Erma Jean had mentioned that she met one of my seven sisters and we were identical twins. Confused, I simply replied, "Really. Hmm, that's interesting." As it turns out, my dad was a musical savant but had a "player's" streak. Evidently, he and my mom had a one-night affair after one of his concerts. To my knowledge, she did not know that his wife worked on the same floor as my mother, but in a different unit.

Prior to my birth, my father was on parole for an alcohol abuse related crime and was kicked out of his house with his wife and six kids. My sister Cindy was born a couple of months before me. He absconded

176

parole and fled to Florida. In exile, he would never see his seven kids again and it wasn't until 1976 that he and I met.

On a wet and overcast Friday evening in March, the day had finally arrived. Remembering my manners, and with a limited knowledge about my mysterious father, my mom and I grabbed a booth near the front door of the restaurant. We sat and she tried to make sure that my nerves were calm; they were. I was really relaxed because, in my head, Daddy Green was my father but this was the man that "made me." I didn't have the emotional tie to fret the encounter.

Then, after nearly five minutes, my dad, Bryce, entered. The front red door opened and a dark haired balding man, standing around 5'9" and weighing about 220, entered. I jumped up and walked to him. I extended my hand and said, "Are you Bryce Cole?"

He said, "I am. You must be Shawn?"

Then I extended my hand to him, shook it, and wrapped my arms around him and said, "Hello, it is nice to meet you. Please, my mom is sitting over there."

Surprisingly, my mom was not nervous and incredibly gregarious in their greeting. As they laughed and hugged for a moment, they both sat across from me. Mom sat on the inside of the booth and Bryce on the aisle. Fortunately, and in hindsight, the man I talked to was a harbinger of my appearance when I was 48 years old. He, my oldest brother Bryce Jr., and I look exactly the same. It was unmistakable that he was my father. Though I was ready to eat, I did not mention it until asked. When Bryce said, "Are you ready to eat?" I said, "Yes, please."

As always, I ordered a sirloin steak and fries, as my dad ordered Chop Suey. As the night ran on, and Bryce continued to ask about school, my friends, and life in general, he said, "Would you like to do something after dinner?" Nervously, I looked up at mom and she nodded affirmatively. I said, "Yes, I would like to go see the movie E.T."

Bryce turned to my mom and she said, "Sure, we can go to the movie."

At that time there were two major theatres in Toledo, the Showcase Cinemas on Monroe and the Secor Theatres on Secor Rd. As fate would have it, we went to the wrong movie theatre and the only one starting at the time was the first showing of a movie called, "Rocky." Having never heard of it, and given that it was its first showing, we sheepishly purchased three tickets. To our great surprise, Rocky was an Academy Award winning movie that propelled Sylvester Stallone into superstardom. For me, the theme of the movie gave me the greatest hope that I would overcome my runt size to become the second baseman for the Cincinnati Reds. Rocky gave me hope unlike any other movie I had seen in my lifetime and it was the only one that I ever saw with my dad; it is a fond memory for me.

Though the next few months swirled by swiftly, as he tried hard to get into my mom's life. He promised to buy me a piano on his first visit to our house on Utah Street. When he left, I started jumping for joy as he was going to make my childhood dream of playing a piano come to life. By now, I was tired of getting beat up by neighborhood kids for playing a violin and always admired Seksom Suriyapa for his incredible piano playing prowess. Sadly, after Bryce left, my mom dashed my hopes by saying, "Your dad has good intentions and probably would love to buy you a piano but he is unreliable. He has a sickness that makes him get excited and think he can do great thinks but he is not capable. Shawnee, so you don't get hurt, don't get your hopes up. Okay?"

"Okay, mom," I sadly replied.

A few days later, he asked mom if he could take me to lunch and being an eating machine, I said, "Yes." Mom kindly granted us permission. As we walked to the "hole-in-the-wall" restaurant on Fassett Street resting between Toledo Tent and Huss Variety Store, he stopped me and said,

"Can I ask you a question?"

Standing in a vacant lot some 25 steps away from the local fire department, I said, "Yes, of course."

At that point, he pulled out a diamond ring and said, "Could I be your father?"

I hesitantly said, "Sure, you can be my father but you *are* my father."

Then he followed by saying, "I mean do you think that your mom will marry me so I can be your real father?"

Unprepared for such a deep and adult like question, I said, "I don't know, you have to ask my mom. But, in all honesty, I don't think she will say yes. She's used to being alone and I think she likes it that way. I hope I haven't hurt your feelings."

He responded, sadly, with, "Oh, ok, let's go eat."

When we entered into the dingy mom and pop restaurant without a name, I ate two cheeseburgers, fries, and milkshake as Bryce slowly drank his coffee. I reminded him of the piano and told him that, "Mom might like it if you get the piano."

He responded by saying that, "The piano was a promise that I made to you."

"Ok," I said.

Soon after, there was a period of time in which he called and tried to become a part of our lives. I saw him five or six times in 1976 and into 1977. Along the way he introduced us to an old man that lived near Waite High School in a ghetto. His name was Woody Garfield and was a larger than life personality. He was a Purple Heart Award winner from WWII and had escaped a Nazi prison camp, Stalag 13, made famous by the 1970's television show, Hogan's Heroes. He escaped by crawling

Dear Mama: Lessons on Race, Grace, and the Wisdom To Overcome

under a fence while weighing roughly 70-80 pounds.

Woody was a great storyteller and comedic entertainer. During a dinner in which he made homemade fries, he entertained us with comedy and knife throwing. Gray, robust, and humorous, we were entertained for hours. He told me of his relationship with my father and how his grandfather (or maybe great grandfather) had been President of the United States. When we left dinner and headed for home, I was electrified. We had had a great evening and my mom, intoxicated, laughed hysterically at Woody.

Unfortunately, Woody began to obsess over my mother calling our house at all times of the day and night. He asked her on dates, dinner, and even threatened to come to the house. He became a stalker and at that time mom terminated all relationships with him and my father. Mama told my mother that if he ever showed up to the house to let him know that "*I will **beat the cow-walking piss out of his mouth*** and then shoot him." The calls ceased.

The next time I saw my dad, I was picking him up for release from the State Mental Institution near the Medical College where mom and Jean worked and the pizza parlor where I had been created. Oddly, he had requested (and mom obliged), that I go into the hospital and get him. As a kid, seeing all of the people with "mental illness" was scary. The building resembled a horror fortress from the movie Salem's Lot, and was intimidating. When I went to the front desk to ask the nurse where to get my father, she pointed to her left and said, "He's in there."

Unlike meeting Bryce at Golden Lily, this time I was nervous. When I entered the room and said, "Bryce, I'm here to take you home." He slowly sat up in his bed, groggy and wearing a hospital gown, looked at me and slurred, "Okay." Mom said that because of the severity of his mental illness, he was given electroshock therapy, and I believe, a lobotomy. Though those forms of treatment were no longer widely used at the time, and in fact illegal in many states, he was given one.

180

When he stood, it was like seeing a zombie. It took him nearly 20 minutes to change into his clothes, pack his sparse belongings, and get into the wheelchair. We dropped him off at his brother's home in Swanton and parted ways.

In reflection, I always thought that my father was a decent and caring man, but his serious bi-polar disorder and alcoholism sealed his torments. I have learned from my five sisters (Susan, Cindy, Susan, Marie, and Sally) and two brothers (Bryce Jr. and Michael) that my father was a good man, but badly troubled. He was known to disappear for days, weeks, and months without notice and only reappear sporadically. Their mother was a stalwart that raised my half siblings. For me, however, meeting my father, while worthwhile, set in motion another series of confusing contradictions on family, love, and mental health.

Most detrimental to my development and adulthood was the idea that I believed that he had abandoned me and his family when he found out he had impregnated two women at the same time. The sense of loss was crushing and the feeling of worthlessness omnipresent. It wasn't until 2012 that I learned from my mother that he didn't abandon me, rather "[She] kicked his unstable ass out of my life."

181

Chapter 31.   Tornadoes, Sump Pumps, and Jiffy Corn Muffins

Nearly 30 years after my father's death, a tornado bounced through our neighborhood.   Shortly after my retiring as a professor from the University of Louisville to pursue a sales position at Southland Log Homes, a cold front moved through the city.   On my first day on the floor as a sales agent, the storm rolled through the city and found our Winchester neighborhood.   Watching the rolling clouds swirl, I saw the funnel cloud begin its descent; I ran to the basement.   Sure enough, it sounded like a train.

When we came from the basement, there was no damage to our house, but a mysterious puddle of water, six feet in diameter, sat under the dining room table.   The doors and windows were closed.   All that we could figure was that the wind had blown the rain under the dining room door and onto the floor.

The tornado had dropped into the back yard of a neighbor down the street and bounced several times, over the expressway, and back to its unsettled sky home.   No houses were destroyed but many trees were downed.   Fortunately, I was able to navigate my way out of the neighborhood, through the timbers, for my first day at work.

No one was hurt.

When I had returned home, collateral damage had impacted the house. The fallen trees had taken out some of the local power lines and left the neighborhood without electricity.   When I went to the basement, I saw two feet of water on the ground; all of my childhood memories had been destroyed.

Baby photographs floated in the murky water.   A library of over a thousand books was destroyed.   My yearbooks from Kindergarten through 12th grade, my only reminders of my school friendships, were stuck together.

As I cleaned the mess, a few miscellaneous items in plastic containers survived without harm. There was magic contained therein. One unassuming envelope lay at the bottom of a plastic container holding some magazines with my idol, Dr. J., Julius Erving, on the cover. He was a childhood hero of mine for his ambassador role as an athlete, and an ethical enigma for me in my adulthood. The manila interdepartmental envelope held some letters that my father had written to my mother in the 1970s. I read with curiosity and excitement.

There were several messages that have had a profound impact on my adult life. 1. He wrote the song, Ma Cherie Amore" for his friend "Stevie." 2. He thought my mom had done a great job at raising "our boy". He always says, please and thank you." 3. He had a brother that was a property manager of an apartment complex in Swanton. 4. He always "loved you, Susie." 5. He was sorry that he couldn't buy me a piano. 6. There was a newspaper article reporting how he had committed suicide by jumping from the High Level Bridge during a police pursuit.

Though I have never tried to confirm that he wrote a song for Stevie Wonder, it rests well to think that my father had accomplished something so important in his life. Further, his notes to mom showed that he was capable of love and an endearing man. I didn't know him well, but I knew he was decent. His death showed that he was quite troubled.

I remember learning of his death in 1977.

On a mundane school morning, my little black radio played the news from WOHO, AM radio. Every morning I listened to the news to see if anyone had been murdered in my neighborhood the night before; if so, I had to prepare for the questions and subsequent ridicule that would follow at school. While eating a ritualized breakfast of scrambled eggs with a plate of Jiffy Corn muffins on a saucer, the news played.

That morning, the news cited that a man had been dragged from the Maumee River that had died from an apparent suicide. My mother approached me and said, "Shawn, that man was your father."

With a momentary pause, my reaction was pretty simple. I felt saddened about the death of my father, but not emotionally attached to it. While I stared at the Zenith radio with its coat hanger for an antennae and knobs that were barely still attached, the power of the moment was lost. I can remember saying to myself, "Hmm, that's too bad, he was a pretty nice guy." Beyond that, I also remembered a zombie looking up at me from his State Hospital Bed. So my response was certainly muted.

As I continued to eat breakfast, I envisioned him catapulting from the top of the High Level Bridge to the depths below. I wondered if he was scared while plummeting toward the water. Was he worried about it being cold? Did he scream? Questions rained.

The vision was vivid. I imagined that he had climbed to the top of the bridge and dove off in a swan dive sort of motion and flipped a few times before his body unified with the river. What did it feel like, I wondered, as his face danced with the falling rain in his descent? What was his last thought? Did he jump because my mother had turned down his marriage proposal? Who was to blame? Was I to blame? Did he feel guilt over the piano? Was he concerned about betraying his wife and seven kids? I wanted to know and needed to know what was in his head when he took his final step toward death.

I turned from the radio back to my corn muffins and remembered that I hated butter on my muffins; it made them soggy. Why did my mom put butter on the muffins? She knew I hated butter.

Then it dawned on me, in 1976 I was talking about reproduction with my friend Jamey at Centennial Park during school hours and in 1977 the authorities were dragging my father's suicidal remains from the icy Maumee River. Life, I surmised, was curious and a complicated mess.

In hindsight though, the newspaper reported that my father jumped from 10 feet and split his head on the footers supporting the bridge. It makes me wonder if he was jumping to avoid capture and a return to the mental institution, or something more insidious. The truth behind his death has long been lost to history but it remains a question of significance for me. I think he jumped to avoid capture and accidentally died when his head hit the bridge footers. I hope the police did not throw him over the side. He did not commit suicide. Of that I am certain.

185

Chapter 32.   Never Trust a Snaggle-Toothed Bastard

Erma Jean was a fantastic emergency room trauma nurse.   She could make life and death decisions with acuity and had earned a legendary reputation on her emergency ward unit. Motorcycle injuries served as a warning to only ride in a car. On a daily basis I heard stories pertaining to the loss of limbs, decapitations, and disembowelment.   The grotesque stories from the trauma unit served as a lesson on staying safe.

Erma, however, who absolutely loved children, could not stomach child abuse cases. Never having children of her own, (except for the rumor that her brother, Leo, was actually her son and Mama raised him as her own, which I never believed), she passed those cases to others. Her emotional attachment to children generated such intense anger that it was feared that she would attack an alleged perpetrator with violence, gunshot wounds, murder, and suicide attempts were managed with emotional detachment and a velvet glove. While there she developed a deep and comprehensive relationship with doctors, police officers, and nurses alike.

Jean and her best friend, Lillian McDonald, were Euchre card sharks and outwitted the police on slow nights while at the hospital. They had developed an intricate system of signals that Officer Kalipitro and his partner could never unravel. It was nothing for Jean to gently slide her index finger across her diamond ring to call diamonds, or flatten her left hand on the table to call clubs. She and Ms. McDonald were amazing card players and Erma Jean was a card-counter; for that reason, she refused to play poker due to her fear of addiction.

She was not hesitant to bet on Super Bowl games with the police and doctors that she knew. For some reason, she routinely won around a thousand dollars each year, especially during the Steelers incredible run in the 1970's. Her love for Terry Bradshaw and Franco Harris was true and Jean was also a ruthless competitor. Every time Mean Joe Green, Jack Ham, Jack Lambert, or L.C. Greenwood sacked Kenny Anderson of the Cincinnati Bengals, she would say, "Bury him, bury him, dig, dig, dig." Her loud and boisterous voice quaked the living room. Honestly, I laughed every time she roared, though it was frustrating to me as a Bengals fan.

Fortunately, Erma Jean loved Ohio State football with Woody Hayes, Archie Griffin, and Cornelius Green at quarterback; we agreed on that. Aside from their matchups, with Ohio State, we also cheered for USC. Lynn Swann was magical and became her poetic favorite with the Steelers. His two catches against the Cowboys in the Super Bowl were a lifelong memory for her. She missed the Immaculate Reception in 1973 when Franco Harris made perhaps the greatest catch in NFL history, following a devastating shot by Ohio State legend Jack Tatum on John Fugua. After the ball caromed off of Tatum's shoulder pad Franco picked it up off the ground and raced for the game winning TD as time ran out. Though I hated Pittsburgh, I went crazy knowing that I had just seen history.

Aside from Erma Jean's love for football, she had a very good eye (though sometimes overbearing), for reading people. Evidently, Mama had trained her into understanding subtle body language cues. In that regard, she was very difficult on my mother regarding her taste in men. As a matter of fact, it was Erma Jean's overprotection of me and moralistic control of my mother's dating behavior that led to the long Cold War at 1315 Utah Street. My God, every night was the same. "Bitch." "Mother fucker." "Wake the fuck up..." "Go to Hell...."

Most days, I would find a way to escape to the "Park" to get away from the screaming and insults. The shit that they would say to each other was nothing short of brutal and typically below the belt. Erma Jean would tell my mom to quite sleeping around like a common whore, while my mom got on her case about her weight and being her personal chauffer (Erma Jean refused to get a driver's license until 1978). In reality, Jean was too big for my mom to fight and on a few occasions tried and lost.

In 1976, aside from the springtime appearance of Bryce Cole, my mom had a reverend friend who lived next door named G-Ray. As a matter of fact, we were bookended by G-Ray's on the left and right. G-Ray on the left went to prison after his daughter found pictures of him sodomizing his mentally challenged son, J. The shock of the oral copulation shook the neighborhood as G-Ray was known to be the neighborhood handyman. He was a slow learner with a red mustache matching his hair and once had crushed my beer can collection as an accidental but kind gesture of goodwill.

For years, I traveled to local factories and neighborhood homes, asking for returnable pop bottles to get a dime each and for cans to earn money. G-Ray had gone into our garage one early morning with J. and I heard my cans being crushed. I was devastated when I sprang out of bed to see my mint condition Frankenmuth cone top get smashed under his G-Ray's right foot. All of my Zodiac and Billy Beer cans (named after President Jimmy Carter's brother) were already flattened. Later, we were all the more traumatized when the news of the "nice man" next door being sentenced to prison. It hurt me to my soul to know that J. had been forced to perform oral sex on his father; I was sickened and worried about the implications.

I have never surmised as to whether or not my mother slept with G-Ray Smarty-Pants. G-Ray Smarty-Pants lived on the right of our house and preached at a local church. He was kind and a master of puns, and loved to do imitations of Groucho Marks as my mother played along spending hours together engaging in their silly game.

As a "Tween," I found the "punny" banter funny but aggravating. Erma Jean found it to be inappropriate and enraging. I think there was more to the story than my 10 year old eyes understood. Further, it was odd that they would get drunk on Crown Royal.

During the G-Ray period, I continued to live with Mama Green, though my mother had moved to the day shift. By the spring of 1977 Erma Jean had moved upstairs, finally, and I had my own room on Utah Street. It was cool to be there as I got a color 12" Sony TV that Christmas, and secretly watched the 1977 NBA championship between Julius Erving of the 76ers, against Bill Walton of the Trailblazers.

In any case, G-Ray would stay late into the evening, posing serious television viewing issues. Given that my room was across from the bathroom, I had to turn the volume down as low as possible and stand right next to the television to hear it (the games were played after my bedtime). If I had been caught it would have been serious trouble, probably worthy of an ass-beating. Honestly, I would have happily accepted a "whooping" to see those magical plays of the Doctor slamming over Walton and Gross in the championship. His play was legendary in that series and confirmed his status as the "greatest basketball player" of his era.

During the early spring, G-Ray Funny-Pants had convinced my mother to allow him to take pictures of me. I had thick black hair and slightly bucked teeth, but was regarded as a "cutie" to the girls in my neighborhood and the nurses that worked with my mother. One even proclaimed to my mother that I would assuredly grow to be a "playboy" someday. G-Ray Funny-Pants took pictures of me in front of the trees, on the porch, and one classic with a truly poor and broken girl named Carol. She was a pretty blond haired girl but was always filthy and poverty dirty. She never had shoes on her feet and had the ring of poverty around her ankles. In the picture, our heads were turned in opposite directions, disgustedly - the picture was magnificent.

G-Ray Smarty-Pants developed the photos in his own dark room. Whenever he left town, and knowing my passion for earning money, he would pay me $.25 for watching and caring for his gold fish, Goldie. On

189

the first occasion, he invited me over to his apartment, the upstairs to the Strock's house, and showed me how to feed and care for her. Though nothing ever happened, he always asked for more photos and showed me his dark room.

In that spring of 1977, he ran a church-related day camp with arts and crafts. The highlight was a trip to see the Detroit Tigers against the New York Yankees. As always, Rodriguez hit a home run and rookies Alan Trammel and "Sweet" Lou Whitaker played like giants. On the way home, as G-Ray Funny Pants drove the bus, his pants flew out the window with his wallet, money, and license. With slight cursing, he looked out the window, tried to turn around but was never able to recover his money. Soon after, my mother's pun partner had left town.

While he was in town, Mama Green continued to tell me, *"Never let anyone in your house when you are alone, even if you know them."* The last we had heard (but not confirmed) about G-Ray Funny Pants, he had been indicted for statutory rape. To this day, I wonder if he masturbated to those photos he had taken of me. Did he have sex with my mom while thinking of me? When the Catholic Church scandal broke in the 1990s, I thought of G-Ray Funny-Pants with nausea. I can remember Erma Jean's loudest argument with my mom, saying, "Stay away from that fucking priest. He's a pedophile." Long after Erma Jean had died, my mom confessed to me that Erma Jean was right. Even so, their battles were agonizing.

"Leave that bastard alone, he can't be trusted with Shawn," Erma Jean would say.

Mom would retaliate with, "You are not my mother and can't fucking tell me what to do."

"You don't even care about your son. All you care about is fucking these men in your home and getting drunk. Quit being such a whore." All the while, I'm eating my liver with gravy and mashed potatoes that she had cooked; I focused intently on the giant spider entrapping Gilligan and the crew on the deserted island.

Mom, not one to back down, would respond with, "Go to hell, you fat ass bitch."

And finally, Jean would say, "I would go to Hell except you're blocking the goddamned way." Sadly, their zingers and bitterness destroyed me and my esteem. Both were protecting me and asserting independence but each word made me feel empty. I hated home and shriveled up when there. I disappeared into a darkened mental abyss. By 15, I wanted to commit suicide.

No one at school or the playground could see the scars. The bitterness turned inward and sports were my only sanctuary. My prowess with a baseball and basketball produced popularity, showmanship, and an avenue of escape. Everyone knew my passion. My days at school were spent trying to find a way to get out of class and into the gym; I wanted to be a professional athlete. That was my only goal and God knows I practiced. I wanted to escape the arguing and parade of men. I wanted peace. I wanted some sort of salvation. I wanted the arguing to stop.

By Christmas, 1977, my mom had been dating J. Pipefitter. I was disturbed by the idea that he was married with four children, though he treated me well. J. was a foreman at a local industrial site and earned $800 per week, which impressed Erma Jean immensely. I don't know why she liked the Pipefitter so much. He seemed nice and kind enough, but was a cheating drunkard.

My mom had a string of boyfriends, too. One was a young blond haired man who liked dogs. One morning he woke up, with his clothes in a pile in front of the couch, as I sit on the chair staring at him. Mr. Blondehair was sitting in my Abbott and Costello viewing seat and tampering with my 7:00 AM show of "Meet the Mummy." I can remember him saying, "Good morning, Shawn" as he fumbled to find his underwear.

191

Mom's boyfriend, Lake, found himself in the same situation. Given my gregarious nature, I would hold conversations with the men on the couch. All of them were uncomfortable, naked, and in a hurry to leave. E.S., the plastic surgeon, was nice and treated us to Earl Cousinos steaks for Thanksgiving, where I had a traditional Thanksgiving dinner followed by a sirloin steak and baked potato. Both were astonished, and my mother embarrassed, when I polished off the meal and wanted more.

Erma Jean liked him pretty well, but Mama wasn't a huge fan. I remember watching the Cowboys beat the Redskins (or the team with the stars on their helmet vs. the team with the Indians on their helmet, as Erma Jean knew them) in a tremendous end of game touchdown. When we went outside to play catch he did not like that I jumped to catch every pass as he said, "Why do you jump every time to catch the ball." And I simply responded, "Why does it matter if, I catch the ball?" Shit, I was only 6, what did he expect?

Mom later dated my baseball coach, Ed. Unfortunately, knowing about the dark and dirty side of sex from the guys at the playground made it hard for me to accept Ed. The thought of my mom performing oral or anal sex, sickened me. Though he was always respectful of my feelings, it was weird. Erma Jean, the guardian to the gates of hell, was disapproving of him and the ensuing arguments were fierce. Coincidentally, mom was dating the Pipefitter the entire time.

J. Pipefitter had purchased an electronic football game as my Christmas gift. By this time, he had taught me how to shoot craps and play billiards. He was 6'4" and had grown up in inner city Detroit with Detroit Tiger great Willie Horton. J. Pipefitter had told me that he had purchased the football game for me but destroyed it on the train tracks when my mom refused to marry him — even though he was married with two sons.

His destruction of the gift angered me mightily. While J. Pipefitter was spending all of this time with my mother, getting drunk and sloshing his

192

words, invading my home, he couldn't give me the game. We lived broke most of the time and even Chris and Brian had the electronic football game that they generously shared with me. Fortunately, I had received a small colored TV from my mom that more than made up for the loss – yet, I was not pleased.

In early March of 1978, J. Pipefitter came to the screen door at the front of the house. It was around 2:00 PM and mom and Jean were at work. As always, I was playing with my baseball cards, memorizing the statistics of all of the players that I owned.

"Hi Shawn, can I come in," he asked.

I responded with, "No J., you can't come in. My mom will be home in a couple of hours and you can come in then."

"But you know me and I have brought this new electronic football game for you," he taunted.

With temptation in my heart, I said, "No, no one is allowed in the house if my mom or Jean are not home. So, thanks for the game but you will have to come back later."

"Okay then, but I will be returning the game to the store," he replied.

I simply said, "Okay." All I could think about was the start of baseball season, anyhow – I didn't care about the game then. All that mattered to me was playing baseball.

During that spring, George Brandenbarry had stopped coaching for Oakdale and moved to Navarre School. Having played for Oakdale for two years, illegally, by using Mama Green's address as my permanent place of residence, George threatened to report me to the city if I played for Oakdale. I refused and chose not to play baseball at all that summer. Boonie, the greatest pitcher that I have ever met, left Oakdale for Navarre and I refused. After battling depression for missing my

193

summer activity, Erma Jean finally said, "Shawnee, I think you should play for Navarre." Mom and Mama Green agreed.

I sent message through Boonie to George to ask if I could play, and was greeted with open arms. Kenny Paszko was the new coach at Navarre. Having had a reputation for being a top-tiered second baseman by kids from the neighborhood, Oakdale, and from Brandenbarry, the starting spot was mine. When I showed up to practice, my long-time friend and neighbor, Billy Mills, was playing second base and gracefully moved to center field, which showed off his cannon arm quite nicely. With his son, Kenny Mike at shortstop, Mr. Paszko said, "you can't play second base by sitting on the hill. Get your glove and let's see what you can do." The night before, David Martin and Danny Wamer rode their bikes all the way to Hathaway Park to tell me "thank you" for joining the team. I said, "You're welcome and I can't wait to play with you guys."

It was such a warm and unexpected welcome.

Soon thereafter, on a Saturday afternoon, I was doing my usual baseball card filing and memorizing. Mom was preparing to go out with the Pipefitter for dinner that night and Erma Jean was sitting on her rocking lawn chair on the front porch. Mom and the Pipefitter had been drinking the entire afternoon and were drunk on Erma's gin and tonic mix.

"Knock, knock," the Pipefitter said as he entered my room. "What are you doing?" he asked.

I said that I had just put my baseball cards away and was heading up to the Park to play some baseball. As he approached me with his bloodshot and drunken eyes, he said, "Shawn, you're quite a smart and handsome young man. Did you know that I love you?"

"What are you talking about?" I asked.

Before I could respond, he had pressed his 6'4" frame against my body to hug me. Standing 4'9" and weighing about 100 pounds, he flung me easily onto my bed. My practice of slipping between the wall and the bed to avoid burglars was useless.

"You know," he said, "I really wanted to give you that game the other day but you wouldn't let me in the house. But, I'm here now and wanted to tell you that I find you so handsome. I love you, Shawn."

When I said, "Get off of me," he pressed my face into the pillow on my bed. He held my neck down with his forearm so that I couldn't move. I tried to squirm out and kick but he was too big and strong. Then he rolled me over and started to kissing me on my mouth and slipping his drunk gin-tasting tongue in and out of my mouth. He then covered my mouth and started kissing my neck leaving a brutal series of love bites, etching into my skin a pattern that looked like a winter scarf.

Then he threw me on my stomach and yanked on my belt to unfasten it. After a great struggle, he won. Rather than crying, I tried to free myself, but just couldn't. I fought. I twisted. I squirmed. He finally got the belt off and pulled my jeans down to my ankles. I could feel his 6'4" adult penis on my back rubbing up and down. I couldn't see it but felt its hardness. He assaulted me that day and life, as I had known it, ended. The notion of trust was destroyed and all of Mama's sayings about distrust rang true. My innocence was lost, my pride stolen, and worst of all, I learned that I did not own my body. My body separated from the experience and hate seeped into my thoughts.

Fortunately, my dog Zeus heard my cries, scratched on the door, and spooked the Pipefitter into quickly placing his penis back into his pants. My spirit, laid naked on the bed, and my soul had been severed. I laid there for a minute, an hour, hours maybe, wondering what I had done to deserve this shit?

What would have happened had I opened that door two weeks earlier?

195

The shame retarded my growth.

The notion of sexuality became monumentally more complicated than it already had been; I slammed close the doors to my own Temple of Pain, forevermore.

When I finally came to the porch, and faced my tormentor, he and my mother were sitting on the glider holding hands. Mom was snuggled up to his chest and they both had a drink on the adjoining table. Erma Jean rocked and joked with the mother fucker that had just molested me. Couldn't they see? How did they not know? As I walked out the door to go to Boonie's house to play baseball, the Pipefitter just looked at me, smiled, and said, "Hit a homer, Shawn." I looked back with a stare to freeze Hell and said nothing.

When I arrived at Boonie's house, my friend Deanna was already sitting on the porch. She had a major crush on me and routinely offered me any intimate experiences that I desired, but I always refused. Typically, and truthfully, I had told her that I was interested in playing for the Cincinnati Reds and replacing Joe Morgan at second base, and was in no hurry to have sex. Boonie, my friend until death, always shook his head in agreement with my dreams.

Her response was a simple, "Oh yeah." Then she chased me into the side yard where she emulated the schoolyard game of "boys kiss the girls." Finally, she caught me and we began to play wrestle in the spring grass. While rolling around she mounted on top of me. With horror, she looked at my neck and immediately jumped off, saying, "I thought you didn't want to have a girlfriend."

"I don't want a girlfriend," I said nervously.

She called me a liar and said, "Then where did all of those hickey's come from on your neck?"

My response was quick. "Well, there's a girl at my school who did that while we were messing around."

Horrified and crushed, Deanna left. She never asked me for intimacy again and a short time later was dating a mutual friend. We remained friends but our relationship was not the same. Boonie just laughed, thinking that it was the girl at school that had left the scarlet markings.

When I left Boonie's house, not desiring the humiliation of playing at the Park, I went home. Finally, walking as a zombie and confused by the day's events, I walked onto the porch where Erma was still in her rocking chair. She looked at my neck and said, "What the hell is that?"

Knowing that hickeys were considered the mark of Satan in her eyes, I told her the truth. "While mom was getting ready to go on her date with J. Pipefitter, he came into my room and attacked me. Zeus stopped him."

Her response changed my life forever. "That's a fucking lie, that fast ass hoe did that to you, didn't she?"

I responded by saying, "Remember when mom was in her room and J. Pipefitter went back to go to the bathroom? He came into my room."

I didn't know why she protected him so vociferously but, again said, "You're a fucking liar." "Mama Green has told you to *'Stay away from those fast ass hoes'*, and now you are marked". Mom didn't believe me either.

I refused to tell Mama Green because she would have shot *the snaggle-toothed bastard* to death; she would have believed me without question. She had always said, *"There is nothing in the drugstore that will kill you faster than me when it comes to my baby,"* and the Pipefitter would have, without a doubt, been killed. So I stayed away from her until the hickeys healed. Sadly, she spent days wondering why I didn't come to see her, and I used baseball practice and school as my excuses. She believed it; my new teammates thought the marks were

197

from Deanna.

Kids at school laughed at me. One girl at school got the same excuse as did Deanna, and it was then that I learned to wear the "mask." People wear masks, theoretically, to present a virtual self so as to protect the authentic one. After that spring day, I became a master of illusion, magic, and control of my presentation of self. My sexuality was destroyed and made dirty, and my understanding of kindness was shattered. From then, I would swear by Mama's idea that I should, *"Never let the left hand know what the right hand is doing."*

It was so confusing to know that I had a pedophile who lived to the right, the left, and one that dated my mother; I guess my days were numbered anyhow. In remembering Pock Face, I was dumbstruck by the volume of pedophiles that lurked in my everyday life. It felt like a trap; it felt normal.

I have never been the same.

In the aftermath of the Pipefitter's wrath, baseball became my entire life. Every moment of every day was spent practicing to become a better player. I practiced and practiced and practiced. If Chris and I weren't playing catch or going to the park, I was playing one on one strikeout with Boonie. In my head, baseball was the only avenue to dispel the demons from the Pipefitter's assault.

Fortunately, our baseball team was incredible and our championship season cured my pains. We were a diverse team in terms of beliefs, talent, social class, and ethnicity, and gelled as brothers. Somehow, the convergence of talent and hunger to win was brought to life through a team chemistry that was unreal.

As our undefeated season for the Braves continued and our legendary pitcher, Boonie, reached mythical heights, the fans clamored to see our team play. Boonie's mom, with her cheer of, "Whiz 'em, Boonie, whiz 'em!" led the fervor. Mama Green was quite the queen bee for the players; my mom and Erma never missed a game and the adult post-parties were frequent, long, and strong. The Navarre Braves of 1978 were sensational.

I played the role of Joe Morgan and met with Boonie often on the mound to call out pitches, keep him calm, and often to have casual conversations about after the post-game, to out-psyche the opponent's batters. With an All-Star catcher in David Martin, the "Bunt Master" playing third base, Mike McDougall, Rocket-armed Kenny Mike at Shortstop, Wamer at first, The Tomahawk swinging slugger and missile launching arm of Billy Mills in Center field, and Diggs in right field; we were loaded. Everyone played a monster role and each player contributed to a true team of destiny.

After beating the Goliath of Toledo Pee Wee baseball, the Walbridge Bears, in a classic 3-2 victory where Pedro Garcia hit an unexpected game winning double, the stage was set. In the championship, we played against Larchmont who had an ace pitcher, John "Spiderarms" Keller. In a defensive struggle, Mike McDougall hit a triple and ate dirt when sliding into third base. Injured but determined to finish the game, he scored the winning run on a bloop single (by Boonie I believe), in a made for television 1-0 victory. Navarre, who was a traditional doormat in baseball just the season before, had won the city championship! I increasingly forgot about the Pipefitter.

We paraded around the '05 honking and celebrating for hours. We rubbed the victory into the face of Walbridge by driving through their neighborhoods and ended at Ede's Ice Cream with a donation of a monumental $3.00 per player. I had six hot dogs, a milk shake, nachos with cheese, and a banana split on the greatest day my childhood life.

As we entered into the regional tournament to determine which team would go to the Little League World Series in Williamsport, we were blindsided by a rule change that killed our efforts. After playing a season where stealing was impermissible, it was permitted in the regionals. With two days to learn how to lead off, steal, pitch from the stretch, and cover the steal, we experienced imbalance. The night before our first game against West Virginia, we were pummeled 13-1 as our power hitting team went dry and our defensive prowess deserted us. David Martin hit a ball with a bat that bounced back and crushed his nose -in that instant, we lost our catcher and our chemistry. His replacement from Garfield, Steve Teneyck, was a hitting master and terrific catcher, but was not a part of the family, yet, and his presence was dry.

When we lost in the second day of the double elimination tournament, we were crushed. Hearing the man in the stands say "that little second baseman there [me] was the best in the state and would be a professional player if he grows" was rendered meaningless after two errors in two games. However, Coach Paszko asked if we wanted to play in the 75 team Keiser Tournament starting the next morning; we decided that we did not want the season to end and reluctantly agreed. As I cried after the game, Mama and Erma Jean hugged me. I felt I was to blame for our losses and I was devastated. Mama simply said, "it's a team game and not about you. It's not your fault." Yes, she was right but I knew, in my heart, that it was my fault.

In the Keiser tournament, we lost the first game of a double elimination. It was then that I pulled the team together and said, "Guys, we are better than this, we've been through too much, and it's time to play! Let's play Navarre Braves baseball and win this tournament." We won 13 games in a row and on the final Sunday, Boonie pitched a triple header and threw a one-hit shutout in game three to win, 1-0. He was named MVP of the tournament and we went back to slaughtering teams. It was here, however, that scouts had noticed that my glove and bat were phenomenal, as I made several diving catches. In fact, I turned a crazy double play on a bunt that Steve fielded near the plate, threw it, reluctantly, to me at first, and I gunned down the runner heading home from third for a game ending double play, winning the game, 1-0. The Navarre Braves were back and our coaches, Crooks and Kenny, jumped with joy as we accepted the tournament trophy from Herm Kander, scout for the Cincinnati Reds, as he gave "the best team in Toledo" the 1st place trophy.

In reflection, the spring and summer of 1978 was surreal. From sexual assaults to baseball championships, the distrust in individuals was confirmed as the value of teamwork was established. All of the lessons on strength and perseverance paid off in both positive and negative ways. I learned that summer that I may be short in height, but my hustle would be unmatched by anyone and I would always stand tall. It was the happiest summer of my life – and the most destructive one. My life was changed, forevermore, and rife with internal contradictions and confusion. I trusted virtually no one and my childhood was reborn, dead.

Chapter 33.   The Blonde Beauty From Around the Way

Erma Jean used to give Troy his allergy shots in the kitchen at the house on Utah Street. He used to live in the grey house around the block with his beautiful blond-haired mother.

Though I do not remember the mothers name any longer, I remember her beauty well. She was always willing and quick to shout a "Hello" from her porch whenever us kids had a bike race up and down Felt street. Troy sometimes played at the Park and was friends, I believe, with a former teammate over in the Oakdale school district.

In mid-July, shortly after our city championship season had ended, I was invited to join their family for swimming. It was a typical four foot above ground pool, common in working class neighborhoods. The cookout during the day had the common hamburger and hot dog fare with baked beans and Coke. The adults, as was common in the 1970s, drank "Bud."

After dinner, Troy, his sister, and I began swimming. There were eight kids or so in the pool after having played multiple rounds of dodge ball. Just after dusk, Troy's mom had him get out of the pool and dry off. After a little water volleyball everyone except Troy's mom, her friend, and I were in the pool. The three of us tossed the ball around for a half an hour or so. With the water being just below my mouth while standing flat footed, we started to splash fight.

The waves in the pool showed that Mrs. Beautiful was not wearing a bra. Her pink round nipples showed through her shirt and I looked with the excitement of a teenage boy seeing his first pair of tits. They were perfect. Her breasts stood to attention on their own merit and were about a 36 C in measurement. Mrs. Beautiful's friend was heavy set with long black curly hair.

As we had played for a while they asked if I knew how to float on my back. I said, "No."

At that time, Mrs. Black Hair put her arms under my shoulders and said to "relax and breathe deeply and slowly." Mrs. Blond Beauty put her hand under the small of my back and at the bend in my knees. As she gently let go of my knees I could feel her hand just gracefully moving around my back. So she stepped to the front of my feet as she let go of me and said, "Relax."

Being poor at relaxing, my feet continued to sink. Eventually, when my feet would sink she would gracefully bring them up. Her hands rubbed the back of my calves and I could feel myself popping a boner in my trunks. At some point, she had straddled me to the side and put her breasts on the side of my cheek and said, "How does that feel."

"Great," I nervously returned. She seductively moved back to the front as her friend continued to hold me and let my feet sink. She said to, "Just relax."

I guess no one could see over the wall but it was a sensual evening. Just as my feet had begun to sink again, she raised my left leg up and in between her legs. She held it there to teach me to "balance." Before long, she was rubbing my foot and leg in between hers. The friend just held me. Then, she inserted my big toe into her vagina and moved it slowly around. My boner stiffened.

After rubbing her chest on my cheek we left the pool.

She and her friend led me inside saying, "Let's dry off and get some warm clothes." When we got into the bathroom, with people in the living room and kitchen, she pulled down my swim suit. Her friend wrapped a towel around my torso while rubbing on my nipples. Mrs. Blond Beauty then took her hand and started to pull on my penis. "Let's warm that up a little bit." As it grew from its cold and shrunken pool state, she caressed it with love and tenderness. Her friend pulled me against her chest as Mrs. Beautiful stroked my penis to climax. Then she said, "Can you relax now?"

"Yes, ma'am," I said.

In reflection, I never told Jean, mom, or Mama Green what had happened since I liked it and yearned for more. I didn't understand it, but it felt really good. Every day I dreamed of going swimming with Mrs. Blond Beauty but she soon moved out of the neighborhood, without any warning. I knew the event was wrong but it felt much better than being forced into submission by J. Pipefitter. My desire for non-intimate sexual contact grew after that but had to be buried due to Erma Jean's puritanical control. "Everyone else was having sex," I thought to myself, but Erma Jean generated an unhealthy fear of intimacy. I yearned for sex but turned it down; I was confused and petrified by it. I liked Mrs. Blond Beauty's tenderness and the "one shot and over" approach but hated Pipefitter's force, control, and domination. The stage was set for a life of confusion and sexual distraction.

Yet, I always wanted to feel her chest with my hands.

Chapter 34.   Pagliaze Pizza, Social Class, and Lessons on Tolerance

Living on the East Side was a significant disadvantage for attending Maumee Valley Country Day School. Though my extended family was superb at channeling resources into clothing and food, there were language, consumption, and cultural capital differences prohibiting me from excelling academically. Though Maumee Valley espoused a highly tolerant culture, the differences in social class and race were quite manifest.

By the time third grade had fully engaged, a community of brothers and sisters had been formed among students who would, ultimately, graduate from high school together. Though my mom and Erma Jean were professional nurses, Mama was a cook at Waite High School (though well respected, angelic, and giving) and Daddy was a pure hearted truck driver, while the roles of parents at MV were different. MV parents were comprised of doctors, CEOs, university professors, business owners, and a plethora of other occupations. Happily, neither the parents nor fellow students treated me differently as I was a recognized athlete and funnyman; I could only tell differences in class when I visited their homes.

The first time I spent the night elsewhere, I stayed with the Katzners in Bowling Green, Ohio. My best friend, Jamey, had an older brother named Jody, and two sisters, Sylvia, and Kelley. Jamey, who was at least 8" taller than me, took me to the basement to play Nerf basketball with a square box as a rim. There were two rooms to the side, and games lined the right wall. It was here that Jamey and I constructed, choreographed, and prepared our "Rubberband Man" Gong Show dance to the Spinners classic; we received a standing ovation in our third grade talent show in both performances. The experience created a lifelong friendship.

205

On the magical day of my first overnight in second grade, as we approached the garage his dad pulled out a garage door opener, pushed a button, and the door opened. I was in shock sitting in the clean, smoke-free, van that was sturdy and rang of family. There was no arguing. No one bossing the others around or demeaning their personhood. No one said, "Shut the fuck up, you dumb ass bitch." No "mother fuckers." The van was loaded with respectful conversation; questions about school, and laughter.

When we pulled up to the driveway I noticed that there was a basketball rim attached to a backboard on the side of the garage. All I could think about was, "Man, they must be rich. My rim doesn't have a net, it's broken and leans to the side, and they don't have to navigate their dribbles around tree roots." Though our playground rim at Hathaway had a steel chain that made a swish sound, typically there was only a bare rim. I quickly asked Jamey, "Can we shoot outside on your rim?" Jody joined us. Though I had to really use all of my strength to get the ball in the hole, given my tiny stature, I could make shots. I dribbled well, especially on the flat driveway. Over the years, Jamey helped me fine tune the rotation on the ball for my jump shots as he was a fundamentally gifted player.

When we went inside and I could only look around and stare. I was shocked at the interior's newness. There weren't any gray and dingy walls; the carpet was fresh; there were bathrooms on the main floor with two upstairs; everyone had their own bed and bedroom. The front room had the baby grand piano of all of my dreams. My only musical goal in life was to play the piano like Mama Green and their piano was like looking through a window at the department store and seeing the dream, but not being allowed to take it home. Jody and Jamey taught me how to play chopsticks and over the weekend I was permitted to go in the room and play privately.

The living room was huge. Dr. and Mrs. Katzner had their own desks.

They had a leather wrap around couch that sat in a squared formation in front of a large colored television. As we were watching an episode of Gilligan's Island and sought to change the channel to the news, Jamey picked up a remote control and turned the channel. I just stared in disbelief. "What in the world is that?" I said to myself. "You mean to tell me that they don't have to hold a coat hanger to get reception? They don't have to turn the knob on the television to get a new show? Wow, this is incredible."

In terms of eating, Erma Jean was adamantly opposed to allowing me to eat at other people's houses. She would say, "We have food and it is just as good as theirs." So, when the Katzners took me to Pagliaze Pizza for dinner, I was afraid to order anything besides water. Though I continued to crack jokes and tell stories of my playground, I did not have the social dexterity or awareness to know if my trepidations were noticed. Dr. Katzner, however, in his ever gentle and coaching style simply said,

"Shawn, do you like pepperoni."

I said, "Yes, it's my favorite."

He replied with, "Do you think we should get a pepperoni pizza? Does that sound good?"

I politely said, "No thank you. I'm not hungry."

Dr. Katzner was a philosopher who played a long term role of making me consider ethical thinking in my approach to daily questions and he kindly said, "We will get a pepperoni pizza and you may have some if you like."

He softened the experience and ultimately ordered me a Coke to drink along with everyone else. In those days, however, refills cost a quarter and he shook his head at me and said, "Please, Shawn, have another Coke with me."

207

When the pizza came he said, "We would like it if you ate some pizza with us."

My internal red light was fully engaged; my stomach was saying green light. The fear of reprisal said, "Red light." Gently, Dr. Katzner said, "Your mother knows you are with us tonight. It's okay."

Typically, at my house we always brought pizza home with us as Jean was too self-conscious about her weight to enter and eat in public. She hated when people stared at us and snickered at her weight. Mama loved the thick and nasty frozen pizzas that were wrapped in plastic; it was like the old generic beer that simply had the word "beer" on its side. So, when the pizza came and Mrs. Katzner put the first slice on my plate, I waited for everyone to have theirs, and then I took my first bite. Not being prepared for the heat of a fresh pizza, and being used to those that had been brought home and cooled, the cheese slid off the sauce, slipped under my chin, and burned the shit out of my face. Not knowing what to do, I slurped it in and burned the upper roof of my mouth. After making a comical face in response, everyone laughed. Sylvia turned red as Jamey and Jody burst out laughing. Yes, it hurt but it was, admittedly, funny to see.

After I let it cool down, I noted that Pagliaze Pizza was my second favorite behind Geno's Pizza, resting across the street from Maumee Valley Hospital where my mom and Erma Jean worked. For the next eight years, whenever I spent the night with the Katzner's in Bowling Green, we ate pizza.

At night, I slept in a sleeping bag in Jamey's room. But, when he handed it to me with a pillow I was rendered helpless. I had never slept in a sleeping bag, as I was accustomed to a roll out bed in the living room or sleeping with my mother next to me as Jean snored in the room across the kitchen. Unrolling and unzipping the bag was an adventure in patience and humility. By the time I figured it out, Jamey was snuggled up in his bed as was his brother Jody. Across the hall next to Kelley's room, Sylvia was fast asleep.

Prior to breakfast, everyone took a shower. To save time, Dr. Katzner told me to use the master bedroom bathroom as he and Mrs. Katzner went downstairs. I had never seen a shower; all I knew was how to take a bath. I looked at the knob and couldn't figure out how to turn on the water. Once it was on, I had no idea of how to make it come from the monster that dangled from the sky. I considered sticking my head under the faucet which was my common practice; the challenge of doing so demotivated me from washing my hair and I often went to school with greasy hair. Thank God, I was athletic; the "wet head jokes" were deflating. Instead, I tinkered around for a few minutes until I figured out how to get the water to flow from above. After messing around with the water temperature, which ultimately was a cold shower since I couldn't figure out how to make water hot, I uncapped the Prell Shampoo and lathered. I was taking my first shower.

Afterwards, when I walked into the kitchen, Dr. Katzner had noticed something out of the ordinary. With everyone sitting at the table, he kindly looked at me and said, "Shawn, have you forgotten something?"

I said, "No, I don't think so."

In response, he gently patted his bald head. When I touched mine, I was mortified to notice that I had not rinsed the shampoo out of my hair. I thought it would simply slide down into the tub since I was standing. After crossing my eyes and patting again, I said, "I meant to do that. I'll be right back." So, I raced back to the bathroom and rinsed.

By the time I made my way back to the table for breakfast, I had already noted that the kitchen had a microwave and a toaster oven. I had heard that microwave ovens existed, but never saw one. Later, when we ate lunch, Jody and Jamey warmed up leftovers in the microwave and asked me if I wanted to eat too. Out of embarrassment for being clueless to the operations of the system, I declined. They had a toaster but warmed bagels in the toaster oven and put on cream cheese. I had never eaten cream cheese and did not want to taste it. Erma Jean's voice rang in my ears, "Never eat at someone else's house." Ultimately, Mrs. Katzner made me cinnamon toast, which was foreign as well, but I ate it ravenously. As I became more comfortable, the family sat back in amazement at my capacity to eat. My imitations of Fred Sanford's "Oh, I'm coming to join you Elizabeth. Oh, it's the big one," left everyone laughing. Finally, Jody could only say, "Man, you should be a comedian" when I broke into my Gene Gene the Dancing Machine imitation from the famous Gong Show variety show.

The whole morning, I conjured up images of Mama saying, *"You have a million dollar personality, no one can take that away from you."* In the face of obvious blunders, I simply went on about my business using humor as salve on what I imagined to be my exposed wounds. I had learned that morning, that even in the face of embarrassment and shame, humor can be used as a tool of salvation and that by being myself, I could be accepted. It didn't hurt that the Katzners absorbed me into their family system as a full-fledged member.

Sitting at the kitchen table with the huge bay window looking out into a corn field was a delight. We laughed and bonded as brothers and sisters. After a series of ringing stories about Mama Green, I felt I was a part of the family. Over time, their kindness was a window into the possibility of living in peace, though I knew that I was eventually going to return to a home of terror. The uncertainty of verbal violence, emotional examination, and threat of alcoholic explosion made me impotent as the clock ticked towards my inevitable departure.

Finally, the doorbell rang. My mother was there, waiting for me to leave. Dr. Katzner invited her in while I gathered my stuff and he said to her, "He was a terrific guest. We hope to have him back soon and often."

As I put on my shoes and gathered my bag out of the hallway closet, I

210

walked towards mom. After she had said, "Thank you for having him over to your wonderful home.", she put her arm around me and walked me to our maroon Buick Special.

Erma Jean waited in the passenger seat and I slid into the back through the driver's side door. As I entered I noticed the gray cloud of cigarette smoke and realized I was going home. "What could I expect when I got there?" I sat and contemplated in the back depressed, knowing, for the first time, that I was different. It was hard to recognize that my street was filled with broken sidewalks, dilapidated homes, throwback technology, and that I lived in a war zone. Having a taste of peace left me sad, anxious, and desperate for a different way of life. I loved my mom, Erma Jean, and Mama and Daddy Green; they were my world and I was hugged and held daily. Unfortunately, there was enough terror and fighting that it neutralized my ability to engage in love.

Seeing that I was visibly saddened, Erma Jean asked me, "Did you have a good time?"

"Yes," I said.

As I expected, her first question was, "Did you eat well?"

Reluctantly, I answered, "Yes. We had pizza and cinnamon toast."

She responded with a trap question, "Did you pig out?"

Fearful of a wrong response, I said, "No."

Now I was feeling the interrogation. "Did you rip and run through the house?"

A positive response was trouble. "No," I replied.

Mom intervened with, "Did you make me proud?"

Giving my customary answer laced with fear I said, "I always try to make

211

you proud, mom."

"Always make me proud," mom extolled. It was her mantra and it had the deep and clandestine aura of control.

Erma intervened with, "Do they have nice stuff?"

"Yeah Jean, they have a basketball rim and backboard attached to the garage." I said, excitedly.

"Um hmm," she replied, unimpressed.

"They also have a piano and taught me how to play chopsticks," I said proudly.

"Well," mom said, "I would like for you to use our family violins and learn how to play that. It's a beautiful instrument."

I replied with zeal, "Can we get a piano. I would really like to learn."

"Sorry, Shawn," she said, "We just don't have the money. These violins have been a part of our family for generations and it's a beautiful instrument. I used to play, you know."

Disappointed, I simply said, "Okay, mom."

Then Jean asked a battery of questions about the house, the number of rooms, the carpet, the kitchen, the location of the washer and dryer, and the cleanliness of the house. When she was done, she turned to my mom, I think to soften the social class differential, by saying, "He's a professor, she stays at home, and their money is through inheritance. They don't have that much." I sunk sadly in the back seat thinking about how my new "family" was being derided. Inside, all I could think was, "How dare you belittle my sense of peace at the Katzner's house?" Here I am going home to a center of terror and Jean wants to minimize this wonderful experience of calm.

212

She looked back at me in the car and, in catching me off guard, said "What's wrong with you? Is this how you're going to act every time you go to someone else's house? If so, then you won't go at all."

Mom, being insulted by Erma Jean's pressing control, said "That's my son and they said he acted like a little gentleman and that I should be proud. Don't you, Erma Jean Bennett, tell him what's going to happen if he acts like that."

Jean responded, "If he's going to act like he's spoiled or superior to us because he stayed with a friend, that is not acceptable. I'll paste him to the wall!"

Mom yelled back, "He's my son!"

Erma replied with a "Humph."

In the back seat, I sat saddened by the realization that war is stronger than peace. The remainder of the ride home was without a word and I ended up at Mama's house knowing that Jean and mom were going to square off in a battle of wills that night. They did.

Two days later, while I was playing wiffle ball with Chris in the backyard, Mama Green and Daddy Green showed up at the house. Mama walked with my mom toward the gate, opened it, and Mama smiled at me as she held a brand new basketball rim and daddy carried a white oval shaped backboard. Chris and I jumped up and down in the excitement that I had a real basketball goal. We hugged, we danced and I broke away and ran to Mama to give her a big hug only to notice one tear rolling down her round left pink cheek. Daddy smiled and said, "This is for you; you make us proud."

We put the backboard and rim on my bed and I just stared at it. Sadly, no one ever put the set on my garage but Chris and I hung the rim on the oak tree in the backyard, on the opposite side of the plant where we used to urinate to "water the plants." We tried to make a basketball

213

court by digging a hole and putting four bricks into the ground. For a week or more we went up and down alleys collecting bricks to build a basketball court that was never finished. The rim, ultimately, found its way to the alley where we hung a makeshift backboard on a telephone pole; seven years later the unused backboard found its way to Mama's new house in the basement storage. However, to this day, I truly understand the meaning that "it's the thought that counts." Mama and Daddy Green showed that love can fix sadness and war can be relinquished to a secondary status with it.

When I arrived "on the hill" later that weekend, I thanked Mama and Daddy for the basketball set. Kindly, while helping Mama cook dinner that evening, we had a chance to talk frankly. I can't remember if we were eating salisbury steak, pork chops, fried chicken, or homemade vegetable soup, but she said that Erma had called and said that "Shawn is depressed after visiting his friends from school."

Mama's response was useful. Erma had the tendency to respond with disdain to situations that could be deflating. My friends had treated me like family and, yet, Erma leveled insults in an attempt to keep me grounded. In the light of such sentiment, Mama simply said, "Sometimes, Erma *don't know her ass from a hole in the ground.*"

"Listen to her, she has a good heart, and loves you. But, sometimes she is as *full of shit as a fat dog is fleas.* Don't worry about Jean," she continued, "*She'll give a dog's ass a toothache.*"

"Baby," she went on, "talk to your Mama." As the smell of food filled the air, I responded.

"Mama, are we poor? Why is there so much fighting at home? The Katzners have a remote control to turn the television channels, a shower, and a microwave oven and they never argue. Everyone loves each other and it makes me sad because we don't have those things. I know you love me but why do my mom and Jean fight all the time?"

It was clear that I was starting to see the world differently. The normality of living in a shack and a violent neighborhood were clearly different than what I was experiencing in school. Once, after playing at the Bright's house, the owner of the Toledo Goaldiggers hockey team, my friend Blaze walked into my house, with my mother present, and said, innocently, "Shawn, I didn't know you were poor?" I shook my head, stared at him for a second and responded, "Neither did I."

My mother shrunk and left the room. Later she cried because her life path had been such a devastating one and she was giving me the best life that she had to offer, and this "rich" kid came in the house and stole all of her efforts. I remember consoling her, "Mom, we're not poor." She said, "We are poor but I chose to be so you can go to Maumee Valley; I don't regret it."

Erma Jean was always kind in her giving. She bought me clothes so I could fit in and be recognized as worthy. She washed our clothes, cooked, and protected my image. Some neighbors thought she was our maid, when, in fact, she was a LPN nurse and used her money on my clothes, food, and detergent. So, she took any, and all, social slights as a matter of insult.

Mama said, "Maybe we don't have a lot of things; that may be true. But, I want you to remember that you are surrounded with a lot of love. Daddy loves you. Leo loves you. Jean loves you. Your mom loves you, and so do I. Just remember that even *rich people can be unhappy.*"

Finally, and in terms of money, she reiterated her lifelong mantra, *"If I have a dime, you have a nickel."* That sentiment always made me feel secure and it helped to eliminate my issues with social class. Further, when Mama would come to Maumee Valley with me for parent's day, she was received as a queen. Ned "The Claw" Wickes loved her and thought she was hilarious; the kids would swoon when Mama showed up. Her splash came at my e

215

ighth birthday party at Stroh's Ice Cream. As we were playing "bounce the ball into the gallon ice cream container," the kids missed every shot. Seksom missed, Jamey missed, Bill missed, Ron missed, George missed, Jeep missed, Steven missed, Brian missed, Matt missed, Joe missed, Doug missed, and David missed. I missed. She walked up and said, "Baby, give me that ball." She bounced the rubber ball off the floor, ricocheted off the display case, and straight into the container. One shot and bam, she made it. Everyone broke into a laughing roar, including the employees. "That's how you do it."

In any case, she never hid behind race or social class. Mama was consistent across social situations and was a model of comportment. Every one of my friends who knew her, loved her; they feared her, but they loved her. Nonetheless, it was her words and actions that always reinforced my confidence and esteem. Her pure existence taught me that, *"Honey attracts more bees than vinegar."* I learned to be kind, to care, and to never be afraid to be myself.

In reflection, growing up relatively poor and in a uniquely arranged family situation is an interesting experience, as a child only knows their surroundings. Socialization can either build or break esteem. As a process, I learned that as obstacles come forth and messages get mixed, it is the consistency of love and its affirmation that matter. My experiences of seeing into the world of the wealthy and educated were invaluable.

In essence, Mama was teaching me the difficult concept of C. Wright Mills' Sociological Imagination. That is, people are more similar than they are different. Race and social class are irrelevant for those who are unhappy, depressed, or lack internal self-esteem. It was apparent that the most important message from Mama to me was, *"Be you; be yourself."* Everyone faces adversity and theirs are as important as ours and ours is as important as theirs. At the end of the day, Mama said, *"It is not my job to judge others, I leave that to the Lord."*

It was clear that I was as important as anyone else but not better. I was guided to *"not to judge another because you have never walked in their shoes."* Tolerance was built into my heart, care was cast in my soul, and socially constructed and arbitrary differences were regarded as irrelevant. The only thing that matters is, *"Don't be nobody's sucka; don't be nobody's fool!"* She added, *"Never turn your back on a person in need, they may be your guardian angel."* In other words, simply love.

Chapter 35.   Baseball Is Just a Game

Aside from Mama's advice and my mother's ongoing search for self, sports dominated the kid's lives in our neighborhood community. We played all year round, and it didn't matter where we were or the time of day or night. Hathaway Park was our neighborhood's "Field of Dreams." As kids, me and my best friends in the neighborhood, Chris and Boonie, played something all the time.

Hathaway Park was a seasonal experience, starting with baseball and basketball in the spring, baseball through the summer, and football in the fall. In the winter, most of the kids played hockey with the orange ball and makeshift goals; I rarely played and opted to practice basketball in the snow and ice instead. However, I never missed the opportunity to play tackle football, baseball, or strikeout. Because of my size (Chris was even younger), we had to learn to be quicker, craftier, and more elusive than our counterparts in order to compete.

Boonie and I had a jump on Chris due to his age; Boonie was bigger and stronger than me, setting up certain advantages as well. Nonetheless, playing with older guys was a lesson in perseverance, persistence, and patience. Chris and I practiced by playing catch in the side yard every day before we rode our bikes around the neighborhood and to the trails. We played with a baseball for a few hours and tossed a football for a few more. In addition, I had a "pitch-back" machine which was an angled bouncing net that returned a ball to the thrower. It had a rectangle target in the center to practice accuracy; Chris had a Johnny Bench "Batter-up" that we used to learn how to hit. Chris' dad, Whitey, spent considerable time teaching us how to throw, catch with two hands, bat and other fundamentals. He had played minor league baseball for the Tigers but turned down a pro offer to stay home with his wife, Sue, to parent his children.

Neither Chris nor I were permitted to cross the street (though we could travel to the dangerous world of the playground without adult supervision) and that forced us to play in my yard. In addition to catch, we loved playing "pickle." It was a game where there were two bases at the end of the yard and a baserunner. The object was for the baserunner to get from one to the other without getting tagged. Shawn and Billy Brady would come over from across the street; Billy Mills and his sister Sundai (who was so pretty that every boy had a monster crush on her), and Chris' little brother, Brian (when he was old enough) would run bases. After a couple of hours of playing in the persistent sun we would shift to playing "Five Dollars."

In Five Dollars, a group of kids would stand in the outfield by the garage as a strong armed participant would throw pop-ups. The object was to muscle in and make the catch before anyone else could. Catching the ball in the air was worth a dollar; one bounce was worth $.50, and two bounces was worth a quarter. Dropping the ball, even if it was due to interference by a competitor, was worth the loss of a dollar. We played for hours.

When everyone would leave for dinner, Chris and I continued. We would throw pop-ups off the top of my house and play the "Ball off the Wall" game on my backyard patio. As we got older, Chris and I turned the game into a competitive one. Just like at Mama's house, we would stand with our feet just in front of the sidewalk by my front porch and whip a tennis ball or rubber ball off the wall at his house in my side yard. The opposing fielder had to field it to earn points. To say the least, the game required the reflexes of a cheetah. In the end, the never ending practice made both of us All-Star players. We never played on the same team because of our age differences, but we were both gifted defensively. Chris played first base and pitched for Good Shepherd and I played for various teams.

When I was six, seven, and eight years old, I played for the Maumee Valley Country Day School Mini-Mohawks; at eight, I joined Chris to play

T-ball at Oregon Coy where me and his cousin, Jeff Keels, dominated; at nine years old there were no teams for me to play for and it was awful. Though I practiced at Mama's and up against the wall at home, the playground was a sanctuary. However, I enjoyed the safety of playing for sanctioned teams. I didn't have to worry about fighting other kids in order to get chosen for a team; no worries of knives being pulled on me with a death threat. There were no concerns about pigeon decapitations, nunchucks, or drugs. Sanctioned sports, though more sterile and less creative than the playground, provided safety.

In the summer of 1976, while sitting at home as other kids played for Navarre, I wasn't permitted to play because I went to a different school. Erma Jean contacted her Aunt Pauline, and asked if her son, Ray, could help me find a team. Within an hour, he had called his former baseball coach, George Brandenberry, and secured a tryout with the Oakdale 76ers. The school was out of my district so I had to use Mama Green's address as my homeaddress to circumvent the rules.

Though the season had already started, I was given a tryout with the team by George as a favor to Ray. My mom drove up to Oakdale School just as practice was ending. My mom and I sat by the backstop when George, who looked like a cross between Herman Munster and Frankenstein, said, "Grab a bat and let's see what you can do."

I hadn't had any warm up swings and he was throwing heat. Fortunately, I had been playing against the older kids for years and knew how to hit a fastball. The bats were aluminum and had grips on them and I wasn't used to the feel in my hands. The old Willie Horton bat felt entirely different with its rough and splintered edges. As I stepped to the plate, David Lozano turned to Mr. Wallace, the assistant coach, his two sons, Mike and Tim, and said, "Who is this clown?" As everyone was picking up their bats, Ray said, in the background, "Just take your time and hit the ball." Dean Street, Croak, the Rowlands, Tommy and Billy Carr, and Clarence Carter all looked on. Then George threw a fastball on the outside corner of the plate and "wham," I crushed the ball to right center field just short of the wall at Oakdale School. I looked back and heard Lozano say, "What the fuck?"

The next pitch was a fastball down the middle of the plate and I ripped a line drive straight into center field only to hear Lozano say, "Sign him up, George."

As everyone looked on at this puny runt sized stranger rip the ball, George said, "Let's see if you can hit a curve ball." Wham, I pulled the curve down the left field line with a one bouncer onto the pavement. George looked at Mr. Wallace, then to Ray, and said to my mom, "He's on the team. This kid can hit." So, instead of me going home with mom, I was invited to ride in George's station wagon with about eight other kids and we all celebrated. His daughter, Peggy, was kind enough to rest my head on her swollen chest.

All of the hitting stones with a broomstick, playing with the "batter-up," getting molested two years before at Weiler Homes, paid off with three hits on three pitches. Ray gave me a high five, mom hugged me, and George raved.

When we stopped at the house on Utah Street, he said, "Ms. Schwaner, we're going to have him bat at clean up. With his ability to hit, he will be knocking in everyone." I was voted MVP that season though we were only a .500 team. But, man was that team talented and boy did we play well together. During that summer, I started spending time at Warner's House reading the sports section every day. While at the Lozano's for tortillas on the stove, we would grab all of the guys and play baseball at the Park on Oakdale. In the summer of '76, I played baseball everywhere and my 7 year old sidekick, Chris, was right there. Eventually, Boonie was coming over too and his talents were immediately noticed; he was a phenomenon.

221

Gary Allen Fine's classic study, With the Boys, documented our history perfectly. Playground sports were dominated by childhood creativity and the construction of ground rules. Sanctioned baseball was dominated by adult rules and regulations and the parents were ferocious, loud, and vociferous. By 1977, Boonie came to Oakdale to play with the PeeWee league team, the A's, as coached by George. I had told George that Boonie was a star and he was on the team without a tryout.

Mr. Wallace split from George and coached the Oakdale Vikings. Off the field, we were all best friends. On the field, we were fierce competitors. The A's had a slight edge having Keith White, Kenny Ewing, Duane Schaffer, Jesus, Boonie, DiMaccio Sifuentes, Brian Whitman, and me on the team. The Vikings had amazing talent with the Rowlands and Wallaces, Jessie Pettaway, and Lozano. The As won the league that year because we were able to beat the Vikings twice while riding Boonie's arm. Similarly, we beat the perennial league champions, the Walbridge Chargers (who were the secondary team to the legendary Walbridge Bears, who played in the Little League World Series one year), because Boonie and Keith White were ace pitchers.

Boonie was a legendary type of pitcher who, by all intents and purposes, should have been a major league player. By age 11, he was throwing an 80-90 mile an hour fast ball, had a three foot breaking curve ball, and knuckle ball with control (that he only threw on rare and special occasions in actual games), a rise ball, a drop ball, and a screw ball. Because we were such close friends, and knew each other's tendencies so well, we were brothers on and off the field. Because of this, George had given me permission to call out the defensive alignments from second base and signal the pitches into Jesus. I was truly the field general and mimicked my game after Cincinnati Reds All-Star, Joe Morgan, the shortest player in Major League Baseball but a two-time league MVP.

As a coach, my brain developed a complex thinking system of strategic formation. Fortunately, our new head coach, Ed Rangle, and his assistant, Ray Castro, were given free reign by George. By the end of the season, we were 13-1, after losing to East Side Central – a perennial powerhouse, who won the league championship followed by the Chargers and the Vikings. Unfortunately, we lost in the first round of the playoffs to the Walbridge Bears, a team that would become our mortal rival. Though we ended up becoming friends with some of their players, as Boonie and I were extroverts, we maintained great disdain for all things Walbridge as that rivalry was deeply entrenched in our souls.

Boonie, however, was very successful in his acquisition of Walbridge women. He dated Liz, who was known as 3T (Tan, Tits and Twat), and his ultimate love, the beautiful and sultry Wendy. Boonie was the ultimate lady's man. He had taken his childhood sexual victimization and released it externally; I had only begun to meet my tarnished destiny at that time and was not interested in dating.

Baseball was my refuge. It also promoted intense social bonds within the community. Our parents came to every game. Mama Green and Erma Jean would sit with Mr. and Mrs. Boening and around 50 other fans; the crowds grew as we won more, and Boonie's notoriety grew. My 4'8" and 80-90 pound frame didn't strike fear into any opponents; my surprising bat and incredible though flamboyant fielding prowess earned respect from teammate and foe alike. Most important, baseball brought our parents and provided escape from their despair, pain, or poverty. They yelled at the top of their lungs, yelled at the "blind" umpires, and chanted names like, "Boonie, Boonie, Boonie,"…."Little Joe, Little Joe, Little Joe." And we thrived.

And, my goodness, each game was met with an after party. First, the kids celebrated with Ede's Ice Cream and then the parents came to our house for adult parties. Erma Jean loved to get everyone drunk. Mrs.

223

Sifuentes always brought me six tacos where the meat was held together using mashed potatoes; Theresa brought homemade tamales, and we had a festival. Gang member's parents, the police, coaches, nurses, and doctors came to the massive events. Us kids played Battleball outside, Nerf basketball inside, "up and over" on the coach (modeled after USC and New England Patriot star, Sam "Bam" Cunningham), and whatever else we could think of. Sadly, mom typically passed out and on one occasion we draped her with a bunch of stuffed animals and she earned the nickname (from Boonie) of Fruit Cake, later shortened to Fruit.

The league championship party at Ed Rangle's was a blowout festival. He had everyone over to his house that rested on the corner of White Street and Girard, two doors down from Oakdale Avenue and his oil refinery factory, Unicast, where he worked. Mama Green brought home brew and wine, and the food exploded with culinary love. The kids earned their trophies as Boonie was given the MVP. I was runner-up followed by Keith White.

As always, I was the last to leave the party with my mom and Erma Jean and helped with clean up. When the party had ended, Mom and Jean went to Utah Street and I rode home with Mama. When we left, Ed and his wife were left at home with Ray and Theresa Castro and one other woman. No more than three minutes after the party had ended, the other woman's husband came into the house, furious. As he stormed into the kitchen, with his .22 gauge shotgun at the ready, he turned to his wife and pulled the trigger. While she dove to the floor, Ed Rangle's wife stood frozen and her head was shot off her shoulders and sprayed along the cupboards behind her. She laid dead and Ed's life, fundamentally, ended.

Soon, thereafter, mom called me at Mama's to share the news that Ed's wife had been murdered. She was shot at point blank range in the face and her head was blown apart. Everyone fell into immediate shock; the players were crushed and confused; parents yelled in pain; and baseball was rendered meaningless. We lost the playoff game to the Bears the following week and it didn't seem to matter.

Baseball, we learned, was only a game; life, we learned, was a precious gift.

In reflection, the summer tended to be a time of community and fun. Kids played baseball and the issues of race and social class were insolvent. The baseball bond built a community where everyone got along. Though we learned that the difference between winning and losing may be driven by chemistry, we were impacted with the notion that life itself is fleeting.

No one could have predicted the nature and direction of a "man's" murderous rage or how it would end the life of an angel. The polarity of balancing lessons of winning with the vicissitudes of life and death, was indeed a challenge. Though we all grieved and banded together in unity, Ed, our coach, mentor, and friend, was destroyed. Everyone, including Mama, went silent.

225

Chapter 36.   Zeus

My mom and I had begun to move closer to each other after years of guidance by Mama Green. By 1978, Erma Jean had moved upstairs into her apartment and I reclaimed my own bedroom. It simply had a dresser, a rickety metal bookcase, a stand up armoire for a closet, and a bureau. The side window was in front of our gate which petrified me. Due to the broken wooden planks in the fence behind our garage, it was used as an escape route for criminal felons fleeing police chases through our yard.

My fear of intruders and Mama Green's training promoted a desire for safety. As such, I took all of my games, monopoly, Life, and the like, and lined them up beneath my bed as a wall creating an illusionary fortress. Then I would lay under the covers and practice rolling off the bed, between the wall and mattress, to the floor where I was shielded by the games. Since I didn't have a gun on Utah Street, and because of the threat of neighborhood violence, I practiced safety and escape techniques. I yearned for solace. Enough people had been shot and killed at Chardee's Bar, in the back alleys, and in nearby homes that it was always on my mind. Pock Face, The Pipefitter, and Little Crazy Joe haunted my nights.

The foot chases by some of the older kids near Fassett Street worried me. Motorcycle gang shootouts with police was like a scene from the movies. On numerous occasions, Chris Strock and I were lined up against the wall at Chardee's and pelted with ice balls filled with rocks. There were countless times where older kids, strangers to us, would throw us up against a wall and punch us in the stomach without mercy. I quit playing the violin because of being chased for carrying it when I got off the "Monkey Vomit Country Gay School" (the derisive name given to it by the neighborhood kids) bus. Gladys Huss, the owner of the two local convenience stores on Fassett Street, fortified her windows with metal bars. I always wondered how she could live in her own self-designed prison, until I realized the threat of violence warranted such adaptations.

To say the least, my neighborhood scared me. In 1979, a sweet 13 year old girl, Cricket Segura, was sexually assaulted, mutilated, tortured, murdered and left on the railroad tracks near Weiler Homes beneath the Fassett Street Bridge. Sexual assault was widespread. My best friend was raped by his older brother; the older brother raped a girl down the street; the girl whom I deeply loved as a teenager was sexually abused as a child; Teen prostitution was apparent; the Cat Lady was a prostitute for the professional wrestlers that came to town. Further, drugs were everywhere. Though it always felt normal, as we didn't know much better, the fear of violation was omnipresent. It was, at times, truly a scary place.

Once while watching the horror movie, "Carrie," starring John Travolta and Sissy Spacek, our house shook as if an earthquake had struck. Towards the end of the movie when Carrie had burned everyone alive in the gymnasium housing the Senior Prom for having dumped a bucket of pig's blood on her Prom Queen dress, she walked to the cemetery. As she was walking, a hand came out of the ground and grabbed her leg to pull her down into the depths of Hell. At that exact moment, our real life house shook. Given my mother's paranormal beliefs, she screamed aloud. We found out later that a motorcycle gang had been in a shootout with the police between Gladys' Variety store and Mullins' Field. At some point, the gang blew up a police car with a bomb and the neighborhood rattled; my school bus stop was at that spot.

In spite of our trepidations, Chris and I managed to deal with our fears in creative ways. Every once in a while, the same Iron Coffin's Motor Cycle Gang, rivals to the Hell's Angels, would race their motorcycles from the end of Utah Street to Fassett Street. Chris and I would have popcorn and Pepsi as we watched. For us, it was entertainment; at my school, it was regarded as weird. So, I tried to learn how to navigate the two worlds carefully and strategically.

Ironically, the violence in my home far exceeded that in the public domain. My mother dating Coach Ed Rangle was cannon fodder. Erma Jean despised the relationship and, ultimately, despised Ed as well. She found it atrocious for him to seek refuge with my mother and for her to share it. My mom had a nurse's warmth when it came to other's pain. She was gentle, soothing, caring, and humorous. She was distant from me as a parent, but worked hard to find that voice over time. I can remember going to my room and putting my ear to the heating vent to learn about the arguments and to prepare myself for a beating, if it were forthcoming.

Fortunately, Mama had given me a puppy from Tweetie's last litter. He was the runt but still my favorite. He had a little black streak down his nose and a beautiful collie-german shepherd mix coat. My mom allowed me to pick him, after our long time stray dog, Tasha, had died. We named him Zeus after the Greek God of strength. He became my closest friend.

Zeus and I played chase all the time. He would chase me through the house and I would hide from him under my beanbag chair. He would sniff around until I would stick out my Ohio State Buckeye sweatshirt sleeve and he would tear at it growling like a loving mountain lion. In time, we were inseparable. And, when I was afraid of a beating, I would lift him into bed with me and hug him. Sadly, on the days when he couldn't protect me, or when mom had detached her love from me, Zeus experienced the aftermath.

With great remorse, there were a few incidents where I would beat Zeus after having been beaten myself. I would look at him and say, "I thought you loved me, Zeus. Why didn't you protect me?"

No matter how much I spanked the best dog on Earth, he never flinched, bit me, or barked. Then, when I would look into his saddened

228

eyes, I would lay with him in the hallway for hours and hug him. I apologized with the heart of a fallen saint. I was forced to act perfectly all the time as no trouble was permitted, but even perceived slights of disrespect were met with a belt. In time, though, when he scratched the door open and forced The Pipefitter out of my ass, I never spanked him again. My beating him lasted a short period of time in the spring of 1978, one for which I feel a great sense of guilt, but it ended when he had proven his love to me.

Zeus was my protector and an incredible watch dog. He knew all the fundamental dog commands, sit, speak, shake, rollover, and lay down. After the pipefitter incident he was treated as the king until he had his first epileptic seizure, which broke my heart.

In the summer of 1978, George had moved from Oakdale to coach the Navarre Braves. And with that, he forced me to quite with the Oakdale A's, as he promised to report the transgression to the city league thereby banning me and Boonie from playing baseball at all. Instead, I opted to go on strike and quite baseball altogether. I played with Chris, who was playing at Good Shepherd, sandlot at the park, and a whole lot of fetch with Zeus and the wall game with Mama Green. It wasn't enough as I slid into a deep childhood depression. My dreams of replacing Joe Morgan were shattered and I just wanted to cry all the time. I held Zeus and hugged him relentlessly. My dog, my buddy, was my whole life. I wish I had never beat him.

Chapter 37.   A Shattered Knee and Broken Dreams

My dissertation advisor from Ohio State, Dr. Simon Dinitz, once wrote a published article entitled, "Nothing Fails like a Little Success." Though he was writing on the success of juvenile delinquency policies, his suggestions were true for life in general. At Oakdale and Navarre, the skills that I learned from Mama's games contributed to my success on the baseball diamond and fueled my dreams of replacing Joe Morgan. Every dream I had centered around playing second base professionally, as I knew that my skills in basketball would never allow me to replace Dr. J, since I was just too short. However, because of my athletic pursuits, focusing on school was of marginal importance to me. I didn't dig into my schoolwork as I did sports. That was a mistake, as it was a lot to overcome, years later.

In the summer of 1980, the regular core of our Colt League Navarre team were present again. Our team was constructed around a group of players who had grown into a brotherhood after the Championship of 1978. Though we had a relatively slow start to the season with an early loss or two, we were still gearing up for a championship run. The addition of the speedy Clarence Carter in right field, who had moved from Oakdale to Navarre, assured success.

Though public tryouts at Navarre School were rigorous, so the starting line-up had stayed essentially the same. After a debate with one of my heroes and teachers, Laszlo Koltay, about attending 8th grade graduation or playing in a baseball game, I crossed the stage. Though in retrospect I wanted to play in our Wednesday game as it was more directly tied to my lifelong dream, 8th grade graduation, he argued, was a once in a lifetime event. So, after consulting with Al Getman, my fifth grade advisor, my mom, Erma Jean, and Mama, I decided (against my will), to graduate. Becky Raisner, another East Sider, and I excitedly delivered the class gift speech, delivering a magnolia tree to the school. After happily graduating, it turned out that the game was unimportant
230

and Mr. Koltay was right.

Our next game was on Saturday, and it provided our team with two days of practice and fun at the park. Given our rivalry with Riverside, the upcoming game was to be played in Waite Stadium; my excitement was growing with anticipation. That Friday, as the construction workers put yellow and brown aluminum siding over the peeled green paint of my house, I walked under the ladder conscious that it was a taboo – furthermore, it was Friday the 13th. Often times, I directly confronted superstitions and fear by facing them head on…nothing happened.

As I was earning more notice by scouts watching Boonie, I was working on ways to become a better fielder. For weeks I had been working on a play to run back on a fly ball, put my arm across the top of my head so that the glove would bounce with my vision, like a shock absorber on a car, and leap up for the catch. It was a play that would only be used rarely, I knew, but it was effective at Mullin's Field and the Park.

Saturday the 14th was met with a light drizzle, but not enough rain to cancel the game. Boonie and I went through our fourth year ritual of pre-game warm up when infield practice started, and he went to warm up his pitching arm for the game as I started to practice. The anticipation of playing at Waite was exhilarating. After hitting a single in the first inning and scoring the first run of the game, Navarre had taken an early 2-0 lead. In the top of the third inning, Boonie was in rhythm to pitch another gem. As the field captain, I waved a request for Billy Mills to have Boonie throw a low fastball on the outside corner of the plate. I figured the opposing batter would swing late on the pitch and it would be an easy ground ball to second making for an easy out.

Mr. and Mrs. Boening had arrived for the game, Kenny was coaching in a cast and on crutches from his recent knee operation, and Erma Jean sat above the dugout with our other faithful fans. Neither my mother nor Mama had arrived, yet.

231

With Boonie's wind up, as expected, he hit the outside corner of the plate with a stifling fastball. The batter hit a soft liner to right center field. It was soft enough for me to run back on it as a second baseman, but deep enough for Mike McDougall, playing centerfield, to come up on the play. As I sprinted into the right field grass in my Thom McCann running shoes, I had the chance to use my newly practiced catching style. To my delight, after calling for the ball three times, I leaped into the air, extended my glove and felt the ball land squarely in its palm. When my left foot hit the ground, my knee exploded in a devastating collision with Mike's rib cage. My shoe slid under his body as my momentum carried me over his and my leg snapped in half in a grotesque exhibition of pain. My glove, with the ball still in the palm, flipped out of the glove and gently rolled out. Clarence picked it up and threw it to second base where the batter stood, aghast.

Though I worked to be a "man" and not cry, the crowd heard a young boy screaming in agony on the grass in right center. In that moment, all I could think about was, "Boys don't cry!" "Shake it off, boys don't get hurt. Shake it off, shake it off, shake it off" is all I could think. As I shook my leg to bury the pain in the depths of Hell, the little bone splinter in my knee was eviscerating my meniscus and my ligaments were shredded to the size of angel hair pasta. As Clarence picked up the ball, I stood up in an attempt to walk and be a "man." Mike was laying on the ground, crying, holding his ribs. *He never heard me call for the ball.* In a moment, I had hit a turning point that changed my life forever; all of my dreams came crashing down. It was over. My knee was destroyed and Joe Morgan's replacement would have to come from elsewhere.

Since Coach Paszko was on crutches, the coach for Riverside came running out into the outfield in an attempt to calm me down. In an effort to avoid crying, I looked at him as he carried my soldier's soul to the West End dug out. I kept imitating Gilda Radner's Saturday Night Live Rosana Danna Danna character famous line:

"Something, it's always something."

Though the coach mildly laughed, he kept saying, "You're going to be okay son. You're going to be okay."

"Something, it's always something." I uttered again.

Erma Jean, to my mother's chagrin, came into the dugout as my leg swelled beyond the size of my baseball pants, "Let me see you walk on it."

With one final step, I collapsed and fell into a wad of chewing tobacco. Erma yelled, "He's hurt, He's seriously injured! He has to go to the hospital, now!"

Erma Jean broke out her scissors from her purse and cut the pants from around my knee which had swollen to the size of a volleyball. Mr. Boening ran into the dugout, picked me up, and carried me up the long hill and took me to his green van. My teammate's eyes, and those of Riverside, dropped to the ground as I continued to scream out in pain.

"Hold on Shawner, I'm going to get you there."

Mr. Boening drove quickly and with an eye toward deliberate safety to my house on Utah Street so as to ask my mother which hospital she wanted me admitted. Instead, she had arrived at the game, found out what happened, and rushed home. When we parked, Chris and Brian heard my screams, came and checked on me with their dad, Whitey, and they looked at my knee in shock. Finally, mom got home in what seemed like a week, looked, and said,

"Goddammit, why did Jean make him walk on that knee. She knew better. She knew better. Don, take him to MCO and I'll follow."

Mama was with my mom and they rode out to MCO, a 20 minute drive. When we arrived, my mom had already gone into the hospital to tell the trauma unit that I was coming in, as she was friends with those in the ER, and I cut to the front of the line.

After cutting off my pants, and in an attempt to stabilize my leg, they rushed me into the x-ray room. Mrs. McDonald was waiting for me when I was wheeled into a private ER space.

"It's going to be okay, Shawn" as she rubbed her angelic hands through my hair that she loved. I noticed a tear fall to her cheek, and I grew worried. By then, my mom was in the room holding me with the most love that I had felt emanate from her small and delicate hands. Dr. Woods walked in.

"Dr. Woods, can I play in our make-up game on Monday," I immediately asked.

"No, Shawn."

"Well, what about our game on Wednesday? We have a game on Wednesday and my team needs me. Can I play on Wednesday?"

"No, Shawn, you can't play on Wednesday, either."

With tremendous reluctance, given my mother's expertise in orthopedics, he said, "Shawn, this is going to be hard for me to say but you cannot play baseball on Monday or Wednesday. You have experienced a severe knee injury and will likely never play sports again. You are likely to walk with a cane for the rest of your life."

"Noooooooooooooo, Noooooooooooooo, Noooooooooooooo, this can't be. Why me? Why me? Why me?" I yelled out.

In a moment, I thought, all of my dreams had come to an end. I would never replace Joe Morgan, I would never play with Dr. J. I was no longer going to be an athlete and I cried like a parent losing a child. With all of those years of playing "balls off the wall," "hit the stone with the broom handle," "Pickle," "Five dollars"... It was all gone. It was a waste. "Why me?" is all I could think.

Then Dr. Wood turned to my mother and said, "Sue, we need to operate right now. Every moment is going to make the damage worse."

My mother, in a moment of clarity, simply and sternly said, "No, we will wait for Dr. Singh to return on Monday."

"But Sue..."

"No Dr. Woods, and without offense, Dr. Singh is one of the best orthopedic surgeons in the world and he will do this operation. You are excellent and I expect that you will take great care of my son."

At that point, they started pushing pain relievers into my system. It was so brutal that I threw up for two straight days. Because of my mother's great influence in the hospital and her subordinates on the orthopedic ward, I was treated like a king. Kathy, a stunning and buxom blond-haired beauty, was exceptionally gentle and caring but the pain was so great that my masculinity was turned off. I couldn't see her or anyone else.

Mama Green, with tears streaming down her face, rubbed my head with her magical hands. She said little but held me as my mother mobilized the nurses and doctors on her unit to provide the greatest of care. Given the amount of times that I had come to the ward to visit my mom, all of the nurses knew me well. Barbara, the Assistant Head Nurse, Rita, the tea leaf reader, Kathy, the Beautiful, and Mom's best friends, Mrs. Hockett and Mrs. Harris, all came to visit.

When no one was in the room, I quietly asked Mama Green, "Why did this happen to me?" I was hurt, confused, and my dreams were shattered.

She simply said, "God chose you for a reason; it is His will. If it weren't you it would have been somebody else. Would you ever want to wish this pain unto someone else? That would be selfish, wouldn't it?

"Yes, Ma, it would be."

And I quietly accepted that my life's fate had changed forever.

Soon thereafter, the team arrived and they were hardly able to stomach seeing their fallen comrade laying in agony. Boonie was never able to visit a sick person in the hospital, again. Seeing his "little buddy" in such pain was beyond his emotional resources. After the team visited and as I continued to puke, I asked my mom to keep everyone out except for Mr. Paszko and Mama Green. Those were the only two people who could get me to eat during my two week stay.

Monday came, Dr. Singh operated, and upon its completion, he told my mother that it was the worst knee injury that he had seen. The eight-hour operation was geared mostly toward sewing together all of the torn ligaments.

As I realized that I was going to have to focus on reading and studying and find a new dream, my sadness swelled. On Tuesday, Dr. Singh came into my room with my mom and said, "How are you feeling, Chief?"

"I'm okay."

"Chief," he said, "I have a deal for you."

"Yes, Dr. Singh."

"I think you will be able to walk without a cane. I also think that you will be able to play sports again. However, you will have to follow my rehabilitation program exactly and endure some of the greatest pain of your life. There is no one that can do these exercises for you, except you. Only you can decide to play baseball again because it is going to be very painful."

236

I said, "I might be able to play again?"

"Yes, but you have to go through the rehabilitation."

I was sold. In my mind there was no one on Earth willing to hustle, work, and endure pain as much as me. Given my size and level of perseverance, I promised Dr. Singh, "I will do it."

Though I lamented my experience, I learned a great deal about friendship and love. Mama and Mr. Paszko came every day to visit me and I finally had something to eat. Seksom brought me a pizza from Pizza Hut, get well cards streamed in, a few teammates visited when they could stomach it, and so did the love of my life, Lisa. When she entered with her card, her flawless body froze time, her smile filled the room, and her hair shimmered in the light. After all of those visits to see her on Ironwood, her home on Oak Street, and in developing a childhood friendship, she was actually in the room – my room - the most beautiful girl in the world.

My crush for her was well known. As she smiled at me and said, "Hey guy, you're going to be alright," my smile beamed. I couldn't believe that this dream had walked into my room. Then she asked if she could draw a picture on my cast and I of course said "Yes."

On the only spot available for a picture (she was beyond a simple signature), she drew a clown. As Kenny Mike sat in the corner under the television, Lisa drew. At one point, she made a mistake and erased. When she blew the crusty eraser nibblets off, my eyes looked at her thick lips, and as the wind from her gentle breath hit my penis, I popped a boner that sprang to life just to the left of her cheek. Kenny Mike burst out laughing and I ripped the sheets over my erection. Though I don't know if she saw it, I was sitting in the bed red with embarrassment.

However, when I went home, after having grown five inches in height,

237

she visited me the first hour I was there. She came in my room and asked if she could play a record on my player. She chose Michael Jackson's "Off the Wall," and Prince's "I Wanna be Your Lover." She continued coming to the house regularly and listened to music with me. Though I never let her be present during the monumentally painful rehabilitation exercises, she started helping me walk to the playground on my crutches. We were attached at the hip, even after I was named "assistant coach" by Mr. Paszko; he allowed me to be the batting coach and scorekeeper for the team and gave me a green shirt with the word manager on the back. We were even able to get the talented and speedy Butch Tammerine to improve his batting average above .300.

Eventually, Lisa became my girlfriend and it was one of the happiest weeks of my life. She once kissed me in front of my house underneath the tree branch that I had used to practice dunking a basketball. Her lips were luscious, soft, and covered with a gentle moisture. As I turned my head to really enjoy the moment, I heard, "Shawn, get in this damn house right now, and you, go home!" Jean had intervened and Lisa scampered away.

A couple of nights later she and her friend Tina came to watch a movie in my living room. I laid my head on Lisa's lap and felt securely at home as my mother, drunken, was on the phone saying, "Shawn's fine and on the couch with his girlfriend." I was embarrassed and hated that she said it, but being with Lisa was great and nothing else really mattered. At one point she leaned over to say something to Tina and her breast rested squarely on my eye and slid down to my lips. My penis started to harden, again, and I tried to use my cast to hide it. Next thing I know, she and Tina were play wrestling on the floor and when Lisa accidentally pulled Tina's top down, her breast lay exposed.

Unfortunately, I was petrified of Lisa's beauty. We had long been friends but I felt inferior to her physically. As had become our routine, she invited me to her house to watch cartoons. When I came around to the backyard, Lynn, Lisa's older sister, said to me, "Shawn, just kiss her. Do   your   lips   like   this   and ssssssssssssssssssssssssssssmmmooooooocccchhhhh, kiss her."

Lisa blushed and I said, "I know what to do Lynn, thanks." Truth was, I had no idea what to do.

Lisa sat to my left with my cast between us. Clearly, she wanted me to kiss her, but I was afraid of getting hard and wasn't sure how to turn to the left with my cast in the way. So, we fake laughed at Popeye. Though we held hands I knew the relationship was going to end because I was afraid to deal with Jean and my sexual insecurity rendered me impotent.

I stood up, looked at Lisa and said, "I think I should go."

She simply responded by saying, "Hey Shawn, thanks for coming over."

Then she took off her pants, then her shirt, turned to her right and walked to the stairs and disappeared. I stood motionless for about four hours as I drooled over the perfection of her body, the size and firmness of her chest, and the curvature of her buttocks. I just wasn't ready for a queen. Though we never again kissed or dated, we remained best friends for life. We were "05ers." We had endured parallel lives, understood each other without words, and had played a childhood approach/ avoidance dance for years. We were meant to be friends and I happily accepted that those feelings would forever remain the same.

The summer passed and I did my exercises. By the winter I was off of crutches and by the following spring was playing baseball and basketball again. I couldn't jump as high, or run as fast, but I was determined to be the best. I could not, and would not, be stopped. And, true enough, I became an MVP baseball player in high school and continued to be a smooth and creative basketball player. However, I knew once and for all that my dreams would never come to pass as I had no other goals.

So I tried to focus on school and learning.

In reflection, the lessons on facing adversity and working hard were deeply embedded within my core philosophy. I was willing and able to persevere through pain and sexual confusion, while surrounded with love and friendship beyond what I had previously known. I learned that people cared, mom cared, and that Mama had trained me to manage any obstacle. The injury changed the trajectory of my life, and though I now have arthritis and knee pain, my position in life was shaped by one error in communication between a second baseman and centerfielder. *Turning points*, it seems, occur when least expected and preparation for them is a lifelong process.

Life happens and can change, in a moment, without notice.

Chapter 38.   The Morning Childhood Died

"Wake up, motherfucker, wake up!"

And with that startling and painful alarm, the lamp on my dresser came crashing down across the back of my skull, shattering. The clock read 5:35 AM and the fearful sunlight hid in the nighttime air. The attack was under way and the fury of an abused life came screeching upon my soul. Smack, the right side of my face was walloped with the compact blow of seething revenge.

"I said, wake up motherfucker! Wake up!" My mother's rage escalated from, "You spoiled brat!" to "You're going to accept Kenny if it's the last thing you do!" All the while, my mother's tiny fist punched the sides of my face with machine-like accuracy. She had straddled me in the bed, using the covers to immobilize me. Five minutes raged as my ears rang like a police car's beacons wailing in the midnight hour.

Suddenly, and without warning, she ripped the covers off of my bed and pushed me to the floor. This sneak attack left me stunned. "After all I've done for you, you're going to act like a spoiled fucking brat? I want my three thousand dollars back for those goddamned teeth that I paid for." And the punches to the mouth began. Ali's rope-a-dope was my only defense. Though I was strong enough to overtake my mother in a straight out fight, all I could hear in the back my head were Mama Green's words, *"Always respect your mother."*

Then, with the swiftness of a gazelle springing in the open savannah, my armoire was thrown to the ground. My clown piñata holding my treasured Susan B. Anthony silver dollars crashed across the floor; clothes were strewn aside as a tornado destroys a house in the Missouri Flats; my games and bookcase were dismantled with a fury and my room was classified by the "Governor of Pain" as a disaster area.

Mom whipped around and stepped toward me saying, "You don't

241

deserve these games or clothes, you fucking brat." The punches continued. With a right cross, she had knocked me through the doorway and into the adjoining hallway. When my face hit up against the broom closet door, my mother ripped into my back with her nails. She flung me mercilessly into the kitchen while holding my t-shirt.

As she pushed me into the refrigerator and cooking island, she repeated that, "We are poor because of you. You go to Maumee Valley and your grades are worse than Kenny Mike's. I'm wasting my money on you for nothing. You fucking stupid brat. You are going to accept Kenny, you are going to accept Kenny, *you are going to accept Kenny.*"

And with one swipe, her nails had ripped through my t-shirt and into my back. Her claws cut wide a trail of bloodied destruction down the path of my spine with red-hot pain. The blood oozed from the canals carved into my skin. Then, referencing what I had been given on child abuse in 9th grade speech class, she said, "Child abuse! Child abuse! What in the hell do you know about child abuse? I know child abuse and now you're going to know it, too!"

The punches continued. She picked up a skillet off of the stove and cracked me on the left side of my head. I saw stars but wouldn't fall – it would have been certain death. The punches to the mouth continued; "I want my $3000 back, you fucking brat." Bam. Smack. Pow. The attack continued. Dishes flew; pots clanked to the floor, tables were flipped, and the wet bar and bookcase were knocked to the ground. The house looked like it been in a police raid.

The war raged for an hour and a half. I realized that my experience was due to my tyrannical grandmother's punishment upon my mother – it was culminating in my worst hour. My childhood was obliterated and died an agonizing death.

Then, in a moment of a torturer's grace, my mother and I noticed the hundred or so thumb tacks laying on my bedroom floor. I knew

242

immediately that she was going to force me to walk on them. As I slowly and gingerly stepped down onto the tacks with my right foot, and quickly and vengefully turned with Satan's rage towards my mother. I looked her straight in the eye and said, "If you force me walk on those tacks, then one of us is going to die today."

With that, the storm passed to sea and mom walked to the kitchen door to leave for work.

As I stood in the hallway bleeding and hearing bells, I heard Erma Jean's apartment door close. Her slow gait clumped down the stairs in a slow but methodical descent. As mom opened the kitchen door to exit the house, she turned and exploded, "Clean this fucking house before I get home."

At the age of 15, I could have fought back but did not. Ashamed and alone, my spirit stripped of its kindred charm, I stood as a statue, transfixed. "My mother just tried to murder me, but why?" I thought. Was she angry from me shrugging my shoulders on Halloween while standing at Mama Green's house or was it because of her desperate desire to be loved and married? Was it about me or about Kenny? I wondered. Then, it dawned on me, it didn't matter, I was a worthless piece of shit undeserving of life.

The day before, I had been at Mama Green's house. I had spent Friday night there and was going to pass out Halloween candy. This was the first year in which I did not trick or treat and I anxiously desired to share candy with the kids.

When Erma Jean and mom had swung by Mama's home after work, they had forgotten to pick up the Geno's Pizza that had been promised weeks before. When she arrived empty handed, I felt disappointed and discarded; "I no longer matter," I uttered to myself. I felt like mom was trying to force me to love Kenny and my life was tolerated merely to ensure her happiness. I shrugged my shoulders, at Jean, in frustration.

243

When I had shrugged my shoulders at Erma for breaking the promise of Geno's pizza, a demon leaped from my mother's toxic aura as she screeched the tires and abruptly left for home. My upset with Erma Jean for forgetting the pizza was taken by mom as an insult; she had enough.

After she sped away, I went into Mama's humble house and told her what had happened. "Sorry, Ma, but I think I should go home." She agreed and said simply, "Be careful."

I rode my bike home and came in the back door. Kenny Mike, Debbie, and Kenny were already there and preparing the candy bowls for the "Devils' Day" distribution. When I asked mom for a sucker, she spun quickly and stated, "I have never denied you anything! Take one!"

I retreated to my bedroom knowing that trouble was at hand.

Trick or Treating came and went and the bowls were exercised of their bounties. Kenny Mike and Debbie had gone home and only adults were left in the dining room. Having practiced listening to conversations through the heating vent to prepare for coming beatings, I listened intently.

Jim Dalton, Kenny, Denny D., Jack Crooks, Erma Jean, and Brock sat talking. When my mother and friends start discussing my "spoiled personality," she sought disciplinarian guidance and asked, "Should I talk to him? Beat him? What do you think is best?"

I listened for at least two hours when suddenly the majority vote was to, "Teach him a lesson." Jack Crooks dissented because of his "Little Squirt" story (where I stood up for him against teammates after a disrespectful day of baseball practice); as the others concurred on corporal punishment. My fate was set, and these mother fuckers had decided that I should be beaten. I suppose that they had no idea that behind my mother's heavenly face rested a serpent who was ready to strike with an abusive force.

Night fell and everyone left. Erma Jean retreated home and my mother went to bed. I thought I had been spared. The morning's attack stole my heart, however, and given Erma Jean's knowledge and role of the event, I never forgave her for sitting idly upstairs. She could have, and should have, intervened knowing full well that a beating was taking place; she heard the screams and did nothing.

After they left for work, I called Mama Green on the phone. "Mama, can you come over, my mom beat me and I need your help."

When she arrived and came in through the kitchen door, she dropped to her knees. Gun in hand, tears rolling down her broken face, screamed with a mighty howl, "I'm gonna kill that dirty heifer. I'm gonna kill that mutha fucka."

At that point, she saw my ripped shirt, bruised face, and bloodied back. Her reaction was that of a beaten child. "No, no, no, this can't be. I'm gonna kill that dirty heifer. I'm gonna kill that mutha fucka.""

I begged her not to kill my mother and just asked her to help me clean up her tornadic devastation. First, she tended to my back, bloody nose, and face. Second, we cleaned. Finally, she broke down when she saw the tacks on the floor and realized that I had been forced to walk on them. Her anger exploded as if she had seen Mr. Dank's ghost.

I was never the same; it took decades for my mom and I to heal from the attack. Though she came home with extreme remorse and apologies, and Erma stared at me in disbelief, I felt like a zombie stripped of his soul by a mother's rage.

The attack sent shock waves through the staff at Maumee Valley. With a day of healing, I went to my trusted teacher and confidant, Al Getman, and sought solace. The pain of my home life required immediate action. At the Monday faculty meeting, I had heard, he shared the secret with the other teachers so they could be aware that their son, Ween (my high school nickname) had been viciously attacked and needed empathetic understanding so as to save my life.

My grades plummeted yet, my teachers held out their hands in love. MV was a place of learning, consideration, and social tolerance.

By May 1982, I had decided that I was going to commit suicide by slicing my wrist with a butcher's knife and taking all of the pills available in the house. The idea of life was obtuse and I had grown exhausted by fighting, violence, and disillusionment. The beating pushed my esteem to the ultimate brink of self-destruction. First, however, I wanted to watch Dr. J., one last time, as he and the 76ers took on the "Green Ghost" (nickname of the Boston Celtics), in game seven of the Eastern Conference finals.

I laid on the couch with the butcher knife on the floor beside me and pills lined up on the coffee table. Dr. J., however, came out and played a game for the ages, dunking over Parrish, McHale, and Bird on a thunderous tomahawk jam down the center of the lane. The cover of Sports Illustrated highlighted the dunk in their next issue. When the Sixers won and the fans in Boston began to chant, "Beat L.A., beat L.A.," it dawned on me that the Sixers were predicted to lose as they had done the year before by letting a 3-2 lead disappear. When they won, and the Doctor had carried the load, I realized that everyone can overcome an obstacle; adversity is just a part of life.

I put the knife and pills away and vowed that, "I will never be defeated by adversity." The worst day, the beating of '81, was also my best day. I became a fighter, driven to persist against all obstacles. Mental strength became my identity marker – but the desire to die persisted. My life had been defined by the push and pull battle between strength and annihilation; fatalism was my new middle name.

The horror of that day resonates until present day. The combination of a history of abuse directed towards my mother, along with her lifelong quest for true love, exploded with an emotional fury. Perhaps, punishment for shrugging my shoulders was necessary, but a full out attack was not. The moment has scarred me with a degree of Post-Traumatic Stress Disorder that has produced fatalistic and paralyzing effects. Every day I live, I want to die; every time I seek death; I choose life.

Even worse, I learned that the intergenerational transmission of violent components requires conscious attention and dedication to stop. The cycle of the normalization of violent scripts have a life letting power, under the right circumstances. For me, learning how to recognize the urges of violence, and channeling them into appropriate directions, was a youthful quest. I practiced the art of internal and external communication and practiced, as Mama would tell me, *"To look for the good in others as we are all crazy in some ways."* Such a quest, even though inherently difficult, *is* possible and a powerful method for avoiding trouble. As Mama said, *"Maintain a still tongue,"* and persevere.

Finally, it was painfully obvious that while the world was teaching me to "never take candy from a stranger," it was the people that I knew that did the most damage. It took decades to understand how a person can love, hate, and harm the same person at the same time. Sadly, a blurring between love and hate marked my childhood existence; that festered and resulted in determination, drive, and relentless ambition on the one hand, and a death wish idealogy on the other. Others who endured similar experiences have suffered silently, abused drugs, or outright died. These lessons cannot be bought, taught, and only marginally understood. One beating, or perhaps an attempted murder, transformed me and my life in perpetuity. I still hurt today. As a matter of fact, I am among the walking dead.

The date of November 1, 1981 is etched into my memory as

247

permanently as a name on a tombstone. I declare that date was the morning that my childhood died, forever.

Chapter 39. Erma's Deadly Moment

The first time that I went bowling was for Brian Rothman's second grade birthday party at Southwyck Lanes. There were 64 lanes and the building felt like a stadium of bowling. The kids, though, could not pick up the 16 pound balls and were forced to use the little 8 pound ones; we wielded potty style shots at the pins. Though I only bowled a 22, I hit the 7-10 pins on a couple of shots; too bad all of the others pins stood tall. My friend, Seksom, bowled a 25 and looked like a king; Jamey was the Jedi Master rolling a 52.

Having had such a great time, I began to study the game. On one particular day, Mama and I had traveled to the liquor store in Rossford, two doors down from the tastiest pizza place on the East Side. I vividly remember that they had a pinball machine that would pitch a marble down the center of a baseball diamond as the player used the flippers to hit it over the ramp and into the bleachers for a home run. That liquor store was Mama's lottery gold.

Though I cannot recount the number of times she hit the three digit winner, she always claimed to see the numbers in her sleep. Being a big believer in dreams and supernatural phenomenon, Mama only played the lottery when there was a "sign." And, sure enough, she won regularly. One particular afternoon when the sun was stinging through the front window, I saw a free book on bowling written by Mark Roth, Earl Anthony's top competitor in the 1970s. The book was only 20-30 pages in length and showed how to hold a ball, the proper steps to take on the approach, how to snap the wrist for spin, and most importantly, it provided diagrams of how to aim for the arrows on the lane. The book showed that aiming at the arrows 10 feet away from the foul line was easier than aiming at the pins 60 feet up the horizon.

I practiced bowling by taking my Nerf basketball and racing from the dishwasher in the kitchen to the divider at the kitchen door adjoining the dining room. For hours, I would work on release and how to slide, in my socks, to the "foul line." Of course, given the light weight of the Nerf ball, it would hit the ground and shoot to the left like a cannon being fired during a military operation. However, I did learn form and technique. Mama would cook in the kitchen as I would report on the score of the match; one would swear that I was bowling in the world champion's tour.

By time the next bowling birthday party rolled around I broke 60, then 100, then 150. Though a few years would come and go before I joined a league, practicing made a difference. By the time I was 12, my friend, Kenny Brown, and his mother invited me to join a league at the Sports Center on Starr Avenue. Though many kids bullied Kenny and treated him poorly, given his brown corduroy pants and living in a poor home in East Toledo, we were fast friends.

Joining the league was a significant sacrifice. Namely, I had to give up Saturday cartoons, including Hong Kong Phooey, The Great Grape Ape, Captain Caveman, Scoobie Doo, and the Fat Albert Show. No more, "Hey, hey, hey, it's Fat Albert." Or, "Hong Kong Phooey, number one super guy," or "Captain Caveeeeemaaaaaaaaaaaaaan," or "Scoobie Doobie Doobie Do, where are you?" My cartoon days ended and my competitive life escalated.

Similar to baseball, I was the leadoff bowler on the team that was carried by a quiet giant. I had a 150 average which ranked me highly in the league, but Jeff assured us a playoff spot. In the following year, the Navarre Braves shortstop, and my good friend Kenny Mike, joined the team.

His dad, who was our baseball coach with the Navarre Braves, coached us in bowling. Mr. Paszko had been a professional bowler in the 1970s and, just as he was to start touring, calamity struck. While working as a garbage collector, street sweeper, and snow plow operator (his official title was Heavy Machine Operator) his knees were crushed in a freak accident. During lunch, in 1973, he and the crew were eating sandwiches while leaning against a guard rail when a garbage truck slipped out of gear and rolled back. Without the time to react, the truck had crushed both of Mr. Paszko's knees against the rail, shattering his kneecaps. He screamed a perilous screech that scared birds from their nest and bristled his co-workers hair.

By the time the truck was moved, Mr. Paszko had slipped into shock and had no recollection of the event. In a true injustice, Mr. Paszko never won a workman's compensation award. Though he would become a professional softball player and hit a foul tip off of the King and His Court, a famous barnstorming team regarded as the best team in the world, he was a professional horseshoe player worthy of a room of awards; but he could never run again. In spite of the injury, he continued to bowl and carried a 205 average due to his abbreviated three step approach to the foul line. He had a 3/4 stroke with a two foot break. He once had bowled a 300 in league play and had a trophy and Toledo Blade newspaper articles commemorating the accomplishment.

In my quest for perfection, and his ability to connect with me, we began bowling on Sundays with he and his best friend, Jim Dalton. Jim was a motorcycling co-worker who had a penchant for attracting women and gambling with bookies; he too was a magnificent bowler with a bigger than life personality. It was at this time that I began betting $5 per week on a four game parlay, which I only won once. I was well known for my encyclopedic knowledge of Buckeye football and the NFL. Mr. Paszko would often take me to Waite High School football practices where I was often asked to recite all of the starting quarterbacks and running backs in the NFL – I did so with ease.

Soon, whenever Mr. Paszko was near, I could break 200 routinely, having a high score of 256. Sadly, though, if Kenny Mike was not perfect, Mr. Paszko would rip into his pride, leaving in its wake a saddened young friend. Kenny Mike weathered many insults but felt unduly criticized for imperfection. Kenny Mike and I were great friends, especially as a dynamic shortstop-second base duo, but I hated how he bore the brunt of small mistakes.

Outside of the league, and much like any other sport, I think I enjoyed the practice more than the game itself. Whether it was posing in the mirror like Julius Erving coming down the lane for a tomahawk dunk, or playing "ball off the wall," or sliding to the imaginary foul line in Mama's kitchen, I loved to practice. Memorizing where to place the ball along the arrows was so much fun.

By March of 1982, I was regularly bowling with John Bronson, of MVCDS, at Rossford Lanes. Though he was definitely a unique personality with an incredible admiration for Ronnie Simmons, highly regarded as the funniest human being alive at Maumee Valley, John could bowl well. Each Friday, we looked forward to eating a nasty square pepperoni pizza with a coke at the snack bar in between our second and third games. Though he routinely beat me, the matches were competitive. We were two sixteen year olds blowing out scores of or 180 to 185 or 210 to 220, which allowed us to feed off of each other. Though we only rarely hung out at school, Friday nights were ours.

During this period, and following the death of Mrs. Paszko (lovingly remembered as Sharon), my mother, just as she did with Ed three years earlier, comforted Mr. Paszko. Though mutual friends suspected that they had been having an affair, I never sensed that. Mr. Paszko and I, just like me and Ed and me and Ray Castro, bonded well. He was much more like a father figure to me than a baseball coach. He knew how to guide me in hitting, fielding, and how to snap my throw on a double play. Even more, he liked my on-the-field leadership role. He actually named me the team manager when I broke my leg at age 14.

Whenever the Reds (my team) and the Dodgers (his team) played I went to his house to see the game on "cable." In those days, only the

Saturday Game of the Week and Monday Night Baseball were televised. Whenever the Reds and Dodgers played I rode my bike to his house at 909 McKinley, and we watched the game. While sitting on the coach, he would do the nerve pinches, by wrapping his hulking hands around my scrawny knees and squeeze until I gasped for air; sometimes he would dig into the nerves in the shoulder and, "boomp," down I would go to the ground. The pain was met with laughter; all of my teammates loved when he roughhoused with us.

Then, in January of 1979, he had Mrs. Paszko find and order an Oakland Raiders jacket for my birthday. Mrs. Paszko baked a banana cake with buttercream icing that melted in my mouth. Though I was sick on that particular birthday, with my hair greased like a 50's slicker, and my nose red like Rudolph's nose, Debbie and Kenny Mike came over as well. We ate, celebrated, and I went back to bed. Behind the curtains of gossip, it was believed that more was at play between mom and Kenny. I doubted it.

Sadly, Mrs. Paszko had open heart surgery that summer and did not survive. On the day that she died, Kenny was at the hospital and Boonie, my mom, and Erma Jean were at the house on Utah. All of our Navarre teammates were at home praying for her safe recovery; the initial reports were good and we all rejoiced. Within a couple of hours, all of the window shades at the Paszko House on McKinley, Mrs. Paszko's mother's house (where Grandma and Linda lived), and our house had the window shades and curtains roll up without being touched. No one knew what to make of the phenomenon until it was known, within minutes, that Mrs. Paszko had, indeed, died.

The man of steel, as us kids knew Mr. Paszko, melted into a weepy eyed child. Everyone cried and he led the charge. Though the baseball season continued, he fought despondency. Having been so deeply entrenched in the party lifestyle at my house on Utah Street, he became a part of the family. He was increasingly visiting and within six or seven

253

months he and my mother were officially dating.

The underlying currents to their relationships were drowned by riptides of concern, anger, and disdain. Some of his close friends wondered aloud, though they didn't know I was listening through the heating vent in my floor, whether they had been dating beforehand. Some friends, such as Crooks and his wife Karla, immediately and happily accepted the relationship as based in love and respect. Karla grew to love my mother as a sister and they were inseparable until my mother's death in 2014. Though the parties continued, and more city workers could be found at my home, there was growing antagonism and the kids, (Kenny Mike, Debbie, and I) absorbed it deeply. Erma Jean was whispering concerns into my ears; "Grandma" and Linda were whispering into the ears of Debbie and Kenny Mike. Though we thought we were masters of our own thoughts, we were being damaged.

As my confusions grew about mom and Kenny, Mama Green acted as a pillar of strength and buffered me from the growing concerns of Erma Jean toward my mom. Whenever I came to spend the night, which was mainly on the weekends, Mama would say things like, "Jean *is as full of shit as a fat dog is fleas and don't know her ass from a hole in the ground.*" When it was really bad she would say that Jean was either a "*cow-walking lie*" and not to listen to that "*snaggle-toothed bastard.*" By then, Erma and Mama were arguing over the phone about the danger being done to me.

To this day, I do not know if Erma Jean were jealous, truly concerned, or feeling the loss of her best friend. She was aware, as was I, that my mother had always longed to be loved, get married, and feel worthy of affection. Kenny had all of those qualities and had long proved his value in her life by showing affection to me; he visited me every day at the hospital, bought me Christmas gifts and did not throw them on the tracks, didn't promise me a piano and recant. He followed through. In addition, he bought my mom gifts and happily drank Black Velvet

Whiskey with her on a daily basis. They, I believe, loved each other, though in a different way than Kenny did Sharon.

Mrs. Paszko was more like the typical housewife of the 1950's. She was a stay at home mom, cooked and cleaned, and made sure that the kids were always dressed well and fed. Their house was the neighborhood hub of childhood activities. Her love was shared with her two adopted children since she, herself, could not have children. She was, as the old cliché goes, the "salt of the earth."

My mom, on the other hand, was a single mother who worked full-time as a nurse. She was a rebel, attending college at the University of Toledo, and a heavy partier. Though the Pipefitter was still lingering in the background, and actively updated on current events by Erma Jean, my mother was the epitome of Sharon's opposite. She could not cook all that well, though she learned. She didn't like staying around the house much, though she started to. And, she had an insatiable thirst for knowledge which led her towards being the first college graduate in the Schwaner family line, which unfortunately ended without a diploma.

Mr. Paszko, however, liked the energy of my mother, the drinking companionship, and the fact that she was willing to slow down. Just as their relationship began to escalate and J. Pipefitter disappeared into the annals of time, thankfully, a silent jealousy began to emerge.

Many neighborhood kids had long thought that I was "spoiled." I had nice clothes (because Jean bought them as a full-time single woman) and went to a great and expensive school (no one took into account financial aid as the means of my continued study at Maumee Valley). Given the nature of the beatings, the never-ending domestic civil war, the psychological abuse of being blamed for our poverty, and the fact that I was well known as being even-handed and respectful to all of my friends, the rumors reached Erma Jeans ears through Kenny Paszko's social network. She was incensed and when my mother bought me a 2 foot high and 2'6" wide J.C. Penney Boom Box for Christmas. I was

255

"spoiled," or so Jean believed, in Kenny's eyes. If there is one thing that is true (though Erma Jean was one of the funniest people I've ever met), a person was taking their life into their own hands if they insulted, threatened, or put a hand on me. Erma never spanked me but she was clear on the fact that she would if I did one of the following:

1. Told her I was gay,
2. Spoke in a disrespectful tone to her or my mother,
3. Used illegal drugs,
4. Got a girl pregnant

However, hurting me was like hurting her son and she would have none of it. One time, a friend and paper delivery boy that I hung out with at the playground pushed me onto the concrete enough times to draw blood from my knees and elbows. When I arrived home, bleeding, she said, "What happened?" After I told her that two older guys were pushing me down while playing basketball, she said, "Okay, I'll take care of this."

The next day when the paperboy and his buddy came to the house, she kindly invited them into the kitchen. As the paperboy leaned against the dryer next to the front kitchen door, Jean looked at me as my mother peered on,

"Do you see that boy right there?"

"Yes, ma'am," he said.

"Did you know that he came home bleeding yesterday from the playground? Shawn said that you pushed him down on the ground over and over again. Is that true or is he lying?"

Sulking, the paperboy said, "Yes, ma'am, it's true."

At that moment she pulled a gun from her purse and placed it on the kitchen island in front of her customary dining seat and said, "Young man, there is nothing in the drug store that will kill you faster than me when it comes to this boy. If he comes home bleeding again, I will find you and kill you. Do you understand?"

"Yes, ma'am." With a ghost-like look, he and his friend left the house.

A few short weeks later, while playing with the paperboy, his friend, and others at the Park, Boonie's sister, Debbie, came sprinting to the basketball court. "Shawn, you gotta go home now. Erma Jean said she is going to shoot Kenny."

Like The Flash, I took off running. I turned into the alley, ran the 15 house distance, straight up the stairs and into Erma Jean's apartment. Her eyes had red veins in them as her sweat rolled like a waterfall bursting from the pressure against Little Boy Blue's finger. "That mother fucker is talking about you again. He's saying that you are spoiled brat and a fag. His friends, and son, are telling their friends and the kids at Waite that you are gay. He said that he doesn't understand how or why you don't date girls. They're talking about your radio and he's throwing your mother's books on the ground and telling her to stop going to UT. He said, 'it's a waste of time because she has a job.' She needs to be home to take care of him. I'm gonna kill him, baby; I'm gonna kill him."

The entire time she was brandishing the gun in the kitchen and waving it around. I was standing in between her and the back porch leading downstairs. Given Erma, there was little I could do with my tiny 110 pound frame. The more she cried and pushed on me to get out of the way, the more I begged her, "No, Jean, it's not worth it, it's not worth it." After about twenty minutes, she sat the gun down and we embraced each other.

"I love you baby and don't want anything to happen to you. You are like my baby," she said.

257

I had always known that I was the only child that Erma Jean would have in her lifetime. Though she was a perfectionist and watched over every move I made when doing a chore, she was also a rock. She cooked all of our meals, washed our clothes, she told jokes, she took me to Baskin and Robbins to watch me eat three or four Matterhorns (ten scoop ice cream Sunday); she attended all of my baseball games. Jean saved me from many beatings though she also participated in the war, which would emotionally scar me for life.

Thankfully, Jean calmed down. No more than a week had passed, however, when I heard a thunderous verbal explosion erupt from the front of the house. Awakened from a dead sleep, all I could hear was my mom yell, in a drunken stupor, "I'm not quitting school." I crept into the hallway beside my bedroom to see what was going on, just in case I had to calm Jean; I never considered calling the police as it was a "domestic situation."

With a furious response, Kenny replied from the porch, "That's fucking bullshit. You're quitting and that's the end of the story." Then, KAAABBLLLLLAAAAAMMMMM, his fist came screaming through the front door with a Hulk-like force. I called Jean who came down the back stairs in her slippers and night gown, gun in hand. "Get out of here before I shoot your mother fucking brains out."

"Damn," I thought to myself.

Erma said, "What the fuck is going on, Susie?"

She stumbled back away from the door and onto the couch, "Kenny wants me to quit school," she said.

Erma Jean took care of her, getting her ready for bed as I stared like a deer looking down the muzzle of a .12 gauge, muttering "I can't believe this." I wanted to cry but I was too scared; instead, I decided that dying would be a better answer.

258

By the end of that night, I knew that my life was changing by forces beyond my understanding. Physical violence and its threat were becoming more apparent as the verbal assaults escalated. Guns were being wielded and I grew certain that a bloody death was marching toward my house from just over the horizon. In pursuit of "street justice," and to my total confusion, Erma Jean called in her gangster backup from Detroit, J. Pipefiitter.

The growing concern of physical attack against my 4'10" mother by a 6'0" Incredible Hulk figure became a source of consternation. I spent more time with Mama Green out of fear of murder as my mother increasingly grew alienated from me. She thought I was disapproving of her relationship while I, much more concerned about being shot, was thinking about dying all the time. I didn't want to be shot in a crossfire. Ironically, though, I plotted my own death as the war had taken its toll on my esteem, confidence, and well-being. With the growing rumors, my confidence disappeared and I felt like a keyhole in a door with only a shimmer of light. I was growing invisible and Mama sought to heal the wounds; it was at this time that she moved away from the "Hill" to Girard Street.

Anyhow, a few days after the hole-in-the-door incident, Kenny and J. Pipefitter were invited to sit together in the living room at my house on Utah Street. Erma Jean moderated the education versus domestic wife role. Finally, after Kenny apologized for his outburst and promised that it would never happen again, he and the Pipefitter walked out to Kenny's Blue Ford LTD where they hugged. Pipefitter lifted Kenny off the ground and said, "It better never happen again or I will kill you."

Kenny, humbly and grovelingly said, "I promise you, it will never happen again."

After Kenny drove off, and J. Pipefitter came back into the house, my mom and Erma Jean laughed and celebrated that the "gangster" had put Kenny in check. Mom's safety was assured.

259

I went back to my room confused and angry. How dare Erma Jean and my mother allow my molester into my home to protect my mother, the same woman who made me walk on tacks? Here, I never wanted to see that bastard again and instead, they invite him into my home. And why? So that my mother feels protected from a man who just put his fist through our front door? Here he is spreading rumors about me, my sexuality, my radio, and they hail this night as a victory. "What the fuck?" I thought.

Less than a week later, John Bronson and I had agreed to go bowling and do our usual Friday night fun. By now, he had a driver's license but, not me; I was afraid to drive. As was normal, and with mom at Kenny's for dinner and a date, I called Erma Jean to ask if she would take me to the Rossford Lanes. She said, "No, why don't you ask your whore ass mother to take you?"

"Well, she's at Kenny's house," I replied.

"To hell with that, she can take you," Jean replied.

"Gosh, Jean, it's not that big of a deal, I'll just ask Mama Green to take me."

"Don't you dare call Mama when your mother can do it!"

"Jean," I said, "what's wrong with you? Why can't you just take me? It's only ten minutes from here."

"Goddammit, ask your own mother."

Knowing that Jean was growing weary of late, I called my mom at Kenny's house, 419-693-4493. "Hello, Kenny (at Christmas he had asked me to stop calling him Mr. Paszko and to start calling him by his first name) can I speak to my mom?" I asked.

"Sure, Shawner, just hold on a second."

260

When my mom picked up the phone, I said, "Hi Mom. I asked Erma Jean to take me bowling but she said to ask you. Will you take me to Rossford to meet up with John, he's already there."

Mom exploded, "Goddammit, why couldn't "fat ass" Erma take you? She's not doing anything."

"Well, she said that you were my mother," I replied.

"Goddammit, I'll be right there."

Still reeling from my beat down the previous November, I quickly said, "Never mind. I won't go."

Then she slammed the phone down. Assuming I may be receiving another beat down, stupidly, I called Erma Jean on the phone and said, "She's pissed and coming home." Erma Jean made her way down the stairs and started yelling, "What the hell is wrong with your mother? I'm going to talk to her."

"Never mind, Jean. Go home, I'm just not going to go bowling tonight."

Just then, my mother slammed through the front kitchen door, "What the fuck is wrong with you, Erma?"

Jean said, "You don't care about anything except that asshole. All he does is talk badly about Shawn, force you out of school, and he punched a hole in your door."

"Fuck you, you fat ass bitch, you can move the fuck out of my goddamned house."

I tried to intercede and said, "Mom and Jean, it's not worth it, I won't go bowling tonight."

By then, the argument had escalated into a toe-to-toe argument with Erma standing on the spot in which she fell when Martin Luther King

261

had been assassinated. My mother was leaning against the backdraft vent duct where the three foot wooden fork and spoon dangled from the wall. At that time, Jean said, "I'm going home" and walked in front of my mother.

"Get out of this house, fat ass." As Jean walked by mother to exit, mom gave Jean a push in the back.

When fury finds its way into a sullen soul anger,finds its expression on the surface. With one motion, Erma Jean stepped back, and with the celerity of lightning, lifted my mother by the throat toward the sky. When she wrapped her left hand over her throat too, my mother dangled in the air as a ragdoll being shredded by playful Labrador puppy's bite. This was not play and my mother started to froth from her mouth as her eyes rolled back in her head.

"No Jean, let her go!," I yelled with a furious spew. "You're going to kill her!"

Erma couldn't hear me as she said, "Mother fucker, you're going to die tonight, bitch."

"No Jean, let her go!"

I came around the island and dove with my arm around Erma's neck. I tried to take her down but she had entered into an alternate universe and couldn't feel my fight. Her 350 pounds stood like an oak and I could not budge her.

In a snap judgement, I ran to the neighbor's house and yelled, "Whitey, Erma Jean is choking my mom. She's too big, I can't get her off. You have to help."

Wearing boxers, he sprinted out the door, though the grass, and into the kitchen. My mother was kicking with her last breath as her head dangled toward the ground, her eyes rolled back. Whitey ran in and busted Erma Jean's arms with all of his might and ripped my mother from her enraged grip. As my mom fell to the ground barely clinging to life, Whitey held her and said, "Breathe Sue."

Pandora's Box was unleashed as Erma made her final exit. "Your mother's a whore.....She sold herself as a prostitute and lived in the motel next to the bridge....She lived in a storage room in a pizza parlor when you were born; your father was a trick".....and my mother's skeleton's fell one-by-one to the floor. As my mother used to say, "Them bones, them bones, them dry bones" lined the path to exit our Utah Street home forever; we never slept another night at 1315.

In reflection, the relationship between emotional servitude and violent expression are, at times, endemic to relationships built around the "Four Horseman of the Apocalypse." Seeing my mother dangling against a wall, where I was beaten just six months earlier, was a moment of terror. I was certain that I was to be an orphan that night – I was going to grow up with Mama Green.

The thunderous lightning by which the attempted murder occurred has always made me watchful of the slightest gestures of communicative provocation. The aftermath of that night was met with monumental social breakdown and hopelessness.

The venom that Erma Jean spewed left me tangled. For 34 years I thought I was a "trick" gone bad. It's one thing to be a bastard, it's another to be a trick bastard. In any case, it finally made sense when my mother had taught me how to use newspapers to cover up, if I was homeless and living outdoors in the winter. She did, in fact, struggle mightily when she first moved to Toledo, living in motels, outdoors, and selling herself. Her strengths were confirmed and manifest as a survivor of violence borne from a lifetime of hate. This time, though, her temper was in the clutch of Jean's murderous hands. The incident, which justly qualified for a prison term, was handled informally under a "street justice" rubric.

263

For me, Mama's role as a guardian angel was never more important. The darkness of life that persisted from those few curious months took my biological and hormonal growth and bludgeoned them with depression, fatalism, and a death wish. Mama Green saved my life before my birth by thwarting a possible abortion and did so again with the healing power of positive reinforcement, love, and continuous confidence building. Anyone who judges another based upon race, class, or education level has yet to learn about the fragility of life and the possibility of unconditional love. Mama's sentiment that, *"You should never judge another until you have walked in their shoes,"* is the guidance of empathy so deeply needed in the modern day – her wisdom shaped my life.

Chapter 40.   A Homeless Night

Erma Jean had made her way back to her upstairs apartment, leaving in her wake Hurricane Camille's fury.   The three foot wooden fork and spoon that hung, untouched, on the kitchen wall for a decade were lying on the floor next to my mother, who was fighting like a fish out of water, gasping for air.   Whitey stood above my mother like a saint reviving a lost spirit's soul; the dishes and cooking utensils lay on the kitchen floor, curious in their demise.

Jean made her way upstairs as my mother regained life. I stood, solemnly, mystified that these two warring best friends had sunk into the eternally cavernous depths of Hell as my heart sunk knowing that my life had officially ended; Chris and Brian would no longer be my neighbors, the Park would become a memory, and the unforeseen psychological and emotional abuse storm was on the horizon.   Like Mama said, *"If the clouds start to roll, you need to take cover";* I knew that a socially constructed cyclone laid in my path. Mama's role in my life reached its apex in importance at this time.

As mom struggled to her weary feet, I looked to the ceiling asking for God's grace and to give me the courage to walk in the direction of Providence.   Whitey left as my exasperated mother rested her head on her hands beneath the kitchen cabinetry that had been refinished ten years prior. With tears in her eyes, she looked to me and said, "What now, Son Shine?"   Still reeling from my November beat down, I walked to her and embraced her with a hug of solace.

"We can figure this out mom."

First, I gave Zeus, Calee (the Chihuahua) and Caesar (our gorgeous grey and black spotted Great Dane) food and water. "We'll be back, guys." I said. After hugging them I simply said, "Come on mom, let's go for a walk."

We walked the path I had taken when my 12 speed chrome Western Auto bike had been stolen. The path went from Utah Street and took a right on Fassett Street. Mullin's field, named after Mike and Jeff, whose father was the President of the Iron Coffin's Motor Cycle Gang, was on the left of the street. Gladys's "Huss" variety store was on the right and reminded me of the days where I was routinely quizzed by Gladys about how much change I should get whenever I made a purchase; a free pack of baseball cards were granted for a correct response. We passed Vince's Barbershop, the place where I had my first and every haircut as a kid. Littered in the window were the Playboy, Penthouse, and Oui Magazines that Chris and I stared at while awaiting our haircuts. The hole in the wall burger joint where my father Bryce and I had discussed his marriage proposal to my mother (and the only time we had lunch together) rested next to Toledo Tent and half a block away from Huss Variety Store II where soda fountain malts and shakes were trademarks of the "good old days." On the corner of Oak and Fassett sat the Bank and Bar Café where Donnie had fallen from the second floor, through a fire escape, and crushed his skull.

As we turned left, with my arm around my mom, we talked and walked. "Shawnee, I don't know what to do. How can I live in the same house with that "fat-ass" bitch? She's going to kill me someday, and it's my house?" As we walked over the Oak Street Bridge overpass, my childhood flashed before my eyes.

At the bottom of the hill, and just on the other side of Earl Street, was an old run down bar/saloon. It is here where Joe took me and Jerry Berry to meet up with Buster for drinks. Her head was bandaged from a car crash and her profile was as pronounced that night as the one in which I had the nightmare of her hanging herself and telling me in a sinister voice, with her bloodied eyes, "I hate you, Shawn." Of course, given that it was 1971, Jerry and I split a Budweiser. Across the street was the location of the original Taco Village that was a dump and, yet, had the best burritos in Toledo.

266

We continued walking on the bike path to Waite High School where we sometimes practiced for my East Toledo Junior Knothole team. We passed the beautiful Sherry Monk's house. We approached the corner of Navarre and Oak and curiously stood looking at Walter's Pharmacy and pondering how Gloria Steinham had grown up two blocks away and had become the most noted Feminist in America. We turned right where a service station once stood. That spot would be my bus stop soon and continue until 1984. It is there that I first heard two white strangers talking about trying a new drug, crack. Clarence's house was next door to the pharmacy and all I could think about was how great a smile and personality he had in spite of poverty and being the youngest in a huge family. I reminisced about Clarence spreading plaster at my house during the remodeling of '74 when he was seven years old. That discipline won him a full ride scholarship as a defensive back, where he became a captain, for the North Carolina Tar Heels.

Navarre School, named after the War of 1812 hero, was to the right. It was my home school that, to me, was more like a jail than center of education. Though all of my neighborhood friends went there, with the exception of Chris and Brian who attended Good Shepherd, it was a place where only the strongest survived. I believe I would have perished had I gone there even though I would have had a lot of friends. We passed McKinley Street where Kenny and Chuckie Mims lived. My mind, though reminiscing, was clear and focused.

We passed the Bonded Gas Station on East Broadway and turned left. Not far up the street was the old Eastwood Theater with its old fashioned structure and ticket counter. With my mom, I watched the Bad News Bears starring Tatum O'Neill from the upstairs balcony, as well as Herbie the Love Bug, Benji, and the Apple Dumpling Gang. It was a great old theatre that later succumbed to the vicissitudes of pornography and was the place where I first saw a man masturbate in public.

When we passed the new Taco Village, I had an epiphany. That is, though Taco Village had moved from Oak to East Broadway, where I would consume six of the soft fresh tortillas wrapped around the beefy ecstasy, I realized that change was a constant in life. They had moved from one location to another and became bigger and better than they had been before. I could still eat 6-9 burritos in a sitting and leave hungry; change happens while some things stay the same.

Mom continued to cry but had significantly sobered from the Black Velvet icing her veins.

Finally, we crossed Starr Avenue near Murphy's Store, saw Don's drive-in restaurant (home of the Trailblazer double cheeseburger), and Becky Raisner's house attached to her father's church where my bike had been stolen and later dismantled for parts. That incident always pissed me off. After practice at Waite, I had my glove hanging from my front reflectors and my cleats from the handle bars when I stopped for a glass of water. No sooner did we get into the kitchen when I heard the pedals on my bike start moving (someone had snuck up to the garage where my bike was hidden in front of their mini-van). Before I could catch them, they were out of sight. When I got home mom exploded on the news:

"Goddammit, Shawn, how could you be so stupid? I spent a lot of money on that goddamned bike and you carelessly let someone take it and your baseball gear. I should beat your ass for being so stupid."

Though I was angry and crushed by her insensitivity, I simply responded with, "How can you blame me for someone else stealing my bike. They are the one who committed a crime, not me. I am the victim here and you're yelling at me. I don't get it."

"Goddammit, you're going to use your Susan B. Anthony Silver Dollars and buy it all back and I'm not giving you a penny."

268

Erma Jean sat and stared without uttering a word.

I said, "Cool, okay. I'm going to buy a Schwinn Continental bike like the one Ray has, and replace my Wilson glove and cleats myself...no problem." After I spent $275 on all of the replacements, I counted out silver dollars, one at a time, while the counter clerks giggled. By then, in the spring before my greatest beat down, I knew that Erma Jean was right; my mom was listening to Kenny and was trying to make me into a man. It drove me crazy. I thought to myself, "Are you kidding me? With all the drugs, sex, and violence I have seen at the playground and in my home, you're going to act like I'm not a man...bullshit!" Resentment of her detachment to me had set in, and Erma's hateful fuel made for a confusing period of time. Fortunately, I spent the night at Mama's and she said, "That's why you save your change, someday you may have an emergency and need that money."

But, on this night, my memories of war and brutality faded into the background. My mom was scared; she was desperate; and, for the second time in her life, approached the doors of death. She was shaken, and my epiphany of change boiled up to a cascade of wisdom that emanated from of my mouth.

As we sat on the curb in front of Wendy's on the corner of Front and Main Street, across from McDonalds (which had finally served a billion), the car wash, Murphy's, and the nearby Sports Arena, she said, "What am I going to do?"

"Mom," I said, "You and Kenny are in love and it is obvious that you are going to get married someday. You should ask him if we can move in and live in his house. I like him and know that he loves you. Kenny Mike and I are friends and I really like Debbie."

"Do you really think that is the right choice?" she replied.

"Yes, I do"

"I don't know; I can't live in the same house as a man without marrying him."

"Then ask him to marry you. We can't live on Utah Street anymore because I am tired of the danger and all of the arguing. You and Jean just can't get along and it's ripping me apart inside. I hurt, mom, and I want the pain to end. Go ahead and ask him. All he can say is, 'no.'"

"Are you sure that you're okay with it?"

"Yes, I'm sure."

In the back of my head, I just wanted to bow out of the whole picture and live with Mama Green. However, my mom needed me and I wasn't going to turn my back in her darkest hour. Though she struggled with affection, I knew she loved me – she had sacrificed her wardrobe, social life, and prosperity for me to go to Maumee Valley. While sitting in the drizzling rain, I realized that my mother had been the best mother possible given her horrid childhood, and Mama had always said, ***"Never turn your back on a person in need."***

By now, it was midnight and mom and I had been walking and talking for a few hours. So we made our trek back to Kenny's house. We knocked on the door, where Kenny Mike and Debbie were both asleep, and he invited us into the house.

"Sue," he said, "What happened?"

"Erma tried to strangle me," she said as the black and blue marks about her neck were more apparent in the living room light.

"What? She tried to strangle you?"

"Yeah."

"Did Shawner see it?"

"Yeah, he ran and got Whitey to break it up."

"Are you okay?"

"Yes."

"What are you going to do?"

"Kenny, we have nowhere to go. Can we stay here with you?"

"Yes! Of course, you can stay here."

"But," she said, "We have to get married because I don't believe in living with a man unless I'm married."

"Sure Sue. We can get married right away."

I sat there watching the melodrama play out the whole time knowing that life as I knew it was transforming. My friends on Utah would grow away; I would not be able to take the school bus any longer; no more bike riding at the trails; I would see Boonie less and rarely play at the Park or Mullin's Field. No more Gladys at the store or Vince haircuts. One thing was for certain, though, I was going to be spending a lot more time at Mama's House on 1234 Girard.

As I lamented these certain changes, mom furiously turned to me, "You, Shawn Louis, are no longer permitted to talk to or visit Erma Jean. As far as you know, she is dead."

Fearing a punch to the face, I acquiesced by saying, "Okay." Inside I thought, after I saved her life, talked her down from her fear laden tomb, she was going to look at me in anger. Just like the bike, I thought to myself, "I'm not the one who's to blame."

That night, I slept on the coach in front of the tv, watching the Showtime channel movie, "Wild and Beautiful on the Island of Ibiza," a soft core porn movie made for teenage boys. Since we didn't have

271

cable or a shower on Utah Street, I thought to myself, "At least there are some perks to living here."

John Bronson bowled alone that night.

A Letter to Mama

Dear Mama,

I know that you always told me that, *"Things happen for a reason and it is not my place to judge them,"* but it was so hard moving away from the "Hill." When mom and I moved away from Utah Street and you made your way to Girard, your wisdom and guidance made all of the turmoil and challenges manageable. By nature, I am weak and afraid, but with you I am strong and alive.

I don't know if I ever told you "I love you" enough but there are none other who can compare to you. Your protection, your fear evoking strength, and gentle touch blanketed in love were gifts. I loved your pancakes too, as did all of my friends, especially Boonie.

In addition, your wisdom carried me through high school. The challenges and tribulations that you witnessed were significant and were only managed with a deeply held belief that, "I am somebody." Each day I seek the best in others, acknowledge and understand their weaknesses, and suspend moral judgement as, *"I have never walked in their shoes."* I must confess, though, it was hard to do on McKinley, but I tried. Thanks for sticking with me and allowing me to be.

I love you, always.

Your little white baby,

Shawn

SECTION FOUR: BEYOND "THE HILL"

Chapter 41.   Prologue to 909 Crazy Avenue

After the night that Toledo died, the winds of change blew. Mama had moved away from the "Hill" and was firmly entrenched in a life on Girard Street, five houses away from her sister, Pauline. Though I was spending most weekends at her house, my life as a high school student pulled me more deeply into my friendship networks and extracurricular activities. We spoke daily by phone and loved each other dearly, nonetheless.

However, during the transition from Utah Street to McKinley, it was extremely difficult to manage the obliteration of the relationship between mom, Jean, and myself. Though I loved my mother, Erma Jean was instrumental in getting me into MV, feeding me and keeping me clothed. Their war, though painful, did not change my love for Jean or my mom. Sadly, the confusion unleashed by seeing Jean try to kill my mother left me stunned, confused, and invisible. Mama's role, through her consternation, anger, and upset, was to focus on maintaining my esteem. She was right, Erma could *"Give a dog's ass a toothache."* She was also, at times, *"As full of shit as a fat dog is fleas."*

Mama, never knew, however, that by the time mom and I moved to McKinley that I was suicidal at worst and fatalistic at best; death did not scare me. As a matter of fact, the damage from the abuse combined with feeling "stupid" compared to my reference group at MV, always bothered me. I expected that someday I would find myself in a situation where my demise was certain. I avoided suicide but not dangerous situations. I had figured that if I committed suicide, all of Mama's lessons would have been lost and she would not have been proud of me. Death at the hand of another, though devastating, would be better than death at my own.

274

During this most troubling psychological and emotionally destructive period, Mama's words kept me alive. Though Mama, Jean, and Guy loved my stories of danger, they always shook their heads and would say, almost in unison, that *"God watches over all fools."* As I found myself in more crazy encounters, I also discovered that my "silver tongue" and "million dollar personality" provided me with entry into worlds that most fear, distance themselves from, and avoid. In time, I realized the constant and unending edification of my confidence and esteem by Mama Green gave me the gift of tolerance, acceptance of broad differences in race and class, and that I was accepted "as is." By the time I was in high school, my greatest gift from her lessons was the ability to communicate and to genuinely accept people, for better or worse.

Mama squarely played the role of friend and artist in guiding me through the emotional labyrinth. It was during this time that I learned of the brutality of Mr. Dank. She used her horrible stories to keep me balanced, grounded, and cognizant of the idea that *"things could always be worse"* and focused on my accomplishments to ensure that I had earned her respect and that of others, and that I could always keep my head up with that *"million dollar personality."* So, though she protected me from physical violence as a child, now she protected me from the depths of emotional despair associated with the psychological challenges grounded in a re-constituted family embedded in a web of strong and external negative forces.

My future life on McKinley Avenue was, in a word, crazy.

Chapter 42.   Setting the Stage on McKinley

The assault on my mother accelerated the relationship between and Kenny and my mom; it moved at light speed. On the surface, and apart from his fist slamming through the front door on Utah Street, it was clear that they cared for each other and that my mom had genuine love for Kenny.   He was born and raised, and to his great pride, as a "Poleack" in the Poletown" section of Toledo.   Though he had a funny and mischievous side, he was a good man.   My sister, Debbie, and brother, Kenny Mike, were both adopted and Kenny Paul (Mr. Paszko) was a traditional man who went to work while the spouse stayed home, that was obvious.

After moving in, Kenny and my mom immediately shopped for wedding rings; that charmed my mother's spirit. Yes, she was shaken by Erma's attack and, yes, she was the target of malicious rumors set forth by Erma at the Medical College of Toledo, but her new life was well in motion.   My mother, the rock of the orthopedic floor, was living in infamy; disgraced by her drinking behavior and socially eviscerated by dating a man whose wife had just died.   Erma had led a charge to destroy mom's character and her ongoing relationship with the nurses on my mother's unit was used to spoil mom's identity.

Their mutual friend, Maureen Harris, stood by my mother like a rock though she had known Erma Jean all the way back to their days at Oakdale Elementary School.   Mrs. Hockett, McDonald, Jackson, and others bought into the nature and direction of Erma's rumors which ignited a drinking spiral from which my mother never recovered.

Sadly, at the point in which we moved in with Kenny and the kids, my mother was becoming a teaching legend in the nursing school at the Medical College of Ohio, a well renowned head nurse, and was asked by the Director of Nursing to consider a professor role at the college. Her acumen as a nurse and pure genius to understand the complexity of

276

chemistry, anatomy, and physiology, in fact, made her a near literal walking encyclopedia. She knew (and the doctors never contested her), pharmacy and medicine at a level higher than most. Further, she was two classes away from earning her Bachelor's Degree at the University of Toledo. My mother was an intellectual stalwart.

The idea that the self can be discredited and one's identity spoiled through social mechanisms is true. Mom continued to work as I sadly watched her self-esteem depart her soul. Her fall from grace was akin to a Shakespearian tragedy. She maintained a high level of effectiveness as a head nurse but her ongoing hangovers and daily drinking was showing up, surreptitiously confirming Erma Jean's stories. In time, and within a year and a half, my mother retired from the profession that she loved and that had pulled her up and out of poverty, abuse, and squalor. By spring 1983, she pulled her entire $27,000 savings out of the Public Employees Retirement System (PERS) and paid off Kenny's debts.

The pressure of retirement came from the internal collapse of her personhood at the hands of Erma's ruthless rumor mongering and Kenny's desire to have a stay at home wife. He had finished eleventh grade at Libbey High School and went to work for the City of Toledo when he was 18 years old. In my opinion he was intimidated by educated woman (Jean confirmed this). By the end of the spring of 1982, my mother dropped out of the University of Toledo. Instead, she became an expert in conspiracy theory and studied the Illuminati, The Rothschilds, and the Rockefellers until her dying day.

The rumor mill was in full motion prior to our move to Kenny's house. The rumor that I was gay and a sissy were coming from numerous sources that could never be identified. Jean had told me that Kenny was the root of it and that he had told his City co-workers the deceptive stories. He believed, as I was told, that I was a spoiled brat and got everything that I wanted. It was confirmed that he thought spending money for me to attend Maumee Valley was wasteful since Waite was equal in quality and his son got better grades. So, by the time I walked into 909 McKinley, I was shaken by the depth and vicious nature of the rumors; mom was suffering from her own work related demons and had dedicated her life to Kenny. To Mama Green's shock, mom made me secondary in her life in the pursuit of love and acceptance.

I understood that her quest to be loved was immense. She had never had the adult intimacy that she yearned for and I could not provide it. In order to fulfill Kenny's desire for a traditional home, he pressured my mother to redefine her life around the institution of family and not work, as my feminist mother had long been driven to do. She was in the midst of selling her soul to a marriage institution that countered her intellectual proclivities through mounting social denigration and destruction. Mom was well liked, but internally, she was challenged by the demons of abuses past. She opted to give up on her beliefs, fall back on her social skills and humor with others, and build a new life. On the surface of it, Erma's interpretation and warnings appeared true to me and I just ached in my heart. The pain in my soul commiserated with the pain in my mind; confusion was ceaseless.

Kenny Mike and Debbie, however, entered into the reconstituted relationship in the aftermath of the death of their mother. Mom and I stepped into a city worker's lifestyle, which was, in fact, very energized, fun, electric, and qualitatively different from a life with nurses, police officers, and doctors. Kenny Mike had a warm and open disposition and was always a best friend of mine but the notion of being a brother was foreign. He was tall and handsome; I was short and cute. He had great grades; mine were average and slipping. He attended Waite High School; I attended Maumee Valley. Though he and I had no competition with each other, as we had long been teammates on the baseball diamond; it was outside observers that set up a contrived battle.

Girls loved Kenny Mike and always wanted to date him. His long curly locks made him a local East Side celebrity. Truthfully, when W. came to the house one evening, intoxicated, I was enamored when I opened the door and her right breast fell out of her tank top. "Kenny Mike, W. is here." Yes, I was not jealous of his height or looks, but his ability to have girlfriends pestered me. No one knew that the ongoing messages of deviant sexuality, molestation, and condemnation of human expression had ripped away my desire to pursue a girlfriend. Kenny would always advise me to let the girls come to me and never pursue them. Later I learned, that much of his guidance was designed to "make me into a man."

Debbie, who was a true rebel and fierce to fight, had decided to engage in dating, and had a heart of purity that was devastated by her mother's death. As a young girl, 12 or 13 at the time, her role model and soul had found glory in Heaven. Debbie could cook and had a remarkable network of friends, many of whom, may I add, were gorgeous. Being a straight male and living with a cute girl who had a set of beautiful friends was a real test for a hormonal boy becoming a man, especially for a confused one with an unstable sense of intimate self. I always had the desire to date two of her friends, but they regarded me as too "cute" for a relationship. Debbie, however, was confused and in pain and my mother's replacement of her mother sent an electric shock down her central nervous system. Anger seethed in Debbie's heart.

After a week had passed, my mother and Kenny were to be wed at the Family Baptist Church by our family Pastor, Reverend Floyd Rose. Debbie and Kenny Mike were told one day before the wedding and felt crushed, hurt, and confused by the startling news. The small and intimate wedding was and witnessed by Maureen Harris and Jim Dalton (Kenny's working best friend). And in that moment, the legitimation of their union was set and the craziness soon ran wild. Mom and Kenny were married and I was no longer an only child; Kenny Mike and Debbie's mother had been replaced and the subterraneous norms of internal demise were set in motion. The next three years were not

279

physically destructive but emotionally degrading. I needed and leaned on Mama Green more than at any other time in my life; once again, she was saving me from self-destruction.

After the marriage, my mom and Kenny tried to create a Brady Bunch situation, but the external forces of rumor stung the ears of us young and vulnerable children. The difference in an adult perspective as opposed to a child's without experience, was stronger than I had ever imagined or even understood at the time. The old notion that teenagers think that they "know everything" but they ***"don't know their ass from a hole in the ground,"*** was confirmed. Neither Kenny Mike, Debbie, nor I had the emotional experience to fight the perfect storm of the retroactive interpretation and deviance constructing definitions of the adults that persisted in our lives; mom and Kenny were left at the mercy of God's hand in managing us while we all had our own lifestyle and patterns of behavior. It was, indeed, impossible for there to be peace. The rumors gave this ***"dog a toothache."***

In reflection, though we continued to spend weekends and eat together, Mama held me together and prevented me from falling apart with wisdom, love, and grace that shielded me from following a path of self-mutilation. During this period, her anger with Erma Jean was growing explosively as she could see the damage inflicted upon my fragile psyche. Though I was not permitted to see Jean or talk to her, I snuck over to Utah Street anyhow. She was like a surrogate mother and slipped me little pieces of money so I could be independent while she would say, "See, your mom and 'dad' won't even give you money, but I will." Then, midway through the summer she moved out of the house my mom owned and moved into the upstairs apartment above the Strocks, the same home occupied by G-Ray Funny Pants. On one visit, she offered to buy me a used Camaro since my parents were, ***"Too cheap to take care of their own bastard child. You're not a bastard like you are being treated!"*** I never accepted the $12,000 gift but I was tempted.

My emotional self cried loudly as my inner child died. The saving grace was that I could always hear in the back of my mind: *"Baby, you have a million dollar personality that no one can take from you,"* and *"You have more brains than anyone I know."* With those echoes, I would not falter. I fell but I would stand again. I was besieged but would not break. I was, indeed, a wounded warrior fighting for my very existence and Mama was the glue holding this broken soul together.

281

Chapter 43.   Change in the Darkest Hour

The more that the rumors spread, the more the venom stung. As a young and relatively smart young man, it was my perception that I was handling everything well. It didn't matter that my grades at Maumee Valley were sinking like a rock. It didn't matter that my teachers, especially Al Getman, worried relentlessly about my well-being. All I knew was that my knee was healed and I could cling to the professional sport dream. However, all of my life was flipping upside down and change was reconstructing my sense of self and aspirations.

There were two significant changes that sent my heart into the abyss. Though my life up to then had been atypical, there was a lot of normalcy. I loved my mother, and she loved me. I loved Erma Jean, and she loved me. Mama and I were best friends. My childhood friends in the neighborhood thought I was a great athlete, humorous, and smart. At school, my childhood friends thought I was a great athlete, especially in baseball and the basketball game called "21," humorous, and smart. I had great buffers and a strong sense of being; yes, I was often "troubled," as Lisa had observed, but I thought I was special; I thought that I had gifts though I was not sure of their content.

Zeus was still in my life. He was a tough dog and my rock. His epileptic seizures hurt me to my heart and I had allowed him to sleep in my bed with me. Caesar was a saint, and Callee, the enigmatic bow legged creature of humor. At Kenny's, Zeus' sleeping quarters were relegated to the back utility room behind the bathroom; I was told he shed too much hair for Kenny's immaculate house. Though I often went into the room with him and laid on the carpet, it wasn't the same as on a couch, bed, or next to my chair. His dismissal from the central arena of the home ripped me apart and I had no place to file an appeal. I promised to sweep the floor every day, walk him, and feed and brush him but it fell on deaf ears. I could not negotiate a place for Zeus in the house and it pushed me completely away from the family. My parent's

282

decision broke my heart.

Caesar, though he was a gentle soul, was allowed some time in the main quarters but his desire to step over the fence in the backyard and explore the neighborhood presented a liability issue that was beyond our family's ability to permit. We sent him to a farm and I cried internally. The day after being taken to the country, I came home to find him lying in the back yard by the door; he had travelled 13 miles to come home. Kenny, again, took him to the farm and that was the last time I saw him. Calee died within a month. My life with my furry friends was disappearing and the emptiness continued to swell.

More importantly, for the last few months of the school year I had to walk from Kenny's house back to my bus stop on Yondota, across from the grain elevators, near Utah Street. Though it was spring, it was still cold and scary with river rats the size of cats walking by the sewers. They did make for a great rock throwing target practice. Each day as I made my way down Earl Street, near the bar with no name and the factory on the corner, I was fearful of being abducted like Cricket Segura and dumped by the train tracks by Weiler Homes under the Fassett Street Bridge. In response, I smuggled Kenny's "billy club" in my jacket sleeve each day and hid it in my backpack when I arrived at school.

One crisp morning, while waiting for a train to pass my cross walk, I stood on the stoop of the Gargoyle building beside Mullin's Field when a pick-up truck stopped to wait for the same train. The passenger rolled down his window and said, "Hey, man, do you hear bells?" Not knowing what he meant, I said, "I don't hear anything." Just then, he opened the door of the car and started walking towards me. I pulled out the club, shot off running to the right and circled through Mullin's Field to take a shortcut through Rusty's yard to make my way to Clark Street Park and up the back hill to Oak Street to run home. I figured that as many times as I had practiced escapes in my old neighborhood, the man would never be able to catch me. Though he initially ran after me, he stopped once I turned in the alley and ran toward Rusty's house. Rather than

283

running up the hill, I circled up the back alley and came out be Vince's Barbershop and peered to see if the truck was still there. The train had passed and the truck was gone; my fear of abduction was, so I believed, confirmed.

Kenny Mike and Debbie rode the Toledo Area Regional Transportation Authority (TARTA) public bus to Waite and East Toledo Junior High School. Since I was active in sports at school, I could no longer ride the Maumee Valley bus home so I was forced to ride TARTA from Maumee Valley to the downtown loop, near the Nut House on Adams, and ride the 11 back to Oak and Navarre. Arriving home at night in our neighborhood where gangs, drugs, and homicide was frighteningly common, I rode with trepidation. I always had a club in hand, though, when I traveled.

By now, I had lost my overwhelming need of independence. Each day that I came home, Debbie had my monster boom box in her room and no matter how kindly I asked for it, my requests were met with conflict and consternation. Eventually, Debbie had broken the handle and I rarely, if ever, got to use my own radio; after all, the dominant belief in the house was that the radio symbolized me being "spoiled." On one occasion, I asked mom and Kenny to get it back for me because I wanted to make a dub tape of Prince off of the radio. However, it was met with the first fist fight between my mother and Debbie; sadly, though it didn't happen often, there were a couple more brawls. My mom was a fighter from childhood and Debbie was a fighter as well. Beautiful and typically kind, Debbie could and would square off with anyone. Once, a friend of hers had turned and insulted her in front of Navarre School. Before anyone could bat an eye, Debbie had thrown the girl down and was pounding her head, by holding the other's hair in her hand, into the pavement. The mother, who had been sitting on the front porch across Navarre Street by the school, came running to her child's rescue. Debbie grabbed her and started pounding both of them into the pavement; she beat up her friend and mother in the same motion. When she came home, slightly out of breath and agitated, she

284

went to the kitchen, grabbed some guacamole and tortilla chips, flipped on MTV, and relaxed. When she told me of the fight I thought,"Huh?"

Though I always knew that Debbie was a sweetheart underneath her tough exterior, I really didn't relish the idea of confrontation with her. Instead, it was easier to walk by, say "Hello," and go to bed.

Pitifully, I was the first in the house to leave for school in the morning and the last to come home. Mom's dedication to Kenny permeated all aspects of her duty. In the morning, I ate cereal as she would not cook breakfast until it was time for Kenny to get ready for work; he liked his food hot. He typically returned home from work at 4:30 and wanted dinner at that moment; Kenny Mike and Debbie, if they came home, ate warm meals too. Me, I arrived home at 7:00-8:00 at night and my cold dinner would be waiting in the oven on low heat. We didn't have a microwave oven so I just ate the leathery afterthought each day. Inside, I felt like I wasn't important enough for the "family" to accommodate my schedule. I thought to myself, "Don't they know how hard I work in school?" "Don't they know that I am scared to ride the bus through downtown? Don't they know it hurts that I am the only one who does not eat hot food? How can they judge me as a failure in school, gay, and not a man when I am living in a house with five people alone in a desert?" My high school experience became one hidden behind a mask of humor and sports where my pain was invisible and experienced in isolation. No one at school, or in my neighborhood, ever knew the depths of the emotional pain that I carried in my soulless heart.

In reflection, it was the feeling of invisibility that hurt the most. The only way in which I survived this period of time without jumping from the High Level Bridge like my father, or driving Kenny's Ford LTD off the entry way from South Street onto I-75 and into the river, was the thought of being with Mama Green. I realized that attachments to loving souls illuminate visibility into the most darkened internal places.

Chapter 44.   Friends and Families Unite

Seventh grade marked the arrival of some of my greatest long term friends. Tracey Morrow (whose mother became my high school history teacher and college advisor), and Erik Rhee came that year. Tracey dated my long-time friend since kindergarten, Stephen. Erik blended in exceptionally well at MV. He was close friends with Mark, Ted, and Peter Chung who lived in The Colony neighborhood in Rossford. Though my close friendships with Jamey, Bill, Seksom, Jeep, Ronnie, Laura Sowatsky, Brian, George, Matt, John, Pratik, and others persisted, Erik was quiet and laughed at everything that came out of my mouth; we bonded instantly.

I can remember that Erik's hair was so well combed that he quickly earned the nickname Silkience, named after the top selling shampoo. In high school, he had joined my bowling team with John Bronson at the newly built self-scoring lanes in Rossford. Further, he listened to my problems without judgment and knew more than anyone else at Maumee Valley, except for, George Hageage. After I had moved to 909 McKinley, Erik immediately recognized the danger of my transportation experience.

Already famous for eating two 16 inch pizzas during a house party, his mother and father quickly grew fond of the "little boy" who could eat with such vigor. After turning 16 years old, Erik immediately earned his driver's license. As such, it was more convenient for him to drive than to have his boutique store owning mother, private practice running and professor at the University of Michigan father, or the genius inventor and food packaging giant, Mr. Chung, carpool everyone home. With permission from his parents, and out of fear for my safety, Mrs. Rhee had Erik take me home from school every night with a stop for dinner at their house. For over two and half years, the Rhees made sure that I had a hot meal and a safe ride home each day.

As teenagers, Erik, Ted Chung, and Mark Chung had consistent dating lives and an intense cultural influence demanding hard work in school, and a wide range of extracurricular activity. Erik's mom was adamant about the kids doing homework and ensuring their success. Michelle, Erik's younger sister, was grounded once because Brian, the youngest of the three siblings, earned a B on a test. The rationale was that Michelle knew the material and had a duty to make sure that her brother understood it, too. And, man, did they study.

Erik was a machine. He played sports, performed in theater, ran the carpool, and did homework relentlessly. Though I did homework, I was more concerned with dealing with being ostracized in my home, quelling nasty rumors, and living beyond an illusionary curtain. Often, rather than doing homework, Erik taught me to play Lionel Richie's, "Hello," and permitted me to play on their family piano. For two years, I became a family member where Brian and Michelle were my little brother and sister and Erik was everything to me.

Mrs. Rhee, who often spoke Korean in the home (I always answered as if I knew what she was saying), removed the work restrictions on me. Instead, she and Dr. Rhee spent considerable time talking and getting to know me personally. I loved them, just like the Katzners and the Hageages, as the family that I always wanted. Though there were strong cultural controls for work and discipline, there was safety, and opportunity in their home. Erik's summers were spent taking classes at the famed Philip's Exeter Academy. I spent more time in their home than any other place except Maumee Valley. I felt safe there.

Incredibly, the South Korean culture of hard work, drive, and academic success paid off for the Rhees and the Chungs. Ted Chung attended Dartmouth, Mark went to Colgate, I forgot where Peter went to college; Michelle earned a degree from Harvard; Erik attended Columbia University and earned a law degree from the University of Denver; ironically, Brian attended Ohio State and took Introduction to Sociology with me. When Brian moved into his apartment, Mrs. Rhee had learned that I was without food or money, and purchased $75 worth of groceries for me.

In terms of careers, Erik became an attorney; Brian starred in a television variety show in South Korea; Michelle graced the cover of Time Magazine when she was named the Chancellor of the Washington D.C. school system; Ted eventually served, for a short time, as the Attorney General for the State of Illinois; Peter became a Managing Director at Morgan Stanley; and Mark became an Engineer in New Jersey. Though I became a professor, I always felt tremendously inferior to my successful friends.

It didn't stop me from having fun, though. On one Saturday, while I waited for Erik to finish his homework, Brian and I decided to play an impromptu game of "Target." We got some rope, a set of earplugs, and a chopstick. The game was to tie the competitor to a chair in the living room, put a chopstick in their mouth, and count the number of times one could hit the target (the "sitters" forehead) with earplugs. I was first. I fired around 40 earplugs at him from the hallway in front of the stairs leading upstairs and nailed him numerous times to the muffled, "Ugh," sound. When Erik came from his bedroom room and saw his brother tied up and being blasted with earplugs, all he could do was shake his head, laugh, get a glass of water, and head back into his room, dumbfounded. When Brian tied me up, he only hit me 10 times or so. The game was a freaking blast.

The Rhees lived in a beautiful home nestled atop a hill and hidden from roadside view by a mini-forest; the Chungs lived in a castle on the river. Though the families treated me like gold, I always wondered what it would be like to be treated so well at *my* home. Instead, my mother regarded me as a competitor against Kenny Mike (although Kenny Mike himself never did) and conflict raged. Rumors circulated feverishly and Erik helped me make sense of the emotional turmoil. At the end of the day, the Rhee's were a non-familial family.

During car rides home, I would constantly tell stories; whomever we saw, there was a story to tell and it was clear that Mama Green was my world. No matter the story, everyone in the carpool would laugh. The characters in the play were unscripted and real; the places of violence were transcendent, and the abstraction of social class differences were not mentioned. I felt different but was treated as an equal. The Rhee's gave me hope and allowed me to see possibility and safety in a period of emotional turmoil.

Similarly to the Rhees, I was quickly and readily adopted by the Hageages as well. If Erik was my best friend by day, George was my best friend by night. Once we were able to drive a car, George's basement became our sport watching haven as his father's "old school, Heathcliff Huxtable" style leadership shaped our growth into men. While watching The University of Maryland basketball games, starring Len Bias, we learned that a man could, in fact, be kind, mindful, and gentle without being emasculated.

In addition, George's mother, and his quiet but endearing sister, Kara, supported the "crazy man" (me) from the East Side. Just like the visits to the Katzners and Rhees, I was family and always felt reprieve and sanctuary at the Hageages. We ate together, traveled on college interview tours together, and were best friends.

Typically, George and I made our way to the Buttons and Renee's dance clubs. Thankfully, George and I didn't drink alcohol,l but we sure did dance. Aside from our focus on soccer, football, and basketball, dancing was our favorite pastime. Break dancing at Portside with Jenny Campbell and going to the "Mall" were normal fun. George's balance of ethical behavior and morality neutralized my desire to drink, party, and run with the more deviant groups. He unknowingly kept me from succumbing to temptations.

Sometimes it's not so important to explain why people turn to crime; those influences are omnipresent. Rather, sometimes it is important to note and understand why crime-prone potential offenders *avoid* criminal behavior. For me, my bonds and linkages to friends, family, school, and the maintenance of esteem as built by Mama Green mattered tremendously. Mama's messages lived in me and I had surrounded myself with friends that supported my struggles without judgement or pressure. I am thankful for my childhood as it taught me well and provided me with the gift of understanding and respect for others.

Chapter 45.   Where Did God Go?

Mama Green was a deeply devout Christian. From her youth until she died, Mama had maintained her Baptist roots. Though I never attended church with her at Shiloh Baptist on the corner of Crystal and Girard, I knew that it was a lively and festive place. Her sister Pauline and all of her long-time friends, Frank Prater, Galum, Stella, and others whose names I have long forgotten, congregated in the body of Christ.

As a child, I had long been turned off by Sunday school, when I learned at the Lewis Avenue Baptist Church that God was going to turn my "heart black" because I was a sinner. I was afraid of God rather than being "God fearing". Even though we talked frequently about God and His grace at home, I much preferred watching football on Sundays or Julius Erving during the NBA season. Eating cobbler at Mama's house was predictable while church served as her weekly reprieve. Her conviction was contagious but my fearof God was significant to the point of phobia.

By 1979, however, the legendary Toledo Civil Rights Leader, Floyd Rose, had started a radio show called "Save the Children" at his newly opened Family Baptist Church. When I stayed at home on Utah Street, Erma and my mom listened to him on the radio and his words, conviction, and dedication touched me. Erma Jean's best friend, Lilian McDonald, actually attended services regularly and convinced my mom to begin attending the "all-black" church.

On my first visit, I noticed that the church itself was located in a dangerous neighborhood in the West End. Inside the church, however, It was a family sharing the Holy Spirit. As the congregation settled into their seats and Reverend Rose made his way to the pulpit, he would raise his hands, without words. The choir began clapping, chanting, and singing, while emerging from the balcony, up the stairs from the basement, and singing and swaying down the aisles. Their energy and

291

spirit was beyond Glory and the feeling of being touched was profound. People jumped in their seats, raised their hands, shook them, and the nurses prepared for those who fainted. The church was packed; the church was electric.

When Reverend Rose asked if there were any new visitors, we stood. When he said, "Everyone, let's welcome Brother Shawn today," everyone clapped, making my sense of belonging immediate. Everything moved in slow motion and I simply bowed my head and waved with my right hand. I was hugged, embraced, and loved by members of the congregation. The notion of the Holy Spirit was starting to make sense.

Then, Reverend Rose spoke. He delivered a speech on the transformation of America from a melting pot to vegetable soup where all of the ingredients mixed together to fulfill God's Will of togetherness and understanding. His message of inclusion struck me as true to my life. When he was finished, I gave what I could in tithe and my mother beamed with love and pride. We ended the service by shaking hands with those around us and saying, "May peace be unto you." I learned that God was good. Reverend Rose touched my heart.

He was such a great speaker, in fact, that when I took speech class at Maumee Valley with Mrs. Campbell, I modelled my delivery after his style. As a matter of fact, given his leadership in the NAACP, I did an entire month long internship with him during my senior year in January, 1984. Learning about the role of the church and black leadership during the Civil Rights Era was still needed and profoundly important. It fueled my desire to have an impact on community systems, program development, and to do so with an eye of helping people first – his message of feeding the hungry reflected Mama's teachings.

When I would get dropped off at her house after church, Mama would answer my questions about God. The issue that I was never capable of understanding, until I had conversation with my friend Sherry McDonald

292

at Denison University, was how could a loving God produce and permit broad-based pain? I could never understand why all of the spankings, poverty, and domestic war could come from a just and loving God. Mama and I talked through those ideas regularly, but I didn't feel religious when I was alone.

My mom, who happily worshipped at Family Baptist Church (and developed her personhood during this period), always had a secret religious side. My mother was interesting when it came to explaining the supernatural. She did not believe that religion and worship had to occur in a physical building; we were all a part of God. She believed in ghosts, she was convinced that UFOs were real, and in the future, religious beliefs became the basis of her conspiracy theory pedagogy. Ultimately, she used the concepts of Christianity to argue that the Zions controlled the banking system and that the Rockefellers, Bilderbergs, and Illuminati controlled the world. Though these beliefs gained hold around 1983, after she roughly and abruptly retired from the Medical College; in 1980 she chose to follow Reverend Rose. Earlier she had followed the kind, but often derided, Carlo Sommers in a commune-like Fellowship of Love. Carlo's mundane and bland television commercials were the target of ongoing derision, but mom was enamored with his wisdom. I met Carlo Sommers him a few times and I liked him a great deal, but when I heard people make fun of him, my mother's spiritual advisor, I felt ashamed. I never spoke up for Carlos due to the fear of being ostracized.

After mom married Kenny in 1982, religion became a very complicated experience in our house. After Reverend Rose married my parents in March of that year, Kenny began to attend Family Baptist. Born and raised a devout Catholic, Kenny willingly went to Family Baptist Church, walked to the front of the church as an act of conversion to that faith, and ate the bread and drank the wine presented by Reverend Rose. I was there that day and witnessed it, while Kenny Mike and Debbie stayed home.

293

Over time, though, Kenny's conversion caused me to think that religion was not authentic and changed his faith to placate my mother's beliefs. He seemed uncomfortable at Family and it showed as he turned bright red while walking to the front. For me, I felt like his rumor mongering, as revealed by Erma Jean, made his religious conviction inauthentic. The entire notion of living with a step-father who clearly misunderstood me, according to the word on the street, made me disassociate my God with his hypocrisy. In addition, it was no more than a few months later that he had convinced my mother that the church wasn't helping our increasingly dysfunctional home and that her college education was not needed for household success. Around that time my mother dropped out of school, stopped attending church, and quit her job. "How could God let that happen?" I thought to myself.

As mom became isolated from her former life (while developing lifelong friendships within Kenny's social circle, such as with her spiritual sister and soulmate, Karla Crooks) she dove more deeply into conspiracy theory. She had a lifelong ability to allow her obsessions to feed her never ending thirst for knowledge. In the 1970s, she dove into Man, Myth, and Magic; from 1975-1979 she was fascinated with Carlo Sommers; from 1979-1982, it was Family Baptist Church. From 1982 until her death, she bore the paranoia of Illuminati control.

The deeper she delved into Conspiracy Theory, the more her friends disappeared. Erma Jean heard of Kenny's conversion "through the grapevine" and spent most of our visits together noting that my mom was "crazy." Though Mama Green was deeply disturbed by mom's changes and worked extremely hard to keep me balanced, her dismay was apparent. "Why is she doing this?" "Why?" "Why?", she would ask. It was during this period that she shared with me her knowledge of my mom's upbringing, the roots of her newfound perception, and how her new found beliefs were without merit.

In reflection, when it was all over, the inconsistencies of Kenny's religious conversion, my mom's new Christian/conspiratorial fueled belief system, and the levity of Erma's banter tore at all of my religious being. Mama held me. She continued to feed me in body and soul, but my confusions grew. All I could ever say is, "How can a loving God allow me to be treated so badly? After all, I always tried to be the perfect kid, avoid trouble, make my guardians proud, and I received nothing but pain and anguish in return." Though I never heard a suitable response, Mama held me tightly and never let me go. She was still my ultimate source of strength during this dark period of spiritual confusion and psychological seclusion.

Chapter 46.   Sexuality of a Confused Nature

Mama Green taught me about overcoming adversity and only discussed human sexuality regarding Kenny and my mother. It was during this time that I learned of her sexual victimization, assault by broom handles, and the bizarre side of love. I didn't enjoy the conversation, but I listened nonetheless.

When "Crazy Mary" was released from her closet prison on Utah Street, around 1979, she came out as a promiscuous "misfit." She was well known for performing oral sex and surely, many of my friends accepted her invitation. Erma Jean, rightly, told me that if Mary approached me to put my "penis" in her mouth, to say "no." Though my friends were always discussing the virtue and sensation of receiving oral sex I was strongly deterred by Erma Jean's Puritanical moral system. Given my respect for her, I accepted her guidance without reservation. Further, she absolutely abhorred sexual release, due to the high rate of teenage pregnancy in the neighborhood. "You see, Shawnee, if you get someone pregnant, your life will be ruined, forever."

Jean was right in her assessment though she was draconian and undemocratic in her principles. She used strong scare tactics and either joked about me talking to girls or overtly told them to leave from my yard. Erma was a gatekeeper and significantly impacted my view of sexuality by painting a dirty picture of sex in its purist forms.

Meanwhile, the guys at the Park were a deeply inculcated in the 1970s sexuality movement, where male bravado and conquests were consistent. Though it was not expected for me to have sex, it was always an issue that sat on the table. The guys and girls, for whatever reason, continuously asked me about my sexual conquests, and many young girls offered me sex. Though there were some very attractive women in the neighborhood, others had great bodies, and some were "fugly." Whenever girls approached me (as I was never the aggressor), I turned down each and every offer. Don't get me wrong, I had a litany of crushes, especially Lisa, Livia, Deanna, Jamie, Lydia, Kelly, Sylvia, Debbie, Michelle, Michelle, Jane, Julie, Tracey, Tracy, Gianna, Sherry, Dawn, Jenny, Bitten, etc.

When I moved to McKinley, though, Kenny Mike was a handsome teenager who had numerous attractive girlfriends. Though Debbie was younger than myself, she too was beautiful and had boyfriends. Together, the two of them were relationally active, mostly within normative boundaries, while I sat there confused. I was "cute" but closed. I lacked confidence in my appearance and height. My new neighborhood friend, Bill Hartford and I spent a lot of time checking out girls as well as walking to Waite football games to watch Jessie Pettaway (Waite running back) and Clarence Carter (Cardinal Stritch quarterback). Yes, we played basketball at Navarre School where crowds came to watch me play half court games; yes, we went to Buttons, Renees, and Glass City Boardwalk dance clubs; and yes, we hung out with some of my women friends from Maumee Valley. But, I never had a girlfriend while my siblings were loaded.

The sexual pressures were tremendous. Between the activity of my siblings and the conquests of my neighborhood friends, I felt like a loser and unwanted intimately. Though it was true that I had a reputation for being with numerous girls from Waite, it was all rumor. I never had sex with Tammy though she spent an entire afternoon with me while Mom and Jean were at work; Lisa and I never had sex; Deanna and I never had sex; Jamie the Queen and I never had sex; Suzette and I, though the rumors were strong, never had sex. Even though the large breasted, braces wearing, Sherry performed a modified version of oral sex on me at the "Pock Face Factory," we didn't have sex; Sonya from down the street (another large breasted and fantastic kissing teenage woman) and I, never had sex; Jane and I never had sex; I had never had sex with anyone, though the rumor mill echoed loudly. As a matter of fact, when I went to see the movie "Indiana Jones and the Temple of Doom,"

I mentioned to my date that she had gone to second base with Kenny Mike and she responded with a list of my "rumored" lovers, though I had never had sex. Though she and I enjoyed the movie, we never went out again.

I liked girls a lot, to say the least, and had a crush on many, but serious crushes on a few. Between Lisa, Jamie, and the first girl that I ever officially kissed (at Point Pelee, Canada, on the beach at Lake Erie) Livia, sex scared me. I had an interest in experimentation, but I didn't have sex. Yes, I had touched breasts and had been molested on several occasions, but all normal intimate expression was scary and obtrusive.

However, the psychological pressure persisted. Friends at Maumee Valley had significant others and experiences while all my friends from the neighborhood and my siblings all were sexually active. Erma's continuous message rang loudly, so I found myself in countless awkward sexual situations. But, sex was something that I wished didn't exist.

Once, against my will, a girl performed a "hand job" on me while I was watching television at her house. Though it may have been normal teenage experimentation, she did it behind a pillow that I held on my lap as her grandmother slept on the other side of the room. On a separate occasion, my buddy was with his girlfriend and we ended up at the same house. With reluctance, and much pressure, the same woman stripped down my pants and rubbed my penis around her vagina without me inserting it, and the whole time my friend and his girlfriend laughed. God knows that I felt so fucking dirty.

On another occasion, Kenny Mike and I, after watching a mother and her 16 year old daughter prance around their second floor apartment nude (a hot delight for that summer), his girlfriend and her best friend came to the house. After 20 minutes of talk, as Kenny and my mom slept in their bedroom and Showtime played on the TV, we were "kidnapped." The beautiful short, dark haired girl, whose lap I had sat

298

on in the front seat, had slowly placed my hands beneath her legs and made me rub. Though I liked it, and kissed her luscious lips, we didn't have sex when we got to her friend's house. As a matter of fact, the anxiety of having left the television on and leaving the house while everyone slept, petrified me. We got home at 5:20 AM, ten minutes before wake-up time, turned off the TV, and quietly climbed the stairs. I thought about the girl in the front seat and wanted to see her again, but was too afraid to contact her. Towards the end of my senior year in high school, I saw her at Southwyck Movie Theatres while hanging out with Erik, and kissed her passionately in the front seat in remembrance of our summer interlude. My senior prom was forthcoming but I was unsure whether to ask her, Lydia, or Jamie. Erik was puzzled that I didn't ask Julie to prom, given our enraptured bond and his knowledge of my dating struggles, but I was scared and actually wanted to fail, because it was easier to deal with rejection than opening the gates into my heart's chambers. I had to protect my Temple from intruders.

The fear of sex and exposure was not a fear of talking to women. I did break dancing at Portside where some dancers had taught me pop-lock moves that I practiced for hours in my bedroom. At the clubs, I asked everyone to dance, but struck out regularly. The 0-62 rejection record destroyed my confidence, but noy my perseverance. Though I had heard thatthe short-haired girl from the front seat said she would go with me to my Senior Prom, my fear of failure prevented me from asking her. Since my soulmate, Jamie, was dating a guy named Jughead, it was a boundary that I chose not to cross. Instead, I sold out and went to prom with a woman who was later found hanging out with my best friend under the ping pong table at an after-party celebration.

Once, while playing basketball with Hartford and Boonie at Navarre School, I had grown thirsty and there was no water to be found anywhere. The local government worker, Mr. Fedora religiously watched us play. We had exciting games and, eventually, I was able to dunk a basketball on that court. In between games, after finding all of

299

the water jugs empty, Mr. Fedora asked me if I wanted to get a drink of water.

He pointed up to his apartment that overlooked the court, and I said, "Sure, I'll take a glass of water." As I was walking away, I looked back at Hartford who was watching me, and did the "just one second" point with my finger. He nodded, "Okay," with his head.

When I arrived in Mr. Fedora's apartment he asked, "Do you want a beer, some weed, or some cocaine?" I looked at him bewildered and said, "All that I want is a glass of water."

He responded by saying, "Okay." And then, he put his key into the lock and dead bolted the door shut. I was locked in with no exit and the red flags exploded. Then he said, "All you want is water, huh?" Then he came over to me and said, "Let me give you a hug," and he did so long and strong with his 6'3" frame while picking me up off the ground.

When he put me down and headed towards the kitchen, I looked at the door, the window, and scoped out the entire apartment quickly looking for an escape route. In the kitchen rested a butcher's knife, and behind me, a window. The memory of a Fedora wearing man who paid me a dollar for my ice cream push-up as an 8 year old child flashed before my eyes and the brutal murder of Cricket and her abduction from Navarre School flashed by. Mr. Fedora's presence at the bus stop defined the idea of a stalker before the concept was found in the common vernacular.

As he filled the glass with water, I watched to see if he would pick up the knife. If he did, I was going to jump out the window. If he hugged me or approached me affectionately, I would run and get the knife, **"throw my back into a corner"** and slice his neck. So, I watched with my life in the balance, awaiting his decision. All I knew was that I was going home that day. When he approached and extended his hand with a glass of water, I said "I'm not thirsty anymore. I want to leave."

He responded with, "But our party hasn't started yet." I said, "I don't want to party, I want to leave."

"I don't want you to leave." I said," Hey, look, my friends saw that I was coming up here to get a glass of water. They know where I am. If you don't let me go, they will come looking."

Given that he had watched us play 100 times, he knew I was right.

"Please, step back and unlock the door," I uttered. He did. With anger in his eyes, he stepped back.

I ran out the door, down the stairs, and out the front door and back to the basketball court and said, "I got next." I had decided that I would not leave the court, again, under any circumstances. When I was chosen by Wilson to play "next," I looked up to Mr. Fedora's apartment window and saw him close the blinds. I never saw him again.

When I went home, I trembled. I reflected on the idea that he was going to rape me, or at least try to. I wondered if they were going to find me mutilated under the Fassett Street Bridge by Weiler Homes. All I know is that I never shared that story with the police, my parents, my friends, or Mama Green. The shame and humiliation of falling for such a stupid scheme left me dumbfounded and irate with myself. I wanted to die for being stupid; instead, I stared at the ceiling that night as Kenny Mike whispered about his date with W. I berated myself for not listening to Mama's advice. Did I have a brush with death? I don't know.

All I had to do was remember, *"Never go out on the boat with the boys,"* and I would have been fine. Instead, my life was jeopardized for no reason. "Stupid fuck," I thought to myself, "I guess *God does watch over all fools."*

Chapter 47.   Tainted Money Rules

The hospital visits, intermittent beatings, and alcoholism certainly challenged the self-esteem and confidence that Mama Green had built up in me, brick by brick. However, my greatest pain was completely emotionally and psychologically based. From the earliest time of my life, we were poor, but with the resources embedded in Mama's extended family network, we survived. Mom always played the guilt card and hung the poverty blame over my head, however.

Whenever times were difficult, I would hear, "It wouldn't be like this had you not attended Maumee Valley. We could have lived a better life and I could have bought clothes and lived a normal life." Though mom was always proud of my efforts at MV, it was during times of financial peril that I heard these economic woes smothering the life out of my frail lungs. Nothing hurt more than bearing the economic burdens of the household, and after her marriage to Kenny, the entire family.

After her first year of marriage, mom had retired from MCO. The ghosts and whispers of alcoholism combined with Erma's rumors tore her soul's fabric straight out of her heart. Even with the Director's request that mom take a leave of absence, her essence had evaporated. The Ohio Nurse's Association President who had fought so valiantly for nurse's rights was extinct. She felt worthless, and Kenny was now mom's pillar of strength. Mama stood by my mother though it was far less frequently than a half decade before; Karla Crooks, spouse of Kenny's co-worker and friend, Jack Crooks, became my mother's sister and sustained her until death.

At home, the descent of my grades at Maumee Valley was met with competition and disdain. My step-brother, Kenny Mike was earning all As and Bs at Waite High School, as my GPA slipped to 2.4. The rumors were casting shadows of doubt on my already fragile confidence; the Cold War between Jean and my mom shredded my being; feeling like the second coming of a bastard child ate at the connective tissue from my past to my future. Mama's never-ending support, my friends from school, Al Getman and my teachers, insulated me from the fall and provided a safety net from the tightrope on which my fragility teetered. I was near the cliff where one stiff wind would have blown me crashing to my demise below.

Within the home, soft scale skirmishes were launched. Kenny Mike and Debbie both received In-kind payments for their adoption as I was earning around $250 a month for my father Bryce's death. His suicide provided more in death than I had ever seen from him in life, aside from a promise of a piano and a cheeseburger at the "Hole-in-the-wall" on Fassett Street. Kenny Mike and Debbie's aunt and grandmother were pounding them with questions of monetary expenditures. I was really too absent to pay attention or tell their story, but money became a central issue in the house and our youthful detachment was secured. Before I had left for college, the strain and turmoil grew and Kenny Mike moved out; Debbie left when she was only 15.

For me, my Social Security earnings were used for household spending. Then, just after the start of my junior year, I was told that I was being removed from MV and sent to Waite. The argument that mom and Kenny leveraged was that Kenny Mike's grades were so much better than mine that they were wasting their hard earned money on my "spoiled" education. No offense to Kenny Mike, or any of my good friends at Waite, but Maumee Valley was renowned for its intensely challenging curriculum and was, in actuality, more difficult than attending Denison University – a school ranked in the top 100 in America.

The shit hit the proverbial fan. Mama Green begged and pleaded for them to keep me at MV. She was a legend with my friends and they were both mystified and upset. My increasingly close relationship with the Hageages served as a buffer, alongside that of the Rhees and

303

Katzners. Mama, though, was my only "real" fortress of strength when I wanted to cry or even die; she'd say, *"Baby, you have a million dollar personality; God will take care of you; as long as I have a breath, I will be there for you."* Those sayings were reinforced and saved me. I was tired and alone, yet, edified.

Finally, upon special request, Al Getman was given special permission by the Headmaster, Mr. Milhon, to be my high school advisor. After having told Al about the scars left from the November 1, 1981, massacre and my current financial despair, he chose to intervene. About a week after the news of my transfer, and prior to my impending departure, he met with me in the high school library.

"Shawnee my boy, I love you as a son."

"Thanks, Al."

"My wife and I have talked and we have made the decision that you will finish and graduate from Maumee Valley, no matter what it takes."

"I wish, but I'm going to transfer to Waite, Al."

"Shawnee, Mrs. Getman and I have decided that we are going to have you move in with us in Perrysburg and you can attend Maumee Valley. I will either pay your tuition or adopt you so you can attend using my faculty stipend. You will not have to pay to finish attending Maumee Valley. I will take care of you."

"Huh, what?"

"Shawnee, you can come and live with me."

With tears rolling down my cheeks, I said, "Al, I appreciate that but I'm going to figure this out. If I can't, I will call."

After all of the years of financial turmoil and guilt, I had an exit. It was legitimate and offered by my greatest teaching hero. I had never imagined that anyone would actually step outside of themselves with such goodness and allow a broken-winged bird to fly. Al cared for me, and in my mind was not a teacher, but an angel.

His kindness, ironically, crushed me. I was elevated by his care, but cognizant of the fact that my life had spun so far out of control that extraordinary forms of intervention were necessary. It was embarrassing, humiliating, and painful.

While waiting for Erik to complete practice for his role in the Pirates of Penzance, I was given special permission by Ms. Donaldson to use her office phone after school. I called Mama and explained the situation.

"Mama, I'm scared and don't know what to do," I said.

"Let God do his work, use your brains, and you will figure out your solution. The truth lays in your heart. Trust in God."

"Ok, Mama."

Al had called my mom at home such that my arrival home that evening was met with the icy stares of hate. Mom glared through me as Kenny sat back in his chair and turned to look outside. I simply walked upstairs and went to bed. I laid in bed confused, wondering about my place in the world, and whether or not I should continue to live at all.

While I slept, the answer appeared in my dreams like a movie at a drive-in theatre. It was clear, that the Social Security money that was sent to me by the Federal Government was mine and was designed to take care of MY well-being. It did not belong to my mom or Kenny. I decided that I would use it to pay my tuition.

The next morning, I said nothing as I walked to the bathroom to take a shower. After shaving my little peach fuzz, and putting the hairspray in my hair, I walked confidently into the kitchen, looked at mom and Kenny, dead in the eye, and said, "You will no longer be using my Social

305

Security checks to meet your needs. I am paying for Maumee Valley with it and that is my legal right."

Neither my mom nor Kenny responded but the fire blazed from their eyes. I told my mom, "I will not be moving out because I still love you, but I am not going to Waite and you may not use that which is rightfully mine."

As I walked to the corner of Navarre and Oak, I trembled and I reflected. What would Waite have been like? What would Mama do? The grace and kindness that my teachers and friends (and family) were sharing, how would they respond? I felt valued yet ashamed; Mama helped to sift through these complex feelings that would serve me well as a college student and future professor. I swore that the philosophy of real people and real lives matter. It dawned on me that I had internalized Mama's lessons and I was evolving. My natural tendencies were being polished and I was seeing the world through the lens of a giant. I was garnering strength from my Temple of Pain and building one of my own, designed to confidently march in the direction of fate while feeding the hungry along the way. I had become a man.

When I arrived at school, I shared my solution with Al. He walked me into the Headmaster's office and explained the situation. So, on the spot, Mr. Milhon called Mr. Ralston, the Finance Director, into his office and had him look up my records to review my financial aid eligibility and tuition requirements. When he returned, it was clear that my Social Security checks did not quite cover the entire amount due. I panicked and thought I was going to vomit.

Just then, Mr. Milhon turned to Mr. Ralston and said, "I don't care what you have to do, make it happen so Shawn can stay here with his family. I don't care if he has to attend for free."

I cried like a baby because I didn't have to transfer. I had finally internalized Mama's message of strength, used my brains to find a solution, and God put the right people in place at the right time. Though painful in experience, the lessons paid dividends for me and more future students than my feeble imagination can determine.

In reflection, I learned two indelible lessons: 1. Greatness lives in the hearts of others, and 2. solutions to problems exist even in the darkest of times. Mama's lessons saved me and lit my path on an incredible journey. My talents were coming to life and my vision of success was clear. My journey was just beginning and my pain was meshing with my proclivity for tolerance, understanding, and respecting others for their strength over weakness. I was learning to be a professor without having a degree, I was on my way to something special.

Chapter 48.   The Middle of the Pack

Maumee Valley Country Day School was a special place. Few people in America are as blessed to attend one school from Kindergarten through high school graduation. It was apparent from the first day of school that college preparation was the central goal there. Though my mother was fearful of the costs to attend college back in 1971, she believed in the value of education, nonetheless.

Erma Jean had begged and pleaded with my mother send me to MV and give me a chance to succeed. Though my IQ test was below average, my interviewing skills were superb; I graduated high school, though, with an IQ far above average. This increase led me to believe that IQ scores were culturally driven and that it was a reflection of the ability to use an upper middle class vocabulary system.

Mama Green made it clear that her primary goal, especially after Guy had dropped out of college to get married, was for me to graduate from high school. She absolutely loved talking about school, her little school house, and how she had dreamed of two things her whole life: 1. Getting a baby doll for Christmas, and 2. Graduating high school. In 1977, I bought her a baby doll with my own money, and she cried for half an half hour. She held it in the box for hours and even slept with her baby. Our bond was forever forged that night as I had made her dream come true. Sadly,I couldn't get her a high school degree.

I could, and did, work as hard as possible to get an education. Fortunately, and unfortunately, I was surrounded by wealthy and brilliant students at MV. In all honesty, I never reached the top-tier in my classes with the likes of Seksom Suriyapa (Williams College, Insead, Stanford Law School), Pratik Multani,   (Yale and Harvard Medical School), Angie Anagnos, Jamey Katzner (William and Mary), Erik Rhee (Columbia and University of Denver Law School), Judy Schwartz (Princeton), Tracey Morrow (Colby College), John Fischer, Angela

Anagnos, Brian Rothman, Laura Sowatsky, George Hageage, Bill Stewart, Heather Knight, Amy Stein, Debbie and Darlene Bates, Ronnie Simmons, Steve Boeschenstein, Leslie Van Hee, Heller Shoop, Kim Veraneau, Matt Bretz, Stephen Foster, Jenny Campbell, Matt Heidett, John Schneider, Mark Goldman, Wendy Wyeth, Beth Wilson, Becky Raisner, Elisa Taylor, Lisa Talley, Maria Mabry, and Susie Reece Our class was comprised of brilliant students. On one hand, I never had the chance to feel superior as I lingered in the middle of the class rankings for my entire academic career; on the other hand, I was in the middle of the pack at a challenging and rigorously academic school. Somehow, as Seksom always explained to me, being in the middle of the pack at Maumee Valley was held in high esteem elsewhere. It helped my thinking, but didn't convince me.

Early in my school career, I had to cheat a lot to keep up, since I was more serious about sports than school. I wish I had paid more attention, because there was content covered then that comes up, even now. Erma Jean used to embarrass me (out of pride) by quizzing me whenever my friends came over to the house to play Nerf Basketball or football in the living room, especially "Up and Over." It was really important for her to show kids in the neighborhood how "smart" I was; I hated it but understood her needs – I was the closest to a son she'd ever have and she was proud of all of my efforts and successes in school.

In any case, my experience at MV was more akin to being a member of a family than a student in school. The philosophy was clear; build a community of tolerance and critical thinking, and create a structure that fosters a love of learning. They were right. No one ever treated me like I was poor though it secretly crept up once in a while; I was tightly embraced by the Katzners, the Rhees, the Suriyapas, The Morrows, the Hageages, the Chungs, and Bill Stewart and his mother. Though they were never aware of my challenges at home, as far as I knew, they extended a hand of care and love that integrated me into a life that was

309

removed from most of the kids in my neighborhood.

Mama Green really worked hard to help me navigate between the two worlds. Though she always made it clear that I was as smart as anyone at MV, she taught me to love and respect my teachers. She would tell me that I was lucky to be blessed with teachers that care. She would say, "I may have dropped out of school in third grade, but I loved my teacher. They give us knowledge. Your teachers are the best and with your brains you can do anything you want in this life." These positive affirmations and the idea that, *"You may not be rich but you are every bit as rich as the kids at school. You live in a house with love"* drove me. So, although there were crazy events and situations that were, in hindsight, unique and possibly violent, I was held a lot, hugged, and protected.

She and my mother loved my teachers; they were heroes.

Ms. Coffin offered me a spot in the kindergarten class because she saw a diamond in the rough. All the way through kindergarten, even when I was showing the cracks of domestic trauma, she stood by me and edified my position in the MV family.

Mr. Wickes was particularly close with Mama Green. Given their proximal age and similar intimidating demeanors embedded in a persona of caring, their bond was tight. After attending a talent show at MV and meeting Mr. Wickes, Mama said, "Listen to him, he is a great teacher." Recently, he passed away and the accolades of his impact on students over a four decade career confirmed Mama's position; he was incredible.

My fifth grade teacher, Al Getman, was a legend. He was regarded as the kindest, most gentle, and loving teacher at Maumee Valley. He had a spirit of duty that bonded him to all that touched his classroom. He had created the School Within a School Program (SWAS) that was designed to work intensely with students who couldn't keep up or perform and get them to the level where they could succeed. Every day that mom packed egg salad or peanut butter and jelly sandwiches I gave them to Al. In return, he gave me a gift of respect and hope. He would continuously call me a "diamond in the rough" and with focus, would shine brightly. When my personal life fell apart in high school he was given special permission to be my advisor and helped me through that difficult time.

Mr. Koltay was a former Green Beret and professional soccer player from Hungary. He was tough, intimidating, and a gentle soul. Once a year students were able to convince him to do the "phone book" trick where he would tear a yellow pages in half with his bare hands. He taught social studies, but loved to fuel debates. It was a great class where we as students were expected to have a voice. Once Alysha had insulted the East Side and I battled like an escaped cobra. I discussed social class differences and argued that the rich and the poor were much more similar than different and parents loved their kids like others but had to overcome financial barriers to maintain stability. Mr. Koltay never forgot the argument. During a parent-teacher conference he told my mother, who initially felt insulted, that "your son has more street smarts than any kid that I have ever met." Though she was initially insulted, she realized that it was a high compliment that I could blend together and move easily between life at Maumee Valley and the East Side.

Toward the end of Eighth grade, Mr. Koltay had overheard a conversation between me and my friend Jeep "Mr. Anonymous" MacNichol, where I confessed that MV was too expensive and my mom was going to transfer me to St. Johns for high school. Mr. Koltay, also affectionately known as Loz, immediately told the class, "Don't move from your seats." He walked up the hallway and disappeared leaving the class in bewilderment. When he came back, he looked at me and said, "You're not going anywhere. You are a part of the Maumee Valley family and will not be going to St. John's." Jeep and I looked at each

311

other unaware that he had heard our conversation. He had gone to the headmaster's office and persuaded Mr. Milhon to reduce my tuition to the equivalent of a year at St. Johns, and he obliged.

My mom was ecstatic and loved Mr. Koltay. Mama simply said, "God is taking care of you, baby. Don't you worry, just do your best." Mr. Koltay was a hero that put the student as a person ahead of the bureaucracy and showed that each child matters.

In high school, we had a litany of great teachers: Mr. Lundholm tutored me in the summer of my freshman year to help me understand polynomials. He always smiled when I pulled my $10 bill out of my sock (as Mama had taught me to hide my money) to pay him, and we actually watched Princess Di marry Prince Charles on TV. Sam McCoy blended humor together with content and made sure students learned through the value of fun. Mr. Testone, the hard and straightforward New Yorker, always taught from a place of care and called me Le Singe, the monkey. And, at the beginning of each French class I'd hear, "Assayez vous, le singe," and we'd all laugh.

However, once, after the November 1, 1981 beating, I broke down. During an oral examination in his office, he asked me a question that I had mistranslated and in my attempt to answer the "complicated question," I started to cry. The arguing at home had ruptured my self-esteem and the beating had annihilated my being. As I cried, he stopped the exam, sat back in his chair and simply said, "Take a deep breath. You did fine, I'm giving you a B+ and that is really good." After quivering for a couple of minutes and apologizing for my breakdown, we talked. At the end, he asked, "What kind of books do you like to read?"

With projection, I suppose, I said, "Real life stories of people who overcome struggles and adversity."

He shook his head and said, "Read Richard Wright's Black Boy, and tell me what you think."

A week later, I gave him the report and his respect for me grew. He was a school favorite and sent me down a path of reading that shaped my intellectual curiosity. The road to sociology and understanding of race and social class became my cornerstone intellectual interests. I later read and loved Claude Humphrey's "Manchild in the Promised Land," and Ellison's "Invisible Man."

Mrs. Schwartz was a master math teacher. Though I never liked proofs much, she struggled with me to help me learn and appreciate their majesty. After my grades had slipped, profoundly, she adapted. During one exam, she had passed them out to all of the students and I started to laugh out loud. Puzzled as to why I was laughing, she asked, "What's so funny, Shawn?"

I replied, "Why would you give me a blank exam but give everyone else a test with questions."

"Shawn, I'm sorry, what exactly are you saying? What do you mean you don't have any questions?"

"Mrs. Schwartz, my test is blank."

Though I was never able to understand what had happened, there were questions on the test but I couldn't see them. It was, I think, an anxiety attack. So, she accommodated me by allowing me to take exams, alone, in the library. My grades stabilized and the free fall finally ended.

Mr. Fischer was a great and humorous teacher but I could never do what he expected. In my first three years of English in high school with him I earned a C-, C-, and a D+ (after mom and Kenny got married). In frustration, the harder I worked, the more my grades fell. Finally, on one assignment I decided to use a creative and deep philosophical approach by comparing Shakespeare's Puck to Arnold Jackson from the television show Different Strokes; I received an F. I stormed into Mr. Fischer's office, told him, "I quit. Since you refuse to help me, and since

313

the harder I try the further my grades fall, I am not going to attend class anymore. I will be focusing on the classes that I can pass." I walked out, slammed the door, and threw my books angrily to the ground. I felt guilty doing so because his son John (later of Haverford University) was one of my favorite friends and he witnessed the conflict. I had enough of failure, rejection, and rumors. I was done. Relying on Mama's virtue of *"Don't be nobody's fool,"* I stood up to his perceived tyranny.

Interestingly, when I arrived home, mom was not angry, and Kenny was shocked that I had stood up to a teacher. Fortunately, for me, my mom directed her anger at Mr. Fischer, confronted him, got me back into class, and made sure I passed. The ugly exchange really was the manifest presentation of how far I had fallen – ultimately it really was me and my attitude that caused my poor grade and not Mr. Fischer at all.

The pain of being ostracized, stigmatized, detached, and separated whilenat home, and being the target for economic failings was great fuel for my speech class. Mrs. Campbell was a wonder woman who could bring out the best in our speaking and acting. Once, we had to deliver a speech about love, so I spoke on Mama Green. While talking, I started crying when I realized that she had given me life and that I was puzzled as to why I wasn't giving the speech about my mom. I spoke through the tears and saw my classmates breaking down. When I was done, Mrs. Campbell came to the podium, gave me a hug, turned to the class, and said, "Sometimes you can move a crowd when you tap into real emotions and experience." That was a defining moment in my life.

Finally, aside from Mr. Lundholm, who was just a purely great teacher and man, came my hero, Benneth Morrow. Her daughter, Tracey, was one of my best friends as Mrs. Morrow was well aware of my troubles. After I scored a 390 on the SAT verbal test, she came to me in disbelief and gave me an ultimatum. She laid out the ultimatum, "You can go to almost any college in America but you MUST increase your verbal score.

I will not tolerate this performance, Shawn."

My experience with Mr. Fischer had thoroughly destroyed my belief that I could do well in English, so I no longer cared. When I presented my case that I could not write and did not need English, she refuted my claims and said, "You, Mr. Schwaner, are a diamond in the rough and have the ability to change the world. I cannot in my right mind let you fail. Shawn, I want you to listen to me because I know that you can write. You have done well on my history papers and you can do it!"

Having always been taught to respect authority, I said, "Okay, Mrs. Morrow."

"Shawn, I want you to spend the summer reading 3 hours every day. Keep a dictionary next to you and look up every word that you don't know. I want you to call me each day and tell me about what you read. If you follow these steps, your score will increase."

Given her quiet strength, my respect for her teaching and love for her daughter Tracey, I agreed. I read every day and found myself enjoying and energized by it. Though I was spending a lot more time in the dictionary than expected, I ate it up. I actually started reading the dictionary when I went to the bathroom; I read a page a day for the entire summer. And, sure enough, that fall, I scored a 470 on the SAT, and 630 in math. I scored high enough to apply to great schools like Denison University, Albion College, and Miami University of Ohio. With her remarkable recommendation letter that Tracey said made her cry, I got into all of the schools of my choice.

At home, however, the expense of Maumee Valley and my falling grades had created a derisive rift in the house. There was a battle line drawn; "Why does the spoiled one get to go to MV while Kenny Mike and Debbie attend Waite and East Toledo Junior High School?" Mama continued to edify me saying, "You are smart and deserve to be at Maumee Valley. Don't your worry, *God will find a way*."

315

In addition, it was at this time that my mother had dropped out of the University of Toledo, retired from the Medical College, and was falling into the abyss of Conspiracy Theory. Most of her nurse friends had thought she was crazy when she said that traditional medicine was a tool of the illuminati to keep people sick so the Rothschilds could make money. She read 10 hours a day, looking at numerology, charted the paths and etiology of the Freemasons, and even made it clear that the history of America was founded by the Masons and that there was a secret sect trying to create a New World Order.

During this period, she and Kenny had decided that my studies were a waste of time and money and I should attend Waite. Though my mother was very popular, sweet, kind, and a good friend with most of the parents at MV, her personal philosophy toward education had shifted. Suddenly, during my senior year, all I ever heard was that "Kenny, wants you to be more like a man. We need to toughen you up because you will never be ready for the world." After narrowly avoiding a transfer to Waite, my friendship with George, Jenny, Katy, and Bill Hartford grew. George and I became dance club moguls and were, for two years, inseparable. Though he usually drove, Kenny permitted me to use his Ford LTD that leaked oil like a sieve and had a short in the circuits that made the headlights go out at will. Though most of my friend were freaked out by the lights, George and I rolled on.

After years of struggle and a high school enshrouded in painful and horrible context of home, I graduated. Mom, Kenny, Guy, my grandfather, and Mama Green were present when I crossed the stage. My mom had cried when she was invited to the end of the school year awards ceremony where I had won the Bolden Award, one of the highest honors bestowed at Maumee Valley. Though my clothes were too small and my shirt slightly dirty, she arrived, without my knowledge, and cried a river when my name was announced. At the end of the ceremony in the lobby, she hugged me and said, "I am so proud of you," and left crying and shaking.

Mama Green stole the graduation show with her humor. She was treated as a celebrity and enjoyed one of the greatest days of her life and mine. My graduation was her greatest scholastic success and she reveled in the moment.

Roughly three weeks before I left for Denison University, however, the final emotional assault occurred. As my mom and I sat alone in the kitchen nook on McKinley, she said, "I'm proud of you. Are you ready for Denison?"

"Yes, I'm ready."

"How much is your tuition?"

"It's pretty good, I got it reduced to $3,000 a year."

"Oh, that's good. How much do you have saved, Shawnee?"

"I have $1,000 from working as a landscaper for Al and cutting grass for the Rhees."

"Well, how are you going to pay for the other $2,000?"

"I'm going to pay out of your retirement. For as long as I can remember, you promised me that you would pay for my tuition in college, if I finished high school. Remember?"

"Yeah, I remember. But, things have changed. I paid off Kenny's debts and we think that it is time for you to be a man."

"What do you mean be a man?" I fumed. "I have been working as a man to get through high school. I work hard, study hard, and have worked my whole life to make you proud. And, now, you're saying that you're not going to pay. I can't believe this. Are you telling me the truth?" "Yes, it's time for you to grow up and be a man."

In that moment a couple of thoughts swirled through my head. First, all

317

of the rumors that Jean had been telling me about Kenny's gossiping about me being gay must have been true. Second, the last beam of light in my soul turned off and my anger towards my mother lit a crusade in me that I would send myself to college and that "no one would ever stand in my way of achieving my goals." All of the practice in sports, anger from the bastardization of my high school life on McKinley, and the relentless tenacity that drove me, came to the forefront.

I said, "Don't worry, I will send myself to school and no one will stop me."

"I hope so, Shawnee. I hope you understand."

"Sorry mom, I will never understand."

After enraging Erma Jean with a quick visit, I rode to Mama's house. Alarmed and devastated, she said, "You can do it baby. Use your brains and let God take care of you."

And so it was. Mom and Kenny dropped me off at West Hall on the hill at Denison University in 1984, where I met my two roommates, Tony Dorman and Bruce "Duke" Teal. it was the last time they'd visit until my graduation four years later, in 1988. Guy would pick me up and drop me off for all of my vacations and time away from school. My parents traded in their Mustang for $200 and bought a new Buick Regal, as I needed a car desperately to manage the climb on the steep mountain like hill located in the center of Granville, Ohio some 30 miles east of Columbus. It finally dawned on me that I was on my own.

On that first night, after I unpacked the trunk that Mama had bought me for college (the last gift she ever gave me), we spoke. Stressed out but excited about the future, mom simply said, "Your life has brought you to this moment and you can do it. Make me proud, Son Shine."

And mom, as had become customary, slipped me $20 (I wasn't allowed to tell Kenny) and drove off.

318

Section Five: GOODBYE TO "THE HILL"

Chapter 49.   When the Student becomes a Teacher

By my junior year in high school, my greatest challenge was navigating life at 909 Crazy Avenue. Though I spoke with Mama every day and kept her up on all of my day-to-day life, I typically spent the night with her one or two weekends a month. She understood that my pursuit of sport dreams, chasing girls, cruising with George, Hartford, Jeff Neal, and getting into college were taking center stage. Our days together were becoming fewer, and it saddened both of us.

However, we still shared common love. We ate pancakes in the morning and vegetable soup at night. We sat on the porch and spit watermelon seeds and talked about life. Sadly, her short term memory had just begun to show some kinks in the armor. Periodically, I would find boxed goods, such as Zesta Crackers nested in her clothes pile in the bedroom much like she had hidden food in hay stacks as a child. She maintained her gun, kept dogs in the garage, and despised her neighbor, Mr. Tellos, given her disdain for Mexicans. She had the habit of accusing him of feeding her dogs so as to soften them for a break-in. But I knew that "Old Man Tellos" was too aged, respectful, and gentle to get involved with such activity.

When she worked on the plantation, Mama was taught that Mexicans were black once, but had become "diseased" and were not to be trusted. Media portrayals at the time reported that Mexicans carried knives and were likely to stab unwary passersby. When Roberto Duran and Sugar Ray Leonard fought on closed circuit television, a fan had been stabbed outside the Sports Arena by a male of Hispanic descent. All she could say was, "See, I told you so." Sadly, it was clear that hate, when socialized into a human's soul as a child, was difficult to dismiss.

319

In addition, it because of Mama's disdain for Mexican people that I learned how strong stereotypes were at creating socially constructed forms of division. For me, it was confusing to have Mama dislike any group arbitrarily; she reserved her anger for those who were *"cow-walking liars"*, those who treated her like a "sucka," or those who talked behind her back. Her hatred of Mexicans never made sense to me.

After the Duran fight, I had a heart to heart conversation with her and spoke using her words. My socialization was complete. I said, "Mama, you like Ed Rangle and Ray Castro, right?"

"Yeah."

"You like my friend DiMaccio and David Lozano, right?" Again she said, "Yeah."

I said, "You even liked my teammate, Pedro, who is 'piss poor,' and Jesus, right?" Again, "yes."

Finally, I asked, "Ma, has Mr. Tellos ever done anything to you? He has fed your dogs and shared his food with you. Didn't you always tell me that, *"Breaking bread is a sign of love?"* Again, she said, "Yes."

It was funny that I was using her same anti-race analogies that she had used on me while eating pancakes "on the hill" a decade before. I was understanding the notion as sung by the rock band, The Police, that there can be a day when "the student becomes the teacher." It was like David Carradine who played the role of Grasshopper in the TV show Kung Fu, who at the end of the series became the teacher to the Master. Our roles were reversing and I was stunned that I was speaking with her voice; I was becoming. I had identified that, even though there was more to learn, I had taken her lessons and was now emerging as a teacher. It felt odd to become a man; it felt stranger yet to be teaching the teacher. My life as a caring, considerate, and adaptive professor was underway.

Unbelievably, she, and to the surprise of all, promised that she would try to be kinder and gentler to Mexicans. That night she invited Old Man Tellos into house as we ate meatloaf, mashed potatoes, collard greens, homemade cornbread, and caramel cake. He came to the house, broke bread, and they laughed with each other like school children who had just met. When Mr. Tellos died (the man that Mama had long said was as *full of shit as a fat dog is fleas"),* she cried.

The next challenge was dealing with Mama's oxymoronic and far more complicated position on race. Though it was true that she was a descendant of numerous ethnic backgrounds, she had clearly carved out a spectrum of expectations for blacks. Her vocabulary on race was far and away the greatest place of consternation for me. Throughout my life, Mama was lightning quick at calling some blacks "Niggers." I hated it. She once heard a white male call one of Leo's friends a "nigger" at Waite High School and she tore from the food line and got into his face. As she told me, "If I ever hear you call him that again, I will take care of you." Yet, she used the term herself – it was mightily confusing.

When watching boxing, or seeing gang members walk down the street, she referred to them as "jigaboos," "porch-monkeys," "redbone," "yellow," "colored," "negroes," and "spooks." Fortunately for me, I never bought into the logic of her explanations and frankly, refused to support her explanations, too. Since I was older, and she always told me, "Baby, your brain is like an iron lock-box," she permitted me to debate her on this topic.

Though the language system was internally contradictory to her teachings of tolerance and respect, the root of her racism stemmed in a most complicated experience with abuse. It was in these conversations that I learned that such terminology was reserved as a psychological barricade and adaptation to the abuses perpetrated by Mr. Dank. In an effort to protect her self-esteem as a woman, she bought into terrible

321

and racist concepts to protect her inner core. As she explained it, "If I let that bastard be normal, I could not have survived his abuse." It was the use of those words within the Jim Crow South that, "I learned their power and force." As such, "I used those words to lower Dank from human to animal and those words allowed me to survive."

Sadly, the use of her admittedly racist language was a survival mechanism. "When I was young, I was too small to fight him off of me. So, I had to use mental escapes. Otherwise, he would have won." Though I understood, and I had never walked in her shoes, I expressed my discomfort. Mama loved being black, and believed in the work of Martin Luther King, but she still observed a divided world that existed on a more macro-social level. Those nasty and racist terms were reserved for cheaters, liars, and criminals. Ironically, gang members and drug addicts respected her, loved her, and protected her.

In another confusing effort to protect me from a racist world, she said, "Baby, you have a natural ability to be loved by everyone and that is good. However, please, do not date black girls because the world is not ready for it." She went on to explain, "There is nothing wrong with black girls; they are wonderful. But the world does not like interracial dating and I don't want to see you get hurt. When I was young, black men were hung from trees for having white girlfriends, even if it was based upon a rumor only. I won't always be with you, but in order to protect you, I don't want you to get hurt over the ignorance of hate."

She forced me to make the promise.

Thinking about Sonia, who was one of the prettiest and sweetest (black) girls I had ever met, I said, "Yes, Mama." And, throughout my life, and given my ability to comfortably communicate and participate across racial, class, ethnic, and community lines, the socialization had a powerful impact and ranked right up there with *"Don't date a fast ass hoes."* It was just one more points of confusion for me on relationships and dating. However, her advice was given out of love and care and not

322

hate.

In return, though, she had to promise me to quit using racist language. She tried hard but the emotions tied to her anger were, at times, overwhelming and unavoidable. As Alzheimer's disease set in later; her childhood memories found consciousness and her language system re-emerged. It was devastating to watch her lose her short-term memory capacity but interesting that she could remember places, names, and years when discussing her childhood; she certainly could also remember the use of foul language.

Erma Jean made it clear that I was the only person on planet Earth who could affect Mama Green's perspective on anything and her use of language. The ability to articulate complex ideas, even in the face of hate, became my own social skillset. The formal education obtained at Maumee Valley polished my lifelong absorption of a sharecroppers teaching; I was given gifts. I realized that the value of the gifts of tolerance, understanding, and diversity made me into a sociologist.

As college approached, Mama glowed with pride. When Mr. Douglas would come by with his 98 pound, toothless frame, carrying a gun in his pants, she raved with pride. Everyone who entered her home heard, *"I've been raising that boy since he was three weeks and one day old."* As she aged, it was clear that my success, my existence, was one of her greatest sources of pride. When we went to Frank Prater's convenience store down the street, it was the same, *"I've been raising that boy since he was three weeks and one day old."* When she visited Maumee Valley, when Kenny came to her house, when she bought her K Car, when we were in the checkout line at Foodtown, and later Kroger's, it was the same. Each time she repeated her tape-recorded like message, I would look in her tearing eyes and see the whole idea of unconditional love. Even when Alzheimers struck, her mantra changed some but continued as, "see that boy, I've been knowing him since he was a baby."

323

As my departure to Denison University approached, she grew excited. She was proud that I had written my letter about Brian Washington, a neighbor from down the street, because of his ability to overcome injury, socio-economic conditions, and maintain an eye for education and respect for others. He was living in Philadelphia at the time and had graduated from Findlay College with honors. Brian embodied, as she helped me write the personal admission statement, everything that she had taught me as a child. So, when I was admitted into college she felt a sense of success.

She made it clear when I rushed to her house to show her my letter, just as Guy had done some 12 years earlier that she had never been prouder. "Baby," she said, "I always wanted to go to college but had to drop out of school when I was in third grade. I did the best I could do with my limited education. But, you are giving me a gift that I couldn't get on my own. I am so proud and you have grown to be a great young man. The only thing that can stop you from being a success is you. Thanks for listening to your Mama."

A few months later, she called me to her house to come get a special gift that she had bought. She had me sit down in the living room on the couch and said, "Let me get something out of my bedroom." When she returned, she brought out a trunk that was for my belongings for college. She said, "When daddy and I moved north, we packed all of our belongings in a trunk just like this one. You are going to be leaving on a trip that is going to change your life and you need to have a trunk like the one I had. Wherever you go, use your trunk, and remember me. Please, don't ever forget your Mama because, *"as long as I have a breath in my body, I will love you."*

We hugged.

Then she finished by saying, "You are a man, now, and there is nothing more than I can teach you. Go to college, remember me, and never forget, *you have a million dollar personality and no one can take that*
324

away. Go, be great, and listen to your teachers because they will help you to fulfill your destiny."

I promised her that day to always be kind to others and to do my best in school. I put the trunk in Kenny's car, and went back to the house on McKinley. I looked out the window on the passenger side and Mama blew a kiss in the air and waved. As I drove past Tello's house, the Washington house, Galum's house, and Pauline's house, I peered in the rearview mirror and she was still waving. I turned right at Ed Rangle's house, headed toward Oakdale Avenue, and waved to Mama and thought to myself, "I love you, Mama."

This section was far more difficult to write than I had imagined when I started it. The chapter took on a life of its own. Though my goal was to discuss the trunk, I had forgotten that it came about in a context of debate, conversation, and the coming of age of manhood. Though my life on McKinley Avenue was in chaos and enshrouded in dysfunction, I was indeed growing into a man. My ability to look into complex matters was clear, the ability to address conflict with respect was apparent, and I noted that it was possible to influence others.

At Maumee Valley, in the beginning of my senior year, a good friend had gotten pregnant. The unprecedented event at the elite private school was unique. Interestingly, administrators held an open forum of teachers, students, and administrators to determine the fate of my good friend. The debate raged and the reputation of the school was, as it was contextualized, "at stake." After listening for an hour or two, I finally spoke. I simplysaid, "How can we turn our back on her and call ourselves a tolerant environment? Linda is my friend and she is a member of the Maumee Valley Family. She is kind, she works hard, and she respects everyone with humor and a smile. So what, she made a mistake. Okay, that happens. But, in my opinion, if we turned our back to a family member that would make us lower than a single female dog that has to raise a litter of puppies. As far as I see it, this is not an issue at all. Linda should stay at Maumee Valley and it is as simple as that."

The administrators permitted Linda to graduate from Maumee Valley where our school community rallied behind her and did not shun her. When Mr. Lundholm told my mother what I had done during a parent-teacher conference and "how articulately he expressed his ideas," he made it clear that I had talents that would realize themselves long beyond my experience at Maumee Valley. My mom sat humbled and with pride. Mama's lessons were living through me and it was obvious.

I was destined to teach and Mama's message was the core of my educational philosophy. I sit bewildered sometimes, knowing that my greatest teacher dropped out of school in third grade and grew up a sharecropper, an abused child and a bare-knuckle boxer. I am amazed that any person can positively, or negatively, impact the world from where they stand. It's amazing that one person, one life, and one act of heroism can make the world an amazing place. Mama was a hero and she continues to speak.

Chapter 50.   On My Own: An Abbreviated History of College

When college finally rolled around, I arrived at West Hall at Denison University to meet my two new roommates, Tony Dorman from Piscataway, New Jersey, and Bruce "Duke" Teal, from Baltimore, Maryland. I was prepared to be on my own, I thought. Mama had poured a lifetime of love into my soul so as to manage any and all adversity that certainly came my way. Her advice, stories, wisdom, and lessons on perseverance were well established.

Maumee Valley had prepared me academically for the rigor of a top learning institution in America as mom slipped me "pieces of money," and Jean sent care packages. Though I had been surrounded by wealth at Maumee Valley, the socio-economic division at Denison was pronounced, severe, and not as well tolerated as it had been at MV. This shift threw me into an immediate tailspin and, in combination with my severe acne, I was immediately marginalized.

By now, Mama Green's razor sharp memory was starting to show signs of wear and tear. She was hiding food in the "hay" and forgetting where she had placed her money. We believe that she had hidden hundreds to thousands of dollars on the "Hill" and on Girard. My first couple of years hurt as she slipped; it was hard to watch Mama slide from the Herculean mountain of strength to frail human. We talked and she advised but the paranoia developed in her childhood was creeping into the fore. By the 1990s, she was regularly speaking in tongues.

Meanwhile, my background as a kid from the '05, mixed with an African-American heritage, did not find a quick or understood home at Denison. The first year was traumatic, on the one hand, and a growth experience on the other. It was hard to be grouped with East Coast "Old Money," as the cultural climate was different than my MV experience. My terrible acne was so bad that when I touched my face

327

with my hand white heads would burst open; the attractiveness of the student body left me in an inferior status while sexual experimentation was widespread and partying was normative. I just didn't fit in at all.

Sadly, the humor that worked so well in my neighborhood and at Maumee Valley didn't work at Denison. I felt a great sense of isolation. Mama, however, would always say, "Don't forget, you have a million dollar personality and no one can take that away from you. No one."

Fortunately, my roots embedded in the African-American tradition were well served at Denison. Interestingly, my two roommates, who were African-American, both demonstrated the same principles of tolerance, outreach, and community that I had grown up with. Just like my experience with Mama, Daddy, and Guy, Tony stood by my side through thick and thin even when I wanted to transfer to a different school. Duke was my athletic counterpart and was a chiseled David of Michaelangelo proportions. A fighter from the streets in Baltimore, he had Mama's strength; Tony had her compassion and respect for people in need. Together, the three of us were brothers of the thickest blood.

As a poor kid at Denison, I was a work-study janitor in Knapp Hall for the first two painful months of school. I worked from 4 AM until 8 AM as others in the dorm partied until 2 AM. I never slept but I studied hard. Within the first month, I was also working the weekend janitorial crew with Duke, and had a new job as a secretarial assistant in the Sociology/Anthropology office under Elaine Hensley. It was there that I met Len Jordan, my future sage, Bahram Tavakolian, Susan Diduk, Kent Maynard, and had become a member of a new "family." I loved them and they loved me. Elaine learned of my trials in financial aid from her daughter, Christie, who worked with me alongside of Mrs. Lucier, Professor Lucier's wife. She stood by me and loved my Mama Green stories. For a year, Elaine begged me to take a Soc/Anthro class due to my personal background but my fear of writing, especially in that famously difficult writing-centered program, was too intimidating.

Paying my own tuition in combination of being poor/working class was met with derision. Tony and Duke, however, engaged me socially by taking me to the Black Student Union for weekend night parties. Thanks to Mama always saying, *"Don't be a wallflower,"* I was able to dance, acculturate and be accepted as I was; as me. Cookie Baker and Deanna Bridgeforth polished my moves to a never-ending stream of Prince; Aaron Laramore, from Libby High School in Toledo, became a close friend who was my top debate partner. To this day, our debates in our Soc/Anthro classes prepared me for teaching and handling any, and all, counter arguments.

Gina Love became a great friend, though she was regarded as a campus model of beauty and excellence. Beautiful, smart, funny, and charming we clicked from our first meeting. We never dated but we instantly became best friends.

In essence, the cultural history of a shared African-American tradition gave me a pathway of acceptance. Though the acne had disappeared by the end of spring vacation in 1985, I had grown anti-Greek and was deeply engaged in BSU activity.

As the year progressed, the ongoing childhood message of "be patient, persistent, and persevere," became my driving force. The rejection by the girls was crushing, yet I was determined to figure out my place and method of expression. Starting in my sophomore year, I focused on being myself. I had decided not to hide behind intolerance and instead allowed my humor, athleticism, and undying work ethic carry me. As I regrouped, my life shifted, and Denison became a great experience. Len Jordan had taken me under his wing to improve my writing skills and sharpen my conceptual understanding of Sociology. Kent Maynard and Susan Diduk offered to pay my tuition in my final term of study at Denison, when I had exhausted my work study and Fellowship money. Kent singlehandedly convinced me to study for an internship in Philadelphia where I worked as a public relations intern with the

Philadelphia 76ers during Julius Erving's retirement season. Charles Barkley loved my "crazy" attitude, emergent from my experience with Mama.

By the end of my senior year, Professor Bahram had enticed me to consider attending Ohio State for graduate studies in Sociology. He also permitted me to guest lecture in his class as a teaching assistant, where I developed a passion for the classroom. As the year progressed, I began lecturing as a guest in other classes based upon my 270-page senior thesis, "The Institutionalization of Urban Basketball and Cocaine Addiction in the NBA." By the end of the year, I had won the C. Wright Mills Award for outstanding undergraduate teaching.

During my run at Denison, I developed broad and varied relationships that reflected my young background. Sherry McDonald, my love at Denison, spent time teaching me about Feminism and Gloria Steinem. She had taken on an unknowing role of dismantling my confused sexuality and homophobic attitude and put the objectification of women's sexuality into its proper place. Lisa Coleman, her roommate and co-resident assistant, went on to become the chief diversity officer at Harvard; Cathy Dollard became a Provost at Denison; John Hong became a medical doctor and long-time friend and personal confidante; Michael Biederman became a business owner and finance mogul; Scott Leithauser wound up being the CIO at Nationwide Insurance. My friends, like those from MV, became a great success. Susan Meier and Heide Morgan were my secret confidantes and played the role of normalizing my esteem. My BSU brothers and sisters became my heart. People like Scott Cook, Deidra Brown, Grover Alford, Jacque Kemp, David Francis, Sandra Mabury, Candace Bergman, Neal Wilson, and Ron Crawford (among many) rounded out a strong and intimate friendship network. Tony Dorman was my ultimate brother.

One of my most prized and memorable circle of friends that I had at Denison were actually nicknamed "The Family" which was coined by our

'Father', "Smooth", for our never-ending arguing, partying, and family like attachment. We were tight, strong, smart, ambitious, and had a lot of fun. The group was comprised of a dynamic group of people named Benny, Face, Pete, Hand, Dre, Big Thunder, T, Dawg, Brando, Ra Love, Red, Puppy, Pete, and Duke. Our experiences of trial, tribulation, and triumph are a story onto themselves and I blister with pride over their successes in life, family, and career. "The Family" was my true family and I love those men, today, as my brothers.

My success and failures at Denison was a great training ground for my academic, social, and professional life which followed graduation. Certainly, and without hesitation, Denison polished my survivor mentality and prepared me for a life of advanced studies at Ohio State.

Though there were many intoxicated nights and incidents of sexual experimentation, my career at Denison was a beautiful one that had taken the lessons from Mama Green and refined them. Once I arrived at Ohio State my identity as a social butterfly was well mixed with intelligence and an ability to confidently teach from a creative, spontaneous, and unorthodox style. The craziness of the social side of Ohio State was profound; the educational challenge was significant; the bonds of friendship were deep and impermeable. It was the Mama Green stories blended with sociological concepts that provided me with a unique and caring teaching frame in the classroom.

Thursday nights from 1988-1990 were the most exciting ones in my graduate school career. My best friends, including Omar Barriga, Brian Martin, Jim Pokas, Dan Quinn, Mohammed Siahpush, Jay Heyboer, Libby Ehrhardt, Debbie Weingarten, Fast Five Freddie Obligacion, Angela Engle, Libby Douglass, Deborah Brown, Carla Corroto, Kimber Davies, Richard Tewksbury, Ramiro Martinez, Vince Salazar, Kurt Schock, Tony Desimone, Chris Papaleonardos, Elizabeth Michalak, John Reynolds, and Leann Jolly were instrumental in shaping my higher order thinking. There were many more. They challenged me, honored me, and shined

331

the dull, flat stone and exposed the diamond for the first time out of the rough. My Ohio State friends, including Amira, Julie, and French Fry, elevated me to the highest levels that my imagination would ever experience.

There were several teachers who finalized the polishing and made my diamond shine. Those important and memorable teachers include: Joe Scott, Ruth Peterson, Richard Lundman, Elizabeth Cooksey, Bill Form, and my ultimate sage and criminology pioneer, Simon Dinitz. Each one of those professors assured me a great and robust career as a professor.

Sadly, by this time, Mama Green's Alzheimers had degenerated to the point that we were unable to hold a conversation on the phone. After Mama had pulled a gun on Frank Prater to purchase a six pack of Milwaukee's Best, Erma Jean, who was housing Guy as well, assumed caretaking responsibilities of Mama. The only time we could talk was when I was with her face-to-face. Soon, Erma Jean moved to the corner of Emerson and Oakdale where she purchased her one, and only, house.

Erma continued to host major Euchre parties where a broad array of friends congregated. It was an interesting mix of "old heads" and "young heads" and was a place where laughter rained. Mama Green, however, unaware of who was sitting at the table, was disgusted with her "mother" Erma. In time, Mama had become violent and was always afraid of being murdered. Any time Erma Jean would ask Mama to calm down during the parties, Mama would sing Amazing Grace or speak in tongues. However, midway through a game she would simply say when looking at me, "I've been knowing that boy since he was a baby." She never forgot me.

By 1993 I had passed my Ph.D. exam, and in the spring I won the Graduate Teaching Assistant of the Year Award which was granted to the top ten out of 2,650 candidates. Storytelling, mixed with caring for and understanding students, became an extension of Mama Green's *"feeding the hungry"* philosophy. After I told her of the success, she

332

said, "I knew you were the best." Even though she had no short term memory or recognition of friends and family, she always remembered, "My little white baby." When she hugged me tightly it was clear that our bond transcended conventional boundaries as we had merged together as one heart and soul; Mama's lessons were complete and her baby was now a teacher.

Chapter 51.   As Long As I Have a Breath

For as long as I can remember, it was always clear that Mama loved me without conditions. Often, it is easy to gauge emotional conditions as people hold out money, favors, and even love in exchange for love. Mama's love was beyond such trite capacity.

Certainly, many found her intimidating with her *"African Soup Bone* (her balled up fist)*," Bladey Mae*, and *Black Beauty*. Others remember her humor and never ending stories and wisdom. My mother loved Mama as a friend and mentor. For me, Mama was a guardian angel. We laughed together, danced, spit watermelon seeds, and even fantasized over winning the lottery. She taught me that love did not have conditions; it was of the soul. If anyone expressed it otherwise, they were a *"cow-walking lie"* and *"didn't know their ass from a hole in the ground."*

After her memory had all but disappeared, and she continuously asked my name, she always knew that she had known me since I was *"three weeks and one day old."* My life's successes were her appendages; my failures were embraced as wisdom. It was a lot of pressure to be "perfect" in the eyes of a saint, but it was natural. Unfortunately, my "million dollar" personality did not prepare me well for her Alzheimer's disease and certainly not her death. I was present, however, until the end.

In Western cultural lore, death is enmeshed in sadness and despair. Tears and hopelessness tend to cast shadows upon the richness of life. Erma Jean used to proclaim that whites bury their deceased in gloom as blacks celebrate the life of those passing on. It is through the memories of sacrifice, engagement, and the connection to matriarchal strength that binds families together in such cultural arrangements. Though grief is natural, Jean proclaimed that it is the celebration of life and adulation that prevail.

334

Though Mama had been deteriorating for some time, the day of eternal departure loomed near. Erma Jean had called me early on in the sweltering morning of August 11, 1993, from Toledo. She simply stated, "Come home, Mama's going to be parting soon. She needs you here to pass to the other side in peace."

Without hesitation, I called my fiancé, whom I was scheduled to marry two days later. Arriving at her parent's kitchen, Kathy (my fiance's mother) proclaimed that the wedding should be delayed. Julie's family sat quietly in the kitchen holding back the tears for a survivor facing a life changing moment. Their kindness was revealed; their care was evident; Julie held my hand in support saying, "We can wait."

My response was simple and embedded in a complex logic that could only be understood by the woman seeking her Heavenly father. Even though Mama continuously asked Julie if she was "from Toledo," she saw our loving bond. Mama Green loved Julie as a daughter and recognized our love and friendship as genuine. Though I thought Julie was the only woman capable of taking Mama's place; I later found that such guardian angels are, indeed, special and rare. It was my belief then, as it is now, that Mama Green wanted to be at my wedding.

Erma Jean, Guy, and I talked steadily after I had arrived after my eternal two hour car ride. Prince could not hold my attention from the tape deck in the car. The memories of chickens walking on pie crusts, snakes in the trees, dresses opening as parachutes, and perfectly cooked pancakes played in my mind continuously. The smell of friend chicken filled my car. Thoughts of blue hats with peacock feathers and laughter from crowds partaking in story festivals ran as a movie at the defunct Eastwood on Broadway. I could not turn it off; my mind was lost.

I don't remember the drive or pulling up in Erma Jean's stone covered driveway. I just remember Jean and Guy with tears swollen in their eyes saying, "We're glad you made it. Come on back to her bedroom, the time of her going Home is upon us."

The walk down the 15 foot hall took three days, it seemed. Each strand of carpet felt like the mud fighting a car tire in a perpetual battle of wills. The cracks in the wall looked like canyons, swelling from numerous rain storms. I was approaching death for the first time and, yet, I felt a calm come over me.

The only doll that she had ever owned, was the one that I purchased for her for as a Christmas present while living back on "the Hill." It was still in its box and resting by the wall next to her pillow. Her pink nightgown rested loosely around the shrunken body of a brawler long past disappeared. The doll laid in peace on her left hand side, filling the single bed where she now laid.

Guy sat quietly to my right as Jean held one of Mama's hands, and me the other. All of the stories in those hands rested gently in mine, soft, unfettered by struggle and time. Surprisingly, and without fail, the memories of the stories cascaded undaunted. References to Daddy Green, Al Green, and the likes of Mr. Bill, and Prince, the Prater's talking dog, rang. We laughed at the massive barbeques, the fear of homebrew bottles firing their caps, burning coal in the furnace, and a woman named Mama. The stories were heard in Bertha's final hour; she rested peacefully.

We laughed. We sang. We hugged. We acknowledged that an angel was soon to take flight. Suddenly, Erma Jean said, "Shawn Baby, Mama's passing on. Do you see here leg? Rigor mortis is setting in."

At that moment we hugged. Each of us spent a moment saying our final farewells to this giant who had raised us, changed our diapers, fed us, and completed us. We celebrated and felt energized by her passing.

Then I said to Mama, "I will see you in heaven and as long as I have a breath in my body, I will always love you. You will always be my Mama."

At that moment, as it was clear that she knew my voice, as she squeezed my hand three unmistakable times. It was a familiar touch that was used for healing in times of sickness; it provided peace. Then, in a last gasp, with her hand in mine, the life of Mama Green had ended and her legend began. And, with the passing of time, I realize that she lives on in me, in story; as a guardian angel, she continues to cast light on a fool seeking his soul.

Epilogue: Shadows from the '05

My life with Mama Green was true. For ten years we were inseparable and, as Erma would say, "Two peas in a pod." Prior to the onset of Alzheimer's disease, I spent more time with her between 1974 and 1984 than anyone else living; we were best friends; we were one soul.

I confess, here, that I have cut my biographical sketch short because our relationship changed during my life in college. Though she was always my inspiration, the changes in her psychological state made phone conversations more difficult, and often times alive and deeply engaged. In the spring of 1987, while I worked as an intern for the Philadelphia 76ers and developed a bond with Dr. J. and Charles Barkley, I invited a group of friends over to my apartment on Bread Street for Mama Green's pancakes and fried bread. When I received the recipes from her by phone, it marked the last truly coherent conversation of our life together. She always remembered me, but change was underway.

By the time Erma Jean had assumed full time responsibility for Mama after she pulled a gun on Mr. Prater for a 12 pack of beer, her life changed and we all hurt. Though she began to refer to Erma Jean as "my mother," and Guy as "her brother," she remembered me as her "little white baby." It was interesting to all of us that she could remember her stories from the 1920's but was confused about present day. Nonetheless, we loved her terribly.

Not only did she directly impact my life, she did so indirectly as well. In this memoir, my mother was painted as an abuser, and at times she was angry and in the battle to establish her own identity to destroy her demons. However, my mother was also a great woman who overcame tremendous abuse as a child and was, like Mama, a tower of strength. She made friends easily and maintained the relationships well. Even in the last twenty years of her life, as she became deeply involved in the Conspiracy Theory underground movement, and alienated friends, when she was done ranting, and the music played, she danced. My mother was compassionate and nursed the sick inside and outside the hospital, she stood for the equal rights of nurses, and did her absolute best in raising her "Son Shine."

Mom always felt deep guilt and remorse for the November beating in 1981 as it served as a barrier to us fully being united as one. I did forgive her and though we struggled to overcome the alcoholism, depression, and emotional scars, we always rallied around our shared experience with Mama. Mama gave my mother life and allowed us to mend our wounds.

In January, 2014, my mom passed away quietly. I was fortunate enough to be present for her last two weeks of life. When I arrived, she and I embraced as friends where all of our past sins were rendered irrelevant. We laughed and talked for hours and reminisced about home brew, cookouts, and our favorite quotes. Thankfully, my mother and I found the love that had eluded us for years - it laid just beneath the surface the entire time. When she died, I felt terribly alone and I miss her still.

Erma Jean was certainly painted as overbearing in this book and, at times, ruthless. Jean, however, loved me as her baby and had a great sense of humor. She told jokes and stories and was a witty and slippery friend. Erma was a master cook, friend, and loving soul. Jean had a heart of gold and provided for me as her own child. There was never a day when we were together that I didn't get hugged, kissed, and edified. Yes, Jean tried to kill my mother once but it was because she wanted me to have a better life. After 1982, my mom and Jean only spoke to each other once because my mother wanted to see Mama Green before she died. Though the exchange was cordial, it was clearly one of enemy combatants raising a truce to pay tribute to our fallen matriarch.

After Erma Jean died in 2001, she and I had settled a major conflict and we were at peace. In 2004, I finally had a chance to speak to Guy and

339

the conversation lasted for four or five hours. We laughed of Big Time Wrestling on the roll out bed, Erma Jean, and caught up on every detail of each other's life. We had decided that day that we would combine our knowledge and write a book about Bertha entitled as either "Mama" or "Dear Mama." The current title is a tribute to my dear brother, Leo Allen Green, Jr. Sadly, when I called back three months later, his phone was disconnected. He had died of renal failure; I was always happy that we had a chance to talk and appreciate, one final time, our brotherhood.

In terms of personal stories, however, this book only hits the high points, most negative ones that marked turning points, and shed light on the power that Mama had on providing wisdom and guidance on my journey to, through, and out of the '05. I wish I could have told all of the stories about my multitude of friends from the East Side, Maumee Valley, Denison University, and Ohio State. The stories during my college years were amazing, dangerous, exciting, and omitted here. My experiences with Brian Martin, Jim Pokas, Omar Barriga, Jay Heyboer, Mohammed Siapush, Ramiro Martinez, Kim Davies, Carlo Corroto, among many others, marked the best period of my life. I simply chose to focus on the years in which Mama and I spent the most direct time together; her influence, though, was present in college through her epistemological impact on my moral compass and behavior. She has always lived with me in spirit.

I told only a fraction of the ghost stories that Mama, Jean, Guy, my mom, Boonie, and I experienced.

By 1993, I had been so thoroughly socialized to believe in myself, my differences, and my quirky but compassionate personality to use an unorthodox teaching method at Ohio State while attending graduate school. My presentation style was a curious blend of Bertha Green, Rev. Floyd Rose, Len Jordan, Bahram Tavakolian from Denison; and Simon Dinitz, Rick Lundman, and Joe Scott from Ohio State. So, when I earned the Outstanding Graduate Teacher of the Year Award, all of the pain, persistence, perseverance, and patience converged in that moment. When I called Jean to tell her of the award and spoke to Mama, all she could say was, "My baby is the best?" and I heard tears rolling down the curvatures of her shrinking face. She died five months later and that award served as one of her last proud moments.

Her guidance and wisdom has helped me navigate into and out of diverse social worlds. Many friends who encouraged me to write this book, such as Grover Alford from Denison, were always curious as to how I could just as easily blend in with whites and blacks, men and women, rich and poor, straight or gay, use slang or professional language instantaneously. Smooth, a 6'4," huge figure of a man who used silence as a distancing tool, once said, "I liked you because you are consistent. You don't change your behavior and act phony with one group and change for another. You are always the same and I respect that about you." Really, what he was seeing is that I had learned to see the good in others as I *"have never walked in the shoes of another and stand in no position to judge."* Race, class, gender, sexual preference, and age have always been unimportant to me. All humans have something good to offer.

Carl Upchurch, author of the autobiographical, "Convicted in the Womb," a friend, inscribed in his book to me, "Shawn, we need your gifts." Hopefully, I have shared some of them here.

Bertha's philosophy carried me into prison as a corrections officer and teacher with few issues. I was able to party in inner city night clubs typically out of bounds for most citizens; I've been in ghettos, hung out with street gang members, and maintained relationships with formerly incarcerated friends. I've had situations in which guns have been pulled on me, knives swung at me, and numchucks wrapped around my neck, but I'm still here and provides for the testament that, *"God watches over all fools."*

341

I have befriended homeless men and women, CEOs of banks, and have countless number of professional friends while simultaneously engaged with persons who, as Jean would say, *"Don't have a pot to piss in or two nickels to rub together."* And truthfully, I get along with people because they are, after all, people. In this book, as I see it, it was my job to feed the hungry, help others find the greatness that lives within their soul, and to extend a hand to the fallen. I am Mama Green.

My life was not always bad either. As a matter of fact, I loved my childhood. I didn't go hungry, though things were sparse at times. I always had clothes and shelter. Though I focused a considerable amount on abuse, molestation, and violence – as those are powerful forces shaping identity; I also had great experiences. Cooking with Mama in the Mecca was straight joy; playing Nerf Basketball and working on finger rolls was wonderful; cruising for girls with George and Jeff was fun and bonding and hanging out with Jeep McNichol and Julie Mott in the summer of 1984 was unforgettable. Being in love at first sight with Jamie was the greatest instant of affection in my lifetime.

I was able to attend basketball and baseball camps regularly. In 1982, Jamey Katzner, Bill Stewart, Kenny Mike, and I attended Julius Erving's Hoop School in Baltimore where we met Hall of Fame wide receiver Lynn Swann (yes, you read that correctly), Magic Johnson, Marvin Webster, Andrew Toney, and the great Dr. J. himself. Doc's nephew, Barry Bookhard, who produced Julius Erving's 2013 documentary, was the forward on our camp team. I worked for the 76ers in 1987, and Doc actually remembered me from camp as did Lynn Swann at the "Winner's Ball," a night of tribute to Doc.

In terms of basketball, I was able to master the playground game by playing with older kids. Chris and Me often went to other areas and won money because no one thought we could win. In 1978, I was two rounds away from shooting at the national "Hot Shot Competition" championship at the NBA All-star game in Detroit. During the summer of 1985, I actually was able to dunk a basketball until I slipped and hurt my back in the driveway while doing a 180 degree dunk coming from the front of the rim. In 1991, I was asked to be on the Ohio State practice squad to guard Mark Baker but opted not to, so as to focus on earning a Ph.D.

Graduate school was the best seven year period of my life and I only missed three or four home Buckeye games at the Horseshoe in that period. I was actually sitting in the "Big House" (the Ohio State student section) when Desmond Howard threw his "Heisman pose". Honestly, I'm still not really happy about that moment in my life and hold an indelible grudge against the Cleveland traitor. I had a Super Bowl MVP as a student, Deion Branch, and more NFL greats and NBA players than should be permitted for any one teacher.

I have earned three Masters Degrees and one Ph.D. I have won numerous teaching awards in my career, been tenured at two different universities and won a Distinguished Citizen's Award. In spite of living a great life, I have been overwhelmed with turmoil and challenges. Interestingly, and in hindsight, when Bertha shot her step-father she released her demons and permitted heavenly spirits to carry me into life. And, with each day, I know that it is my duty and obligation to deliver Mama's wisdom in both direct and indirect forms to those who enter my "Temple of Pain."

However, the most interesting culmination of Mama's pain, my mother's survival, and my walk in the valley of abuse, struggle, and survival has been the birth of my two beautiful children. Had any one event not occurred or had taken place differently, my smart, funny, humble, and spirited rays of hope may not have been born at all. So, as I think of dogs carrying their puppies to safety, sleeping with a gun under my pillow, a gentle hand caressing my back during times of pain and sickness, and consider the lessons of overcoming adversity and loving others, I do so with cosmic respect. All of these events, I know, occurred so as to provide life for my two incredible daughters. And on the days in which they were born, they had radiated light into my heart and cast two shadows from '05 that gives my life continued meaning. They are my life, core of my existence, and remind me of the value of love as taught by my wonderful and soulful, dear Mama.

Final Thoughts, in A Letter

Dear Mama,

I miss you every day and think of you fondly. You were my world and continue to guide me through the dark times and elevate me into the light. I am, to this day, born a "poor black child" bestowed gifts beyond those that should be legally given freely. I have grown into this man's body and proudly share our story.

I have taken the lessons that you so kindly gave me in gift and internalized those as a moral compass. Though no one is perfect, you gave me life and helped my mother grow so that when she died we reunited in love, as she passed quietly and went Home in peace.

By now, I have taught over 300 college classes and have had around 10,000 students learn about the world, life, and sociological concepts because you helped me learn how to think, analyze, and be comfortable and confident in my abilities in spite of a life of challenge. Your ability and message to persevere has been received. Without you, I could not have been as an effective teacher as my awards proclaim; similarly, my students appreciate your struggles, words, and universal guidance.

Your strength has shined light on my path; your compassion has provided life for those who have less; and your love has provided my children with a life of opportunity and care. My daughters have never met you but your presence endears; your experience has protected them and given them chances that we never imagined.

In addition, I promise that I never let anyone leave my Temple hungry and that my house is a place of comfort and compassion. Thanks to your stories of perseverance, persistence, and patience I have the ability to build bridges over troubled waters and carry other's pain humbly on my shoulders. It is my dedication to you.

I know that I would not be here without you and I humbly submit my eternal love to you. You were a queen; you were a hero; you are life.

345

Mama, you are appreciated each and every day and will exist in eternal Grace. With great deference, I say, "Thank you."

Finally, I end by simply saying that I hope I have made you proud. God knows that I have tried.

Sincerely, your "little white baby,"

Shawn

ACKNOWLEDGEMENTS

Sadly, or happily, there are too many people to thank and acknowledge without a separate manuscript in itself. Suffice it to say that the names mentioned in this book serve as reference to those who made my life happen, blossom, and take form. However, in the aggregate, my friends and teachers at Maumee Valley, Denison, Ohio State, are thanked from the depths of my heart. More specifically, Erik Rhee, George Hageage, Bill Hartford, Debbie Paszko Flores and Kenny Mike Paszko, Tony Dorman, Chaka D, Cookie, Gina Love Walker, The Family, Omar Barriga, Brian Martin, Maria Ligon, Elizabeth Michalak, Jeff Hemphill, Gretchen Sharp, and Julie Fantin are the core friends who lifted me and saved me. Several teachers, including Ned Wickes, Laszlo Koltay, Jerry Millhon, Benneth Morrow, David Testone, Sam McCoy, Chuck Lundholm, Len Jordan, Bahram Tavakolian, Susan Diduk, Kent Maynard, Elaine Hensley, Joseph Scott, Richard Lundholm, Ruth Peterson, and the incomparable Simon Dinitz taught and trained me to be a scholar, full person, and genuine human being. Jamey Katzner, Susan Meier Roth, Sherry McDonald Lyons, Tony Dorman, Ardelia Armstrong Freeman, Melanie Parker, Kara Hageage Noss, Lisa Coleman, Michelle Rhee, Ricky Jones, Gloria Bradley, and Ryan Perez read early drafts of Dear Mama and provided support and feedback that allowed the project to complete. And, finally, I wish to acknowledge the life, struggle, and never ending friendship of my childhood best friend, Daniel "Boonie" Boening. Along with Russell "Rusty" Schwartz, he was my first known friend and continues to be my soulmate into the current hour. Boonie knows me and my life better than any other human being on the planet and I thank him for always being there for me, "Go Bucks!." Finally, I miss you Mama, Erma, Guy, Daddy, Kenny, and mom. You all made life an incredible journey.

To those who hurt me, abused me, or assaulted me... you are forgiven.

ABOUT THE AUTHOR

Shawn Schwaner was born on January 21, 1966 to a single mother, Susan Schwaner, in Toledo, Ohio. Alone and poor, Shawn's mother was facing a crossroads when the incredible Bertha Lee Green (Mama) stepped into Susan's life and offered to raise her unborn child. Through numerous trials, tribulations, and personal challenges, Shawn earned a high school degree from the prestigious Maumee Valley Country Day School which would change his life trajectory and allow him to climb to the highest of academic heights. After graduating from Denison University with a Bachelor's Degree in Sociology/Anthropology and then a Master's and Doctorate from The Ohio State University, he went on to earn numerous teaching and civil service awards as a college professor at the University of Louisville, Sullivan University, and Miami Dade College (among many). He has shaped and molded the lives of nearly 10,000 students in his career with his unorthodox and creative writing intensive teaching style and continues to leave an impact that reflects the lessons on race, grace, and the wisdom to overcome as learned from his life with Mama.

Macy and Madison, I will always love you with all of my heart as you give me reason and hope to strive for a better life each and every day. I love you more than you will ever know!

REACTIONS

I love the book and it is haunting my dreams. The first time I read it I woke up at 3 AM and had to read more. The second time I read it, I woke up at 4AM and had to read more. It takes me back to being that young woman and my early days with Leo. You have given me a voice to my past, too. Thank you.

Gloria Bradley, Mama's Daughter-in-law

I'm still crying, right now. I lived most of this book. I loved Mama Green; I loved Erma Jean; and I loved Fruit Cake. We made it Shawnee, we are good people who made it out of hell. I tried to explain to my daughter the hardships, the pain, the life changing sexual confusion; but like combat, it can't be understood unless you lived it. We are our own heroes that had some very, very special people in our lives. I couldn't be more proud of you, little buddy... God takes care of us fools.

Boonie, my childhood best friend

It's a very good and interesting read!!! That was Aunt Bertha! You told it as it was!

Ardelia Freeman, Mama's Niece